The Best Game in the World

This book is dedicated to the late Bobby Keetch, a friend I was proud to have, his wife Jan, and their family, Nicolette, Christian and Karl.

The Best Game in the World

Fifty Great Years of Football to Euro '96

by

Terry Venables

Century · London

This edition published by Century Books Limited 1996

1 3 5 7 9 10 8 6 4 2

Century
Random House UK Ltd, 20 Vauxhall Bridge Road, London SW1V 2SA

Arrow Books Ltd
Random House UK Ltd, 20 Vauxhall Bridge Road, London SW1V 2SA

Random House Australia (Pty) Limited
16 Dalmore Drive, Scoresby,
Victoria 3179, Australia

Random House New Zealand Limited
18 Poland Road, Glenfield
Auckland 10, New Zealand

Random House South Africa (Pty) Limited
PO Box 2263, Rosebank 2121, South Africa

Random House UK Limited Reg. No. 954009

A CIP catalogue record for this book
is available from the British Library

Papers used by Random House UK Limited are natural, recyclable products
made from wood grown in sustainable forests. The manufacturing processes
conform to the environmental regulations of the country of origin.

ISBN 0 7126 7723 2

Typeset by SX Composing DTP, Rayleigh, Essex
Printed and bound in the United Kingdom by
Mackays of Chatham PLC, Chatham, Kent

Acknowledgements

A book of this nature, covering as it does 50 years of English football history, inevitably involves a lot of people and a lot of hard work. I and my co-writer, Colin Malam, must have met something like 30 times in the year between August 1995 and August 1996 to discuss the major issues of the period, record my thoughts on the subject and then go back over the same ground during the revising process. Obviously, I would like to thank Colin for all his efforts in knocking those mountains of material into shape. Less obviously, thanks are also due to Beata Zabarowska, who spent hours transcribing the tapes of our discussions while continuing to carry out her duties as secretary to Eddie Ashby, my friend and business adviser. Eddie's own enthusiastic support for the project was most welcome, too.

Holding the whole operation together was Jonathan Harris, my literary agent. As the middleman between me and Colin on the one hand and the publishers on the other, Jonathan had more than his fair share of problems to contend with; but he seemed to deal effortlessly and efficiently with every emergency, as did his secretary, Georgina Coombs. Their coolness under fire was particularly valuable during the final period of gestation, when our decision to delay the book so that we could include Euro '96 meant the last chapter had to be written at breakneck speed. Mark Booth, the publishing director at Century Books, and his assistant, Liz Rowlinson, certainly pulled out all the stops to get the book out only a couple of months after Euro '96 had ended on June 30. It was a remarkable effort by them and their colleagues.

In addition, I should like to express my gratitude for the help given us elsewhere in the creative process by Dave Sexton, former manager of the England Under-21 team, Stephanie Pryor of the systems support department at The Telegraph plc, Patrick Barclay of the *Sunday Telegraph*, David Endt, Ajax Amsterdam's press officer, Rob Hughes of *The Times*, Ken Jones of *The Independent*, Alex Montgomery of the *News of the World*, Keir Radnedge, editor of

World Soccer, Jack Rollin, executive editor of the *Rothmans Football Yearbook*, Andy Williamson, assistant secretary of the Football League, and Reg Drury, ex-chief soccer writer on the *News of the World*. If we have left anyone out, we tender our apologies and promise to do better next time.

Contents

INTRODUCTION

No doubt some of you will remember *They Used to Play on Grass*, the futuristic football novel I co-wrote with Gordon Williams in 1971. There was a phrase in that book we used as a theme right the way through. It was: 'We had real players in them days!' We had picked it up from conversations with old-timers in my dad's Essex pub, and it seemed to symbolize all those chats about football, often impassioned and usually nostalgic, fans up and down the land love to indulge in. What this book is intended to be is an extension of those chats and a starting point for many more.

I've always liked nostalgia. I enjoy it as a talking-point, not as an obsession. I don't have a Michael Parkinson-type obsession with the past: I've always believed today and the future are the most important thing. So what I and my co-writer, Colin Malam, have tried to do in this book is combine the three time-scales. We've looked at today and the future in terms of serious business, and at the past not only for nostalgic reasons but for what, in the classic historical tradition, it can teach us about the present.

Older people are always saying things were better years ago, but that has to remain a matter of opinion. In football, certainly, you can't measure improvement or deterioration in the same way as athletics by comparing times in the 100 yards or the mile. Faster does not necessarily mean better in our game, far from it. Everything is relative, too. Wealthy businessman Morris Keston is possibly Tottenham Hotspur's most devoted and famous fan, and I remember him saying to me a few years ago that football was not as good as it used to be. In reply, I suggested that it depends on who you support. 'You are supporting Tottenham and can remember the great "double" team of 1960–1,' I said, 'so if they are not having any success today, you don't think the football's as good.

'But they do in Liverpool and they do in Norwich [they were top of the old First Division at the time and going strong]. If you were a Norwich supporter, you'd think football was a lot better today than it used to be.' Morris still wouldn't have it until Darren Anderton, Teddy Sheringham and Nicky Barmby came into the side at the back end of my time at White Hart Lane. He liked that; and then Spurs had that great run with Jürgen Klinsmann in the 1994–5 season. Suddenly, he was saying football had never been so good.

It was from exchanges of that kind the idea for this book came. I had always thought it would be interesting to write about the game's post-war history and try to link it to the present and the future. So, with the 50th anniversary of the resumption of League football after the Second World War being celebrated this year, now seemed a good time to do it. It is not a conventional history in the sense that it does not examine events in chronological order. It is more a case of one man giving his personal impressions of a half-century of enormous change, the greater part of which he has experienced at first hand as a player, coach, manager and administrator.

Just think about it: the 50 years in question have seen the top-flight professional footballer transformed from little more than a poorly-paid chattel into a wealthy and glamorous figure. He has the introduction of television, as well as the players' union and the stubborn Belgian footballer, Jean-Marc Bosman, to thank for that. Arguably, the influence of the medium on football has been more dramatic than on any other section of English society. At the very least, who would ever have dreamed back in the post-war austerity of 1946 that it would become possible to watch top-class football matches live on a screen in the living room two or three times a week?

It has been an era of terrible disasters, too. Heysel, Hillsborough and Bradford are now synonymous with a tragic and unnecessary loss of life. But they have had their beneficial side-effects as well, as can be seen from the incredible transformation of most of the country's leading stadiums from bleak Victorian fortresses into comfortable, safe, user-friendly palaces.

At long last, it would seem, football is beginning to take the fan into consideration. The process was delayed somewhat by the hooliganism that bedevilled English football in the 1960s, 70s and early 80s, when every football supporter was regarded with deep suspicion. But now, with the hooligans in retreat, the game appears to be waking up to the unavoidable fact that its real owner is the fan.

On the pitch, meanwhile, the English are still coming to terms with the concept that they are no longer the masters of the game they gave to the world, a painful learning process that began soon after the war. Winning the 1966 World Cup and dominating the European club competitions between 1977 and 1984 raised hopes of a revival, but a five-year ban from Europe put us back to square one. In that context, particularly, I have offered my view of the way ahead. It won't be easy to implement because it involves a wholesale reconstruction of English football. I'm not talking about the structure of the game as such, but of the way we teach and play it. I don't see any alternative, either.

Reaching the semi-finals of Euro '96 was a big step forward; but unless we sustain that kind of progress in other ways, our clubs will continue to struggle in Europe and the England manager or coach will have an increasingly difficult task in trying to qualify for, and get results in, the finals of the major international competitions. So I am trying to help my successors here. And, yes, I do have something further to say about my reasons for deciding not to continue as England coach after the finals of the European Championship. There again, I have tried to be constructive and suggest ways in which the process of appointing the national team coach, and supporting him in office, could be improved.

We have attempted to avoid the dryasdust approach to these and other matters by dividing them into themes such as the player, the manager and the chairman. I hope you think we have succeeded, because one of my main purposes was to convey my love of the game and enthusiasm for it. We have also attempted to lighten the tone, have a bit of fun, by selecting the greatest players, teams and managers of the period. No doubt you won't agree with all of my choices. But that is in the nature of things, is it not, when football people get together? Friendly disagreement and discussion always have been and always will be the lifeblood of this game of opinions, this game that still has the potential to be the best in the world. Did you hear what that Jimmy Hill said on the telly the other day? He needs locking up, he does . . . .

Terry Venables,
London,
September 1996

Chapter One

The Player

You can have football without television, believe it or not. You can have football without directors. You can even have football without a referee or a manager. Goalposts are not essential, either, because you can just put your coats down and play. But the one thing, other than a ball, you can't have football without is the player. He (or she) is the most important piece in the whole wonderful, complicated jigsaw that makes up the game. The players are the team, and the team is what makes the game function. Without the team there is nothing, and you can forget everything else.

That is not to say the importance of the professional footballer has always been recognized in the 50 years of English football since the Second World War: far from it, in fact. His history in that turbulent half-century has been largely a struggle for freedom from virtual slavery and for a salary that goes with the ability to attract thousands of paying customers to a place of entertainment. A struggle, too, to overcome the sort of official contempt and prejudice represented by the notorious remark of the former, all-powerful secretary of the Football League, the late Alan Hardaker, that he 'wouldn't hang a dog on the word of a professional footballer'.

Happily, it has been a successful struggle. Professional footballers are now among the highest-paid practitioners of English sport and enjoy a degree of contractual freedom unimaginable 20 years ago, never mind 50. But with freedom and wealth have come new responsibilities and pressures. Television, whose money has played a big part in enhancing the status of the player, not only projects the game on an unprecedented scale, but magnifies every little mistake and misdemeanour. In essence, the professional footballer has become part of showbusiness and is at the mercy of the tabloid wolf-packs who prey on such public figures. Never before has his behaviour in public and in private come under such intense scrutiny. Privacy, as star players like Paul Gascoigne have discovered, is a thing of the past. For all his material advancement, too, the player remains just about the last person the football authorities will consult on any subject. He has a much bigger say now in the running of the game than he did 50 years ago, but it is still not big enough.

I must declare an interest at this point. I was a member of the management committee of the Professional Footballers Association (PFA) for about seven years in all and served as vice-chairman to Derek Dougan while the negotiations for freedom of contract were taking place in the late 1970s. Gordon Taylor, now famous as the campaigning chief executive of the players' union, came on the committee while I was there. So did Ian St John and several other well-known players. Unfortunately, I had retired as a player by the time Dougan, and Cliff Lloyd, the PFA's former, long-serving secretary, finally succeeded in obtaining their members a limited form of freedom of contract in 1978.

Jean-Marc Bosman blew away the remaining contractual restrictions in 1995 by winning a gruelling, five-year legal battle with his old club, RFC Liège, and the Belgian football federation over their attempts to block his transfer to another club. But even before the European Court of Justice ruled that the transfer system within the European Community was illegal, English footballers had been free to move to another club at the end of their contracts and the fees for such transfers, if the two clubs could not agree a price, were decided by an independent tribunal. That may sound old hat now, but it represented a massive advance at the time. As John Harding wrote in *For the Good of the Game*, his official history of the PFA: 'And so, at the 1978 AGM, 80 years to the month after professional footballers first met to form a Union to fight the transfer system and secure freedom of contract, the most significant step along that long and weary road was ratified.'

I think that's overrating its importance a bit in terms of improving the lot of the English footballer. So far as I'm concerned, the biggest single change in the last 50 years was the lifting of the maximum wage in 1961, because it started off the whole process. That was followed two years later by the success of George Eastham, then a Newcastle player seeking a move, when he bravely challenged that holy of holies, the retain and transfer system. Before then, no English footballer, no matter how good he was, could earn more than £20 a week and was at the mercy of his club so far as employment was concerned. You signed a contract with a club as a kid, and basically you were there for life if they wanted to keep you – even if, at the end of the contract, they offered you less money. They could do what they wanted, and negotiation was out of the question. That was it: take it or leave it. It was disgraceful, really. All this, mind you, not long after some leading clubs used to have gates of 80,000. You wonder what happened to all that income. Although admission prices were low by today's standards (about 8p just after the war) 80,000 of anything is a lot of money. Particularly when the clubs paid the players no more than £12 a week, the maximum in the first six post-war years.

So there's no doubt in my mind that, but for the PFA, the players of today would certainly not be as well off as they are. We'd have got there eventually, but it would have taken a lot longer. The English players' union were quite progressive and, in Jimmy Hill, the chairman from 1957 to 1961, we had someone who was volatile, energetic and very bright. Cliff Lloyd was a good foil for Jimmy inasmuch as he was a steady hand and a very fair man. What I liked about Cliff was that if he felt the player was wrong in certain cases, he wouldn't support him. He didn't just support any old flimsy case that came up. The combination of Jimmy and Cliff was a particularly good one. There's no doubt they both played a huge part in the abolition of the maximum wage, which was the beginning of the English player as we see him today. I think perhaps they haven't had the kudos they deserve.

It wasn't just Jimmy and Cliff who did it, of course. It was all the players at the time who stood up and put their necks on the line for the PFA and for the future of their fellow professionals. The feeling among the players then was quite aggressive. So, for all the huffing and puffing of the clubs, they couldn't stop the abolition of the maximum wage going through. The players were even prepared to withdraw their labour, perhaps for the only real time during the troubled industrial relations of English football that I experienced.

It was all particularly relevant for me because, having joined Chelsea in 1958, I got in the first team in 1960. Then, in 1960–1, there was this revolution on the maximum wage. I was only 17 then, and I remember attending the first PFA meeting at Liverpool Street. Then I went up to another meeting in the north because I was sufficiently interested to see what was going on. Not that the success of the campaign made any substantial difference to my bank account. Thinking 'This is lovely', I went in to re-negotiate my pay and came out on the same wage. My negotiations were so poor, I didn't do any better!

Johnny Haynes was the other big story in 1961 because the Fulham inside-forward became the first £100-a-week footballer. This opened the doors wide, and I clearly remember wondering what it would bring us in 30 or 40 years' time. But when Haynes was on £100 a week, most other players stayed on the old maximum wage of £20 for a long while, so far as I can recall. It may have been £25 for the average pro and £30 for the good ones, but it wasn't a dramatic improvement in most cases. Haynes was England captain, of course, and there were rumours that Spurs and a lot of other big clubs wanted to sign him. So Tommy Trinder, the Fulham chairman, decided that, to keep Haynes, he had to break the £100-a-week barrier. As a professional comedian, Trinder was more aware than most chairmen of the showbusiness rule that your star attraction should get star wages. Someone with a more conservative sort of mind would have increased Haynes' pay to just £25 or £30, and Fulham might have lost him. But with Trinder being a showbiz man and understanding that kind of situation, he was streets ahead of most people in football and their narrow-mindedness.

The highest wage I ever earned as a footballer was £80 a week, and I didn't finish my playing career until about 18 years ago. It's not that long ago, or at least it doesn't seem it. I had a bit more offered to me at Crystal Palace – about £100, I think – but then I wasn't playing for long there before I became a coach. So it's amazing how quickly the whole situation has changed in the last 18 years alone. There was no sense of grievance over pay among the players of my generation because we didn't know any better. I think that's one of the reasons our professional attitudes, in lots of ways, have not been as good as those on the Continent. By professional attitudes, I mean the approach to the job. That is to say, keeping your body in good condition and turning up on time for training, for meals and for the team coach. Our self-discipline has not been as tight as the continentals', I believe, because the value of the player was not recognized for a long time. Basically, we were doing it because we loved doing it, not for the money. I think it's only now, when the wages are really going up in comparison to Italy, France, Spain etc., that players are thinking about what they eat and drink and making sure they train properly and look after themselves. That's because they know an extra two or three years on their contract could bring them as much as £1.5 million. What I always say to players is: 'If you owned a corner shop, would you throw all your stock through the window into the street? Of course you wouldn't. So look after your body, because that's your corner shop.'

When people accuse the English professional footballer of being less dedicated than his continental counterpart, more likely to drink heavily in other words, they overlook the cultural differences between the two of them. There's a pub culture in England, let's not pretend otherwise. We are known for our pubs here, and I would say the nearest country to us in that respect would be Germany. I remember Gerd Muller, his country's greatest goal scorer, in Canada, when I was playing there with Tottenham. What a beer drinker he was! I've never seen anything like it. He was a real top man at that. Basically it's a question of what everyone else does around you. Your environment takes over. If you are brought up in a family that's a pub family, as I was, and uncles and aunties come over on a Saturday night after the pub closes with crates of beer and sing round the piano, it's difficult not to regard that as the norm. By comparison, relaxation for a young footballer in one of the Latin countries of Europe is sitting in the sun chatting quietly in family surroundings. If there's any alcoholic drink being consumed at all, you are talking about a bottle of wine drunk slowly with a meal. Everyone wants to talk in company, but different nationalities do it differently. I think the Spanish can do it without any drink at all. We English, on the other hand, actually aim for the pub as if the pub is the reason to talk. It's like the old saying about us eating to live and the Latin countries living to eat. That could apply just as well to drinking.

If the young Englishman of 30 or 40 years ago was only getting £20 a week to be a professional footballer and having to make a four-hour round trip to training by public transport every day, he wouldn't see any real reason to change his habits, I suppose. It was nice, and it was good fun. But if, all of a sudden, you are told that if you change those habits, son, watch what you are eating and drinking and go to bed early at night, you'll earn £15,000 a week, you might look at it a bit differently. I think the penny has finally dropped with English footballers because there is so much money to be made through self-denial. Interviewed not so long ago by the football writer, Patrick Barclay, Chelsea's John Spencer said: 'I . . . realized I'd not been been behaving as a footballer should. Without going over the top, I'd been drinking and eating the wrong things and so on. It's my opinion that a young player at a big club should be totally dedicated. I think you'll find more and more players are avoiding alcohol these days. If you want to stay in the game as long as Ray Wilkins, sacrificing ten years of your life makes sense, especially now the financial rewards are so great.' So they are beginning to realize it's in their own interests to look after themselves and they are working it out. They are getting people to represent them in negotiating contracts with their clubs and with sponsors. They also have accountants to make sure their earnings are invested properly and that they are not exploited financially, which has happened to so many players over the years. It's a definite change of attitude, and it's what they've been doing in Italy and Spain for quite a while. I stick to that view, by the way, despite all the so-called evidence of drunken revelry among the England players during the pre-European Championship trip to the Far East. It was all grossly exaggerated.

My own experience in Spain from 1984 to 1987 was remarkable, not least in terms of one of the reasons for my appointment. Barcelona said they wanted an English coach, and I asked why. The answer, which you get from most directors anywhere, was that their team was losing because the players weren't fit. They said they wanted them fit like the English. Well, the super-fitness of the English is a bit of a myth. I mean, the players are fit, but they are also mentally strong. We keep going even when it hurts. Hurting can be a stitch in your side or a pain in your lungs. It can also be losing 1–0 or 2–0. We'll still keep going at 2–0. The classic example of what I'm talking about was the 1966 World Cup final. England were leading 2–1 when West Germany equalized just before the death. That would have crushed the spirit of many national teams, but not the English. They roll up their sleeves, go out in extra time and win the game all over again.

Anyway, I took the Barcelona players training to Andorra, and they were the fittest I have ever seen. I mean, really fantastic. I still had my old timings of English teams, and the Spaniards were not only quicker but did more runs. They were all-round fitter players because the game was their life and they always did exactly what they were told. They were always on time, certainly. If you had any problems with lateness on the bus or at meals, it was always with the three or four foreign players in the squad. The Spanish boys have great respect for professionalism, and I understand the Italians are the same. They see professionalism as something to be proud of, not just a question of earning a living, and they don't abuse their business. It's taken us a long while to get to the same point, but I think we are getting there now.

Personally speaking, I have no problem with the big salaries footballers receive today. I've got to say I still feel fortunate to have had the times I did as a player. I thought I was far more fortunate than the people who played ten years before us. Great players like Tom Finney and Stanley Matthews didn't get anything like they deserved financially. We were better paid than them, and now the present generation are miles in front of us. It's just the luck of the draw. But there's a price to be paid by today's professional footballers for their wealth. Everything you do is replayed over and over again on television, and the pressure is intense. That's why the players get these enormous amounts of money. I think it's understandable if TV is paying a fortune to the clubs. It's only natural it should be passed on to the players, because without the players the clubs don't get it.

Now we've got another phase of the saga upon us as a result of the European Court of Justice's decision in favour of Jean-Marc Bosman. As you might expect, in view of my PFA background, I'm all in favour of a player being free to move wherever he wants without a fee at the end of his contract. I think it will take the sting out of the transfer market. It will bring £8 million transfers down to about £2 million during contracts because clubs will be reluctant to invest huge sums in players they may get nothing back for. People will object on the grounds that the players who are free agents can cash in by negotiating much bigger signing-on fees, but most of the money's going to the players anyway. The important thing is that you haven't got to find £8 million up front. The clubs will complain that they can't sell their players for £8 million, but they haven't got to buy them for £8 million, either.

At the moment, clubs are spending more than they can afford, and it's going to end in disaster. I wonder how many clubs are self-financing, because that's what's required. Everyone's going to shake their heads because clubs will be worth less as a result of the drop in the value of their players, but I think that might not be a bad thing. It would get some common sense back into the game. I'd want some form of compensation or transfer fee during a contract, but not at the end. It's just the same principle as Chelsea getting Ruud Gullit at the end of his contract and not having to pay a huge fee for him.

People say complete freedom of contract would undermine the whole structure of the game, but I think it's being undermined already by an inflated transfer market. Whereas Liverpool, for example, used to buy four players to strengthen their team, £8 million can only buy them one now and maybe they've still got weaknesses in three positions. They can't spread the load like they did before. The market was top-heavy at £8 million, and it wasn't going to stop there. It's going to go even higher than the £15 million Newcastle paid for Alan Shearer*, unless someone says let's cap transfers – which you can't do. It's almost impossible because the clubs won't keep their word on any agreement of that sort. They've tried it before, but one big club broke ranks and paid what everyone had agreed they wouldn't. So what's the alternative? One solution is for the PFA to let the clubs go and buy as many foreign players as they want. Then they'll get better players for less money, but they are going to put their own members out of work. They can't have it all ways, though.

As when a limited form of freedom of contract – freedom of movement is a better description – came in 18 years ago, the clubs will have to weigh the situation up thoroughly. Before 1978, the clubs owned the players and they couldn't get away. Then they had to make judgments about how long to sign them for. They went for ten-year deals, but realized that was too long and would put clubs like Bristol City out of business. City decided the best way to deal with freedom of contract was to sign their better players on ten-year contracts. Then they got relegated and found themselves struggling to honour expensive agreements on a

*Bosman will not mean a complete end to very big transfers like this. Market forces will ensure they occur from time to time, but the general trend in fees will be downwards.

much-reduced income. The clubs responded to that scare by going for shorter deals, only to worry about the players slipping away too quickly. They've got to think it through, really think about the personality of the player and what he's like. Is he someone you can rely on? They've got to do their homework more than ever now. The whole operation has got to be more professional.

As I mentioned earlier, the independent tribunal came in with our form of freedom of contract. People still complain about it, but you are always going to have that when there is money at stake. The alternative of a multiplication formula, which was strongly favoured in some quarters as a means of calculating a player's transfer fee, could never cater for talent. It could cater for age and for wages, but never for ability. That was its weakness. A rather complicated idea, the 'multiplier' involved calculations based on a player's age, the wages he was earning and whether he was moving up or down the divisions.

I'm in no doubt that the overall effect of the changes has been beneficial. You could argue the pendulum has swung too far in the other direction, perhaps, but let's not forget the player used to be little short of a slave. He was exploited and the only real money-earner was the club. The fans support the club, but they come to see the players. That's what the entertainment's about, just as you go to the theatre to see the actors and actresses. That's what brings you out from home. I think it's getting so huge a lot of people, including players and agents, don't really know what players are worth. They just hear what someone else is getting and say my player's a bit better. They just keep squeezing and squeezing.

The clubs have got to make hard and fast decisions about their budgets. Individuals financing clubs is all very well; but once they pull their finance out, that club's going to be left to its own devices and won't be able to cope. That's what's happened in Italy. Despite all the money they generated, and they took millions and millions of lire through the turnstiles, a lot of them still couldn't pay the wages in recent years. It's one of those lessons you learn as a child: it doesn't matter how much you want it, or how lovely it is or how hungry you are, you can't have it if you can't afford it. That's the way it works.

I don't blame the players. I don't blame anyone who tries to get the best deal they can. Especially footballers, who have such a short career. The clubs are obviously agreeing to these things, but they want their bread buttered on both sides. Tottenham, for instance, said not too long ago that they didn't want to pay more than £4.5 million for a player; but when they tried to sell one, they wanted £6 million for him. If the clubs want to keep the transfer market under control, they've got to do something about it. Complete freedom of contract will bring it down all right. If the players are overpaid, it's the clubs' fault for overpaying them. If you pay them what they ask, you can't blame them for asking for it. They are not paid more than players in other countries. And if they can see Premier League clubs getting more and more money through gates and television, they'll want some of it.

It's sometimes argued that the players have alienated themselves from the fans by pushing up their earnings so high they have nothing in common any more. In other words, the bond was closer when there wasn't such a big gap between what the two of them earned. But I thought the relationship was slightly more mysterious then. There was little or no contact between player and fan. If you were lucky, you saw a star coming out of the dressing-room and you got an autograph. They were just Saturday men, weren't they? You didn't have television, so you didn't know much about them. All you got about these great performers was football reports in the papers. Now, the fans feel they almost know them personally, they are on the television so much. So when they see Alan Shearer, say, it's a case of 'Hello, Al. How are you?'

Even so, it was still big time in the 1950s and 60s to be with a club in the old First Division of the Football League. You had your name in the paper and fame in your immediate area, but you weren't nationally known as players are today. You only saw Sheffield Wednesday, for example, when they came to your ground. They could have been wrapped up in cotton wool for the rest of the year until you played them a second time. But now supporters see so much football on television, they know as much about the opposition as their own team and manager. They actually know how they are going to play and what they are going to do. So it's not quite so esoteric as before. Back in the 1940s and 50s, it was like waiting for the circus to come to town. And there was great disappointment if the opposition's star player – Stan Matthews, for example – wasn't fit or available to play in the game against your team. You didn't get the chance to see him again until the following season.

10

Some say the players and the fans were far closer socially in those days, and there was some truth in the stories that, in the 1950s and 60s, the players used to drink in the same pubs as the fans. But if you had 80,000 crowds, they weren't all in the same pub, were they? There might be 50 or 60 fans and a few players. That was a little bit the case when I was at Chelsea, but more so at Tottenham. Dave Mackay and Alan Gilzean, they were always in the Bell and Hare pub near White Hart Lane. There would be about half a dozen players, not many more. The punters knew they would be there and would aim for that pub if they fancied a drink with them. Later, the Chelsea players became famous, or notorious even, for drinking in the Queen's Elm in the Fulham Road. But that was in the 1970s, when the players started to earn big money.

There was never much trouble between players and fans in those circumstances, so far as I can recall, but I wouldn't like to bank on it today. It wasn't all sweetness and light on the trains, though. Until the main motorway network was completed in the late 1960s, all the football teams used to travel to away matches by train. As a kid, I used to go to Kings Cross to collect autographs, because you might find a couple of London teams travelling north from there on a Saturday morning. As a player, you would find your own sup-porters would be on board, too, and I've seen arguments or even fights break out because of fans abusing players verbally after a bad result. That's one of the reasons teams now travel everywhere by coach. Increasingly, the players have become cocooned in their own little world, away from the pub and away from the train. It's odd, really, considering the fan and the player have never been closer in some ways because of TV, but that familiarity has also helped to drive them apart. There's been a big cultural change over the years, and it's very unlikely now the average fan would know where the players would be after a game, particularly on the London scene. It certainly wouldn't be around the ground.

One of the things I noticed when I went to Barcelona was that they didn't have a players' lounge, as they do at most English clubs, a place where you could take guests and have a few beers after the match. Relaxing like that wasn't discouraged by any means, because the management felt that if players wanted to let their hair down the time to do it was after the game. But as there were subterranean car-parks at Barcelona, you could go unseen to your car and drive off somewhere through an exit away from the fans. So you'd go off to your favourite restaurant, out of town or wherever, with friends you wanted to be with. In other words, you'd be able to relax out of the public eye.

Other high-profile people such as politicians and film stars have no trouble distancing themselves from their public, but most professional footballers are working-class boys. So they gravitate naturally towards their old haunts. I remember going back to one of my local pubs in Dagenham when I was playing for Chelsea in the 1960s and a guy I knew said: 'You're supposed to be in the big time now. So what are you doing here?' It was a silly question, but you can see what they feel. They feel you should be drinking in more glamorous surroundings, and are offended somehow if you're not. Perhaps they also fear you are going to come the high and mighty with them.

One of the biggest myths, in my opinion, was all that stuff about the bright lights of London and how they could destroy a player's career. The reality, so far as players with London clubs were concerned, was that we never went into London itself. If you lived in Hertfordshire, as most of the Tottenham and Arsenal players did, you went to the pubs in Hertfordshire or, if you were really daring, Loughton or Chigwell in Essex. No one actually lived in London. I think Gary Lineker, in the 1980s, was the first player I'd heard of who had set up home there.

Another myth was that the hangers-on were corrupting the players. When I was at Tottenham, the only time we went into London was if Morris Keston, the staunch Spurs fan I mentioned earlier, invited us to the boxing at the Anglo-American Sporting Club at his expense. I thought the players were hanging on to Morris, because he was paying for everything. He was the actual big, wealthy supporter who loved the company of the players, but he wasn't hanging on: he didn't need them. To be honest, they all thought they were going to get something for nothing.

It was far more of an attraction to go to Liverpool, Birmingham or, certainly, Manchester. You could be there rocking the night away until 3 a.m., but you couldn't afford to go into London. People go on about the nightclubs of London, but London was always full of clip joints. It was £300 for a bottle of Scotch, and all that; and as I've said, I never earned more than £80 a week as a player. So it really is an absolute myth about the bright lights of London. If you went out with Denis Law and the rest of them in

Manchester at that time, you'd have a night out you couldn't forget after a football match. In those days of train travel, of course, clubs would stay overnight for an away fixture in midweek.

To be fair, if we had gone into London when we were players, hardly anyone would have recognized us. That's why I think moving to London earlier might have saved George Best's career. He could have lost himself in the capital in a way that was impossible in a much smaller city like Manchester. George couldn't go anywhere there without being pestered to death. People would even slice the tyres of the sports car he had then. He sometimes used to have to jump out of the back windows of pubs or clubs to escape. I was there one night when he did that. He jumped out the toilet window of this pub because he was getting supporters coming in and giving him bother. But you can go into London even now and perhaps go to Knightsbridge and areas like that, the Sloaney end of the market, and they wouldn't have a clue who most people were in football. In fact, I thought that if Gazza had returned to London when he left Lazio, and used his loaf, he would have had no problems whatsoever. If he'd resisted the temptation of actually wanting to be seen in certain areas, he could have lived where nobody knew who he was and gone to private clubs where no one would bother him at all. When Gazza was at Tottenham he didn't live in London. But Lineker, another high-profile player, set up home in St John's Wood and nobody bothered him and his family there. So this time round, I'd have thought, Gazza would have had to live in London itself. He couldn't have gone so easily into the local pubs in Hertfordshire, where he lived before, without someone wanting to dig him up.

The status of the English professional footballer has changed out of all recognition during the period in question. About 20 years ago, Italian footballers were on the same level as film stars in their country. Ours weren't, but they are now. In common with a lot of other people, I've always felt that anything that's going on in America comes here later. And as far as football is concerned, the same applies to Italy. I understand Lee Chapman, the much-travelled striker, is a wine buff, for instance. He developed his palate while playing in France, I am told. That sort of interest illustrates to some extent the change there has been in the lifestyle of the English footballer in the last 50 years. You've got a kind of split area here. There are those who go abroad and make it, and those who go abroad and don't. There are the David Platts, the Chapmans and the Linekers, who actually welcome the culture of the country they are playing in, learn the language and enjoy the way the people live. Then you get the Mark Hugheses, the Gazzas, the Ian Rushes, who say 'I'd rather stay where I am and be up the pub with the boys.' They feel comfortable at home; it's their upbringing and there's nothing wrong with that. I hate the sort of snobbery that says you shouldn't go to a pub or sing in the karaoke. That's what they say about me; but if singing a song is the worst thing I do, it's not too bad. Even so, that difference separates players, sorts them out, and they should look at themselves very carefully before they make the move abroad.

It would be easy to generalize and say that Lineker, Platt and Chapman adapted more quickly than others to life on the Continent because they all came from middle-class backgrounds. But it's not as simple as that. John Charles was as working class as they come, yet no British footballer was more successful in Italy than the gentle giant from Swansea. Basically, it all depends on the individual and his capacity for adapting to change. It would certainly be wrong to imagine English football is attracting floods of middle-class boys because the financial rewards are now so great. The gentrification of the crowds has not been mirrored on the pitch. Basically, the game still draws on the working class for its raw material. It's the ones that are hungry who make it. Like boxers, they are prepared to suffer to get where they want to get. They are ready to fight their way out of the poverty trap. The clubs should be doing more to help by making 15-year-olds into better people. At Ajax and Barcelona, they are taught how to behave and what is expected of them. I don't think clubs here have educated players enough in life after football. They should be taught all the things they need to know, not just for a good football career but for a good life.

When I was at Crystal Palace, I tried to get every player learning a trade with companies the directors were connected with. A couple saw the full course out, but most of them did not. That's because it's too late to be teaching players things like that at 16 or 17. The process has to start at five or six, when you can impress upon them that, if they pay attention to their studies, they can be a footballer or do whatever they want to do. It's got to come from the families, and the schools must educate them to have a good, solid life.

When I was a player, there were always practical jokes, always fun. Then it started getting personal. You hear some of the things people say now and you can't believe it. When I was at Tottenham, some of the things the younger players would say about their wives and mothers were disgusting. I couldn't stand it. It really turned me off football for a while. I love the game, but I didn't need all that. I mean, it was truly awful. Graeme Le Saux, on the other hand, is an intelligent boy and the more of that type of player you can get, the more chance you've got.

I've heard it argued that continental footballers are more intelligent than ours because their football doesn't have to compete with rugby and cricket for the brightest young athletes. That's not entirely true, though, in countries such as France, Italy and Romania, where rugby thrives. The suggestion is, of course, that continental football is able to call on a greater number of middle-class boys, who are more intelligent by definition because they are better educated and brought up. But how do you then explain the intelligence of the Ajax players, many of whom are the children of poor immigrants from Surinam? The answer is that they are taught how to behave on and off the pitch by the thorough Amsterdam club.

The failure of some of our best players to make the same impact abroad as they have here has led to unfavourable technical comparisons between the English and continental footballer. But, if you look back over the 50 years in question, we have been on a par with the continentals, to say the least, for much of the time. That was because of the way we learned the game as youngsters in the streets and in the parks. Naturally competitive, we put the coats down for goals and seemed to know exactly how much space we needed for four-a-side, eight-a-side, ten-a-side or fifteen-a-side matches. Looking back now, it's amazing how instinctively it all came to us. In fact, I think the kids of my generation, those born around the end of the Second World War, were very lucky to have been brought up in that period of time.

What happened next was that people got a bit more prosperous, the streets were no longer empty, but full of cars, and the nights got more dangerous. All of a sudden, worried families didn't want their children out playing football in the streets and parks until darkness fell. Meanwhile, the countries who had lagged behind us in terms of skill, like the Scandinavians, were catching up by providing their youngsters with the proper facilities. In Sweden, Denmark and Norway, you couldn't move for good facilities where the kids were safe. Because of their bad weather, everything was indoors. So they have always been able to train every night in winter; and the security is there, and the parking. Mums and dads have no trouble dropping their children off and picking them up.

In Scandinavia, too, the football authorities got government grants because the government understood how important it was to be good at sports and realized what a massive, world-wide operation and influence football is. That's something our politicians still don't seem to understand. They want to win over the masses for their votes, but fail to woo all those football supporters just sitting there in front of them. In Spain, King Juan Carlos and the President will be at major matches, and the people are impressed by that. So it serves a political purpose. I thought John Major saw it early on when he declared he was a Chelsea supporter, which he is, but he didn't really do anything about it. I don't think Tony Blair is really a football person, but he does seem to have spotted the game's political potential judging by the opportunities he's taken to speak at major functions and attend matches.

What everyone, politicians included, has got to recognize is that the provision of proper facilities is the most important change required if English football is to re-establish itself as a major force in the world. It really upsets me when I hear we have been building on playing fields, which reduces our facilities. Here I am pleading for an increase in facilities, and they are actually reducing them! So the kids sit there, and they've got no playing fields. They've got nothing to look forward to. They can't play in the streets, so where do they go? They feel their lives are useless, and they all sit on street corners. It's an excuse to take drugs and opt out instead of going forward.

A couple of years ago, I had to deal with a demonstration at Lancaster Gate by schoolteachers and schoolchildren against the FA's attempt to replace 11-a-side matches for younger kids with smaller-sided games. But that's not the biggest problem, said the deputation, the biggest problem is facilities. When I asked why, I was told by a teacher from Canary Wharf, in Docklands, that because the Prime Minister had insisted sport be part of the national curriculum, he had to take his pupils by coach to Enfield, in north London, a journey of at least half-an-hour, to find the nearest available playing field. It seems all the outdoor facilities the schools in inner London once had have gone. It's sickening, it really is. What the hell are we doing? Not only are we not leading the field, not only are we not catching up, but our lack of policies, lack of political leadership and lack of desire mean we are actually miles behind.

Facilities, coaching and environment make all the difference because all boys, whether they be from Europe, Africa, South America or Asia, have the same opportunity to make it as a footballer. Any raw material, any youngster brought up in any country has the same possibilities. We get back here to the old question of whether people are natural-born footballers, or whether they progress because of their environment and the competitive element in their neighbourhood. What I am saying is, if we had taken Bobby Charlton at two months and put him in Australia or Weybridge instead of Ashington, would he have been the same Bobby Charlton? He would have had his natural instinct for ball games, but as he grew up in his different environment he would have looked round to see what he would like to do. His father could have bought him golf clubs or a tennis racket, and he might never have kicked a football.

In my own case, I grew up in an area of east London with the likes of Jimmy Greaves, Bobby Moore and Martin Peters. It was unbelievable: Les Allen (the former Chelsea, Tottenham and QPR striker and father of Clive), Ken Brown (the former West Ham defender and Norwich manager) and I all lived in the same road. So it's the competitive element that drives you on. You want to stretch yourself, you want to be better than the next guy. Where we go wrong is in believing that, for some reason, English kids are born with a natural advantage when it comes to football. Why should our youngsters be better equipped than anyone else to play the game just because we invented it 100-odd years ago? What have 100-odd years got to do with the boy born yesterday?

We have to recognize that, if we want to be good at football, we've got to make sure the youngsters are brought up the right way. That's the key area. At long last, we're able to enrol them as young as nine in the schools of excellence; but while that power struggle over age was going on between the English Schools FA and the Football Association – a legacy of our long footballing history – countries like Holland were permitting talented school-boys to go to their local football club at one o'clock in the afternoon for coaching. To be honest, we have had a lot of very skilful players come through in spite of the system, not because of it. I remember when I was coach to the England Under-21 team, I asked Glenn Hoddle what had made him want to master the ball to the extent he could. He'd seen the Brazilians, he said: that was his motivation. He saw a picture of what was wonderful and he wanted to emulate it.

If we are not now producing as many skilful players as the continentals, it's because we have never really replaced those games in the streets and the parks with something that teaches kids the game in the same way. In many ways, we have failed the kids with our coaching. When English fans see the superior technique of players from abroad, they accuse English footballers of not practising hard enough. But the actual practice has to come at a younger age. Results don't matter at that level, whereas a lot of what you've got to do at the top is influenced by the fact that the event is everything. In most sports, the nearer the event, the less work you do. Otherwise, as Bill Shankly and Bob Paisley used to say at Liverpool, you leave it all on the training field. So you've got to be training perhaps two or three times a day as youngsters; but when they make the first team, you have to concentrate on getting them right tactically and physically.

If you leave it to the players themselves, some will always show more dedication than others. If they get an opportunity to go somewhere that's a bit more attractive, they'll take the soft option. But if you just say: 'You're back this afternoon. Who's paying the wages?', they are there. You've really got to command the situation. If it is the case that the English player doesn't come back in the afternoon to work on his skills, it's not necessarily his fault. I think it's the fault of the coach or the club. A lot of coaches in a lot of areas don't do enough coaching. They play games to fill up the days to save them doing coaching. Then we find they are over-playing and they've got too many games on their roster, particularly the youngsters. The good teaching's got to take place at the younger end of the scale; but people don't really understand coaching, so they don't really want to know about it and it's all boring. Especially to directors.

Training routines are basically the same today as they were

when I was a player 20 or 30 years ago. Players train in the mornings and have the afternoon off. At least, I know that's the usual programme for the first teams. With the number of games we play in this country, you don't want to be working the players too hard physically. Some people have their own routines, of course. When I first went to Chelsea, and Allan Harris and I were in the dressing-room cleaning the boots, I can remember Jimmy Greaves, the great goalscorer, would never train as an outfield player – he was always in goal. His God-given ability was such that he was a super player at 17, and football was always a bit of fun for Jim.

There's a story about him I told in my autobiography and I think it's worth repeating here. He was one of the few players who owned a car during my early years in the game. It was hardly a limousine, though. He had a Ford Popular, a little pale blue one, and he used to pick me up in Dagenham and take me to games in it. I remember being on the way to one home game against West Brom, and he took me to a place called the Dinner Gong at Gants Hill in Essex for a pre-match meal. I'd only played about three games for the Chelsea first team then, and was careful about what I ate before a match. So I just settled for grilled chicken. But Jim had roast beef and Yorkshire pudding, potatoes, the works. I couldn't believe what I was seeing. Come the game, we won 6-1 and Jim scored five of the goals. So I began to wonder whether I was doing it all wrong. I suppose I was particularly dedicated as a player, really. I never used to have a drink and fell out with my mates a bit because I wouldn't go drinking with them. I made up for it later in life, but I did try to do everything correctly then.

Jim, on the other hand, was a rascal. But it was very strange with him. He never really cared about football at all, the way he trained and all that, until he was near the end of his career. It was almost as though he realized too late what he had, because he started rowing with referees and getting sent off. Then he got on the drink. You wonder what happened. Being a midfield player, I'd always be round the referee trying to wear him down verbally, but Jim would say things like, 'Take no notice of him, ref. It's not that important.' It used to get me annoyed that he didn't care more about it. But when he realized what he was about to lose, he got angry and aggressive. Something must have happened, because he got bitter. I don't know what it was.

It was certainly a far cry from those early days of ours at Chelsea when Albert Tennant, the coach, would tell the players to do six laps then stand and wait for them to finish. Even then, Jim would shout back: 'Two'll be enough, Albert!' Nobody really cared about improving their game. They came into training just to show they were still in the country, I think. I can remember Bill Robertson, the goalkeeper, saying: 'I'm going out for training, but I'll be back before the door slams!' Then there was the time the captain, Derek Saunders, went out with his tracksuit top pulled right up his neck as high as it would go. It was a Friday and the players used to do what they liked the day before a match, even walk around the track smoking cigarettes. Anyway, when the zip on Derek's top started to come down gradually, you could see he had his collar and tie on underneath! He was obviously after a quick getaway.

Basically, the training in those days was nothing. It was just a practice match on a Tuesday – there were certain people they used to call Tuesday morning players because they were great in practices, but didn't perform if they got into the team – and there was hardly any coaching. It was just running round the track and a six-a-side. There are still lots of clubs who work at six-a-sides and there's nothing wrong with that. It's one way of practising the things you have to do. I just believe there's lots more that can be done, and I think the continental sides have proved that.

Ted Drake, the former Arsenal and England centre-forward, was the manager of Chelsea when I first arrived. He was a charming man, and a man of passion who cared about the club, but I have to say there was very little teaching available under his management. Then Tommy Docherty came in 1962, and he was one of the new breed of managers. The FA coaching badge was just starting to be dealt out and worked for, and Tommy did bring in a type of coaching. He would do bits and pieces, and it was quite interesting. He used to say: 'If you've got any questions, ask me', so I was always asking questions. He didn't really like it, though: he thought you were questioning his methods. But all I was wanting to do was find out more about the game.

It didn't get really exciting at Chelsea until Tommy brought in Dave Sexton as coach. Dave was very good, and that was really the beginning from my point of view. It was the time when Don Howe went to Arsenal and we all started getting involved with seeing what was going on at Lilleshall*. Things were starting to happen. A lot of the time, you played six-a-side because it was easy to set up. Anyone can do that and just keep ticking over. Gradually, however, we began experimenting with set-pieces, working out how to make the most of a free-kick or a corner. Then the six-a-sides started to contain some functional work. Because the players used to think training was boring, the coach had to do a deal with them. He'd promise them a six-a-side in return for doing what he wanted them to do. In future, I think, nothing will be wasted. Everything will be geared to winning the next game. You'll work on the opposition's strengths and weaknesses, and where your own strengths can capitalize on their weaknesses. Coaches will spend a lot of time watching videos, weighing up the opposition and making sure they cut down the possibilities of losing the game.

A lot of English clubs have done athletics work. The ones I was in charge of always did. I learned the value of it from Ron Jones, the former captain of the Great Britain Olympic team, who trained us at QPR. Malcolm Allison also put a lot of emphasis on athletics with his successful Manchester City side in the late 1960s. Now, though, some clubs are starting to employ fitness trainers to give their players the sort of specialized physical preparation they get abroad. Nottingham Forest is one of them. There's also much greater attention paid to players' diets. Manchester United, for instance, were worried because Paul Ince couldn't seem to last the full 90 minutes following his transfer to Old Trafford from West Ham. When they discovered Ince was living on junk food, they called in a nutritionist. He put the player on a diet that obviously helped to turn him into the midfield powerhouse for United we became used to seeing. (I wonder what he would have made of Jimmy Greaves' eating habits!) Nutrition, sports medicine and sports science will play an increasingly important part in the future of English football. Because the fitter you are, the fewer injuries you will get. People think the two are not inter-related, but they are. Fatigue will cause injuries.

To sum up, the English footballer of today is almost unrecognizable from the man with the centre-parting and the baggy pants who restarted League football in 1946. It's much more than a

*A national sports centre in Shropshire.

question of appearance, though hairstyles, playing kits, boots and balls have certainly changed out of all recognition in the last 50 years. The man of the people, who would travel to home matches on the bus and pop into the local for a pint with his mates, is now a man apart. Freed from wage and contractual restraints by his union and the courts, he has been taken upmarket and turned into a demi-god by the projection and vast wealth television and sponsors have given the top clubs and their players. So, still being an ordinary working-class lad at heart, he needs the help of agents and accountants to handle all the money and fame he has attracted. The high stakes he plays for have made him realize he needs to be more professional than ever. If he watches what he eats and drinks, and makes sure he keeps in peak physical condition, he can extend his career and increase his bank balance substantially. It could be argued that he doesn't deserve such big money because the skill level of English football hasn't gone up anything like as fast as the wages over the 50 years in question. Many would contend that it has actually gone down. But I wouldn't blame him for that as much as I would the FA, the clubs and the coaches. That's where the responsibility for the decline of English football really lies.

Chapter Two

Great Players

What makes a great player? Come to that, how do you assess the ability of any footballer, good, bad or indifferent? Is it just a matter of opinion based on experience, or is there actually a formula that could make the whole process a little more scientific and a little more accurate? I happen to think there is, because I was one of a number of people who worked hard to find it. In the summer of 1995, after England had played Brazil, Sweden and Japan in the Umbro Cup, I took part in a brainstorming session in the United States. It was organized by Umbro, the world-famous sportswear company. They invited Pele, Louis van Gaal, the Ajax coach, Shu Kamo, Japan's coach, Peter Gooding, of the American coaching association, and myself.

Combined with Umbro's own top men, it was a kind of think-tank designed to come up with a vision of the game in ten years' time. The idea was to find ways of maintaining football's massive, world-wide popularity: it was an exercise in consciously planning for the future. It's like being in any other business. When everything's going well, you can't afford just to sit back and smoke cigars. All of a sudden, you realize your competitors are coming up in the outside lane, and you have to keep getting ahead all the time so you can kill them off.

Anyway, we really hammered away at the job for four days, and one of the things that emerged from it all was a way of assessing the ability of footballers. We actually got a formula down on paper. It comes in four parts: technical, tactical, personality and pace. Those headings, I think, cover all the ingredients required to make a good player, and you give marks out of ten for each section. Basically, you are looking for a pass mark of 32 points out of 40. Colin Malam and I tried the system out using Tom Finney as a test case, and the old Preston Plumber came out of it with a remarkable 37 points, the highest mark I could recall up to then. Tottenham's Darren Anderton, with 35 points, also did particularly well. Some other current players were not quite so impressive, but we won't go into that here. You might find it interesting and revealing, though, to apply the test yourself to the players in your own local team.

At the very least, it provides a starting point for naming the greatest players to have graced English football in the past half-century. I used a very similar system when I was a club manager. I wanted players on the 33/34 mark if I was going to spend a lot of money on them, and I don't think I made too many mistakes over the 18 or 19 years I did it, provided I had the time to apply my own little test of quality. If you look back at the big buys I made, Paul Gascoigne and Gary Lineker, for instance, I don't think many were too far out. I'm not being big-headed in saying that: I'm simply trying to establish that here is a system for measuring the ability of footballers, quite a difficult thing to do, with a reasonable degree of accuracy.

There is a considerable difference, of course, between being a good player and a great one. Great, I think, is being outstanding in every one of the four categories in the system, although certain players, like Bobby Moore, make up for lack of pace with speed of thought. Certainly, if you can get two tens for technique and personality, it's got to take you into greatness. It's usually the most talented players who have a question-mark against their personality. By personality, I mean strength of character and leadership qualities, not charm. Conversely, those with the strongest personalities often haven't got it technically. Tony Adams, for instance, must get a ten for personality, but you couldn't give him more than six or seven for technical ability. That's not entirely Tony's fault, though, as I will explain later. Tom Finney, on the other hand, would get a ten on personality and a ten on technical. That makes him great. Great in national terms, at least. I think we've got to make a distinction here between national greatness and international greatness. If we are going to talk about the truly great players since the war, I don't think we can look much beyond Pele and Diego Maradona. Maybe Johan Cruyff and Franz Beckenbauer as well, but nobody else qualifies for a level that you have to make greater than great. Monumental might be the word for it: people who are over and above what you would normally describe as great.

Maradona's history of misbehaviour might prompt some to give him a low mark for personality, but he's always been a good team player. At Barcelona, they all spoke well of him, never mind what anybody else said. And when he scored that goal for Argentina in the 1994 World Cup finals, all his team-mates ran towards him like a hurricane, didn't they, when he was going mad to the television cameras? They were all behind him, and you could see he was popular in the team. Overall, Pele was probably the better player; but you could argue that Maradona never had as many top-class team-mates around him as Pele did in 1970. I thought his performance in that game in the 1986 World Cup in Mexico, when he beat all those England players in that run half the length of the pitch, was outstanding.

No doubt some will insist that Sir Stanley Matthews ought to be up there on the very top rung with Pele and Maradona, but I'm afraid I can't agree. Apart from anything else, he never dominated a World Cup with his genius in the way those two exceptional players did. I'm not blind to his exceptional ability, but I do think you have to take into account the way the game has changed, particularly in the 30 years since Sir Stan retired in 1965 at the remarkably advanced age of 50. It is much faster, much harder physically and much more sophisticated tactically than it was when the 'Wizard of the Dribble' was casting his spell.

I mean, you look at that 1953 Bolton v. Blackpool FA Cup final now, and it's like Subbuteo. I'm playing against you, and the others are just standing watching. Then the ball goes to those two, and they play against each other. And the goalkeeping errors! They were unbelievable! The shared memory was that they had real players in those days; but our memories were of growing up, and you are really celebrating yourself and your youth, aren't you? When you get older, you hear these young whipper-snappers talking about their stars and you try to put them in their place by telling them how much better the players of your day were. I'm fairly sure the stars of the early post-war years would have been stars now if they had been brought up in the modern game. But the reality, as you can see in the films of the time, is that their football was actually awful by comparison with today's game.

At the same time, we have to remember that everything is relative. I was reminded of that historical rule by a television documentary I watched on '100 years of the cinema'. They had the actual film camera invented by the Lumière brothers, two of the early pioneers, in the late 19th century. It was just a little box, and they ran it again in a big hotel room 100 years later. You see the great films of today and what they can do – the special effects – and it's fantastic. But it might be an easier achievement than 100 years ago, when the film was all crackly. It was actually a little magical that they could do even what they achieved so long ago. The same principle applies to the 1953 final and today's football. Nowadays, you've got a light ball, boots that are as light and comfortable as bedroom slippers and a kit that hardly weighs anything at all. But in those days they had big, heavy boots and played with a leather ball that got like a lump of lead in the wet. The ball had a lace in it, and the lace hurt if you caught the ball wrong as you headed it. It was all handicaps, really. It was almost as if someone had decided to handicap the players of that era because they were too good.

Their matches were certainly watched by huge crowds. In 1949–50, Football League attendances reached a staggering peak of 40.5 million, which is nearly double the number of people who attended games in the Premier League and Football League in 1995-6. One of the reasons people flocked to football grounds in their thousands then, of course, was that there was no television, or at least not as we know it today. The mass ownership of television sets has made an enormous difference to football in more ways than one. So I thought it might be a good idea to use the advent of television coverage of the game on a wide scale as a kind of dividing line when I was attempting to pick a team of the best English footballers since the war.

Taking the debut of the BBC's *Match of the Day* in August, 1964, as a natural turning point, I chose a sort of pre-television side and then one drawn from the television age. Finally, I took my courage in both hands and whittled down the 22 names to 11, plus five subs. And this is how they look in the most common post-war formations of 4–4–2 or 4–3–3:

Great Players

1946–64 XI

Frank Swift (Manchester City)

Alf Ramsey (Southampton & Tottenham)	Jack Charlton (Leeds)	Bobby Moore (West Ham & Fulham)	Roger Byrne (Manchester United)

Stanley Matthews (Stoke & Blackpool)	Johnny Haynes (Fulham)	Duncan Edwards (Manchester United)	Tom Finney (Preston)

Nat Lofthouse
(Bolton)

Jimmy Greaves
(Chelsea, AC Milan,
Tottenham & West Ham)

1964 ONWARDS XI

Gordon Banks (Leicester City & Stoke)

George Cohen (Fulham)	Bobby Moore (West Ham & Fulham)	Terry Butcher (Ipswich & Glasgow Rangers)	Ray Wilson (Huddersfield, Everton, Oldham & Bradford City)

Alan Ball (Blackpool, Everton & Arsenal)	Bryan Robson (West Bromwich Albion & Manchester United)	Bobby Charlton (Manchester United)	Peter Beardsley (Carlisle, Vancouver Whitecaps, Manchester United, Newcastle, Liverpool, Everton & Newcastle)

Geoff Hurst
(West Ham & Stoke)

Gary Lineker
(Leicester, Everton, Barcelona,
Tottenham & Grampus Eight)

FINAL ENGLISH XI

Banks

Ramsey   Jack Charlton   Moore   Byrne

Finney   Robson   Edwards   Bobby Charlton

Lofthouse   Greaves

Subs: Peter Shilton, Butcher, Haynes, Matthews, Lineker

For the most part, I tried to avoid current players. That's not because it embarrasses me, as the recent England coach, to talk about people who are still active, but because I don't think you can really assess what a player has achieved in his career until it's over. I have made a couple of exceptions. Peter Beardsley gets into one of the English teams and, as you will see later, Paul McGrath makes it into the team of Celts and other nationalities I consider to have been the best since the war. I included both of them not only because I rate them very highly as players, but because they are far enough into their careers for us to make a judgment on their ability and their contribution.

I also have to confess to needing a bit of help over the 1946-64 team. As I was born in 1943, my clearest memories of English football don't really begin until the late 1950s. So there was a bit of a gap in my first-hand knowledge that had to be overcome. I tried to bridge it by taking advice from Dave Sexton, who ran the England Under-21 side for me. Dave is a few years older than I am, and I have always had great respect for his knowledge of the game and his judgment of players ever since we first met at Chelsea. His advice was a great help, although I have to say I didn't act on it all. Neil Franklin, the cultured Stoke centre-half, and Wilf Mannion, Middlesbrough's creative, goal-scoring inside-forward, were two players he recommended strongly, for example; but, in the end, I felt more comfortable going with players I had some first-hand knowledge of in those positions.

As for the team I selected in the end, I chose Frank Swift in goal largely because so many good judges said he was a great goalkeeper. Since he won the last of his 19 peacetime caps in 1949, all I ever saw of him was some old film. But he must have been good if he could keep the great Tottenham goalie and my hero, Ted Ditchburn, out of the England team so often. Call it Spurs bias if you like, but I don't think too many would argue with the choice of Alf Ramsey at right back, either.

I've named Jack Charlton as one of the centre-backs even though he didn't play for England until 1965, when he was 30. But he was a good player long before that, and I have a special reason for naming him in this team, which will become clear later. Jack lines up in the centre of defence alongside Bobby Moore, who won the first of his 108 England caps just before the finals of the 1962 World Cup and whose attributes hardly need repeating here. The back-four is completed by Roger Byrne, the former Manchester United left-back and captain, mainly on the recommendation of Dave Sexton.

Sir Stanley Matthews occupies the right-wing berth as if by right, while Tom Finney switches to the left, as happened so often during their parallel careers as England internationals. In between them are Johnny Haynes, one of my particular favourites in midfield, and Duncan Edwards, a true colossus and possibly the greatest all-rounder English football has seen since the war. They support a twin attack of Nat Lofthouse, the legendary 'Lion of Vienna', and Jimmy Greaves, who won the first of his 57 England caps in 1959 at the tender age of 19.

Gordon Banks is awarded the goalkeeping spot in the more modern English team, but I have to say it was a close call between him and Peter Shilton. I nearly picked the whole of the 1966 World Cup winning defence to play in front of Banks, but I wanted to find a place for Terry Butcher, a defender I rated very highly. So Jack Charlton drops out and Bobby Moore switches to the right to accommodate the left-sided Butcher. Those two are then flanked by George Cohen and Ray Wilson. There's a change of format elsewhere, in that I favour a three-man midfield of Alan Ball, Bryan Robson and Bobby Charlton in support of Peter Beardsley, who plays in the 'hole' behind Geoff Hurst and Gary Lineker.

The choice of the final 16 players was anything but easy. Because of my lack of knowledge about Swift I had little trouble preferring Banks to him but, as I have indicated already, it was more difficult choosing between Banks and Shilton. Banks got the nod in the end largely because he was a World Cup winner.

Right-back seems to have been a problem position for England for a very long time. There are not that many outstanding candidates, although I think Chelsea's Ken Shellito would have been the best if he hadn't got injured. I always thought Martin Peters was a good full-back. He played there in our school team, and that's where I thought he was going to make his name. Laurie Scott was one Dave Sexton came up with, which was a good shout, but I decided to go for Alf Ramsey because of his intelligent play and accurate distribution. George Cohen was probably a better defender than Alf, and his membership of the 1966 team gave him a bit of an edge, but I'll go along with Dave Sexton and pick Ramsey. Dave, who used to watch Tottenham a lot in those days, reckons that, overall, Alf was the better of the two.

Jack Charlton or Butcher at centre-back was a very tough decision for me. I went with Charlton in the end because, again, he's got the higher honour than Butcher. Jack was an outstandingly resilient character and a great motivator of his team, but having had Butcher in the Under-21s and seen his qualities at first hand, he would have been equally good in those areas. Jack gets the nod because he played in the World Cup-winning side, but I don't want the recognition I would give Butcher to go unnoticed.

You will have noticed, I hope, that Bobby Moore appears in both of the England teams either side of the 1964 demarcation line. He does so because I wanted to underline the fact that Bobby was the outstanding English footballer of the last 50 years. It is recognition that he deserves for his great ability as a defender and a captain, and I doubt anyone would disagree with my assessment of him. Needless to say, he walks into the final XI.

Ray Wilson, another member of that 1966 England team, was an outstanding player defensively and on the ball. He had a lot of quality, but Roger Byrne would be rated higher for his cultured play. Sadly, we didn't see what he was fully capable of because he was struck down at the age of 28 in the Munich air crash that wiped out half the Manchester United team in 1958. But he must have been some player to have won 33 caps in less than four years as an international.

Tom Finney beats Stan Matthews to the spot on the right of midfield. Matthews was an outstanding individual of his time and a specialist at what he did. But he was a right-winger, and that was it. Finney, on the other hand, could play right-wing, left-wing or centre-forward, where a lot of people felt he was at his best. He would give you a torrid time in any of those positions, and he had the total respect of everyone of his era. He also had 76 caps to Matthews' 54, which is a rather revealing little statistic.

Bryan Robson gets through as one of the modern players because he was an outstanding captain of his club and his country. As Bobby Robson often used to say, England weren't the same team without his dynamic namesake. Bryan stood alone, in his generation of players, as a captain, a defender, a midfield motivator and an attacking force. But Duncan Edwards was just as good, and possibly even better, at all of those things. For him to have got 18 caps by the age of 21 speaks volumes for his ability. Even though our knowledge of him is limited, everyone who saw him testifies to his all-round brilliance. Although Robson did a multitude of jobs well on the field, I don't think he could play at centre-half or centre-forward with the authority Edwards showed. When I was at Chelsea, they used to talk in awed tones about an FA Youth Cup tie, I think it was a semi-final or final, in which Edwards scored twice as Manchester United's centre-forward in the first half. Then he went back to centre-half and stopped Chelsea scoring when they had the wind behind them after the interval.

In my final choice, Bobby Charlton moves to a wider position on the left than some might expect. But that shouldn't be a problem, because the left wing was where he started his career. Alf Ramsey, in his wisdom, moved Bobby inside to get the thrust he could give a team. Instead of getting crosses from him, Alf wanted the power of Bobby's shooting and his ability to score goals from a distance. Charlton could also change direction and gear at will. His change of pace, I thought, was second to none. He'd go, and you couldn't understand where he'd got the acceleration from.

Up front, Nat Lofthouse has a legendary, untouchable record of 30 goals in 33 games for England. In post-war terms, it's way above everyone else's. He had tremendous power, and those who remember Bobby Smith playing for Tottenham and England in the 1960s will have an idea of the sort of centre-forward Lofthouse was. But he was perhaps even quicker and more powerful than Smith, and an even better header of the ball. His nearest rival would be Tommy Lawton; but because of his ratio of goals to appearances, he would have to have the edge over Lawton.

Because of Lofthouse's similarity to Smith, there's a great temptation to pair him with Greaves, Smith's old attacking partner at White Hart Lane. Theirs was a very effective partnership; so, with Lofthouse being that much in front of Smith, it comes naturally to put the old Bolton powerhouse together with the will o' the wisp from Spurs.

Greaves had this knack of scoring individual goals by taking the ball past people at speed. But Alf Ramsey, in the reality of the World Cup final, put Geoff Hurst in front of him and that may have been because of Hurst's greater tactical sense and team play. Hurst's combination with Roger Hunt worked very well immediately, and Alf saw that. I think perhaps Alf went for that combination, as opposed to opting for Greaves's individual brilliance, because he thought it would work better in the context of a World Cup final where the emphasis might be on endurance for 90 minutes and beyond. You cannot argue with his logic and I'm certainly not disputing his decision. But if you are going to pick an England team at fantasy level, you cannot resist the inclusion of Greaves.

As for the substitutes, Shilton, Butcher, Haynes, Matthews and Lineker, it might look like a bit of a contradiction that Peter Shilton should get the second goalkeeping spot in front of Frank Swift, whom I chose in my 1946–64 team. But Shilton was only a fraction, a whisker, behind Gordon Banks, in my opinion, and probably in front of Swift. Although Banks got that World Cup-winner's medal, Shilton's 125 caps entitle him to the back-up position at the very least.

I've already made my admiration for Terry Butcher quite clear, and I could never understand the criticism of him. Because he was big, people underestimated his pace and his turning ability. His passing was good, too, and he was a courageous guy like Jack Charlton. They were two peas in a pod, in fact. Others may not share that view, but it would be mine. I worked very closely with Terry in the Under-21s and I could see what he did. He was also outstanding in that very, very good Ipswich team of Bobby Robson's, a team talked about for its footballing ability. Butcher was a mountain at the back, and I think that if you asked the players he played with for Ipswich and England, they would back my opinion of him. If you want to talk about a players' player, I think he would be in the top three.

Johnny Haynes was exceedingly unlucky not to get into the final XI. He is just edged out by Bryan Robson because of Robbo's greater leadership qualities and more significant achievements for England. Robson was another colossus who drove his team forward, but Haynes was a different type of player. Whereas Robson and Edwards were very alike in terms of style – buccaneering, good tacklers, good defenders, good strikers and headers of the ball – Haynes was essentially a superlative passer. He could deliver the ball over any kind of distance with pinpoint accuracy and a lot of imagination. You couldn't get the ball off him, either. In fact, Haynes was one of my all-time favourite English players. It could be argued that Robson and Edwards were too similar and perhaps Haynes should have been included to give a better balance. I understand that argument and could make a case for it myself. That's how tight it was in the end.

I don't really have to make a case for Stanley Matthews, inasmuch as he was a legend who would be many people's automatic choice for an all-time England team. But, as happened so often when it came to picking England teams during their era, I felt I had to make a choice between Matthews and Finney because Bobby Charlton was a world-class player who deserved to be in on the left side of midfield. And I just happen to feel that Finney had the edge. That said, what a substitute Matthews would be to send on late against tiring defenders!

What I always liked about Gary Lineker was the strength and clarity of his mind. If he failed to score, he wouldn't let it get him down. He'd make up his mind to go in there again looking for chances. He was unusual in that people with pace often lack a bit of thought, but his pace was electric and his mind couldn't have been sharper. His touch could have been better sometimes; but because of his intelligence, his game improved as he got older. His runs certainly improved, and he knew what he wanted from his game. It was all worked out. He very rarely hit the ball over the bar: it was always on target. When it's there, it's always got a chance of going in. Gary was shrewd; when it comes to a striker thinking about his game, he was possibly one of the best.

Last, but not least, who is going to captain this collection of England's finest? We've got some great candidates in Alf Ramsey, Bryan Robson and Duncan Edwards. Even so, there's only one choice so far as I'm concerned. Bobby Moore went through his career being a captain and is the only Englishman in history to have lifted the World Cup. So I think I would leave well alone. I'm sure Duncan Edwards would have emulated Bobby, and might even have done better. We'll never know that; but what we do know is what we've witnessed, and Bobby Moore was head and shoulders above everyone.

And so, on to the Celts and foreigners who have provided English football with a lot of its colour and excitement over the last 50 years. At one time, every Football League club seemed to have a Scotsman, a Welshman or an Irishman on the books, often a combination of all three, and it's only in recent years that the practice has become less common. That is partly because UEFA, desperately trying to fend off the European Commission's demand for a complete open house in football, stipulated that no team could field more than three foreigners. Unfortunately, they put the Celts playing in English football under that heading as well. So English clubs, particularly those with European ambitions, became less keen to sign non-English players. Manchester United's juggling with all their so-called foreigners has certainly handicapped their attempts to make an impact on the new-fangled Champions League in the 1990s.

Players from outside the British Isles have never flooded into English football in the same numbers as the Scots, the Welsh and the Irish. They have always been there during the last 50 years, though. A lot of South Africans, Bill Perry and Des Horne (Blackpool) and Stuart Leary and Eddie Firmani (Charlton) among them, and couple of Chileans, the Robledo brothers, Ted and George (Newcastle), are some of the names that come to mind from the 1940s and 50s. Then, in the 1960s, Albert Johanneson, a South African, became one of the first black players to appear in the English game when he turned out on the wing for Leeds. Sadly, Johanneson died in 1995 at a comparatively early age. I can't remember too many foreigners being about in the 1970s until quite late in the decade, when Spurs surprised everybody by signing two Argentinian World Cup stars, Ossie Ardiles and Ricky Villa, and Ipswich went for the two Dutch artists, Arnold Muhren and Frans Thijssen.

Since then, of course, the trickle has become a steady stream as English clubs have discovered they can buy decent players abroad at a much cheaper price than in the inflated English transfer market. Not only that, but the increasing wealth of the English game, created by the formation of the Premier League in 1992 and the successful marketing of its attractiveness to television and an array of sponsors, has enabled clubs to buy some of the bigger names in world football as well, very good players like Jürgen Klinsmann, Bryan Roy, Philippe Albert, Dennis Bergkamp, Ruud Gullit and Juninho.

What I decided to do, then, in playing this fantasy football game we've got going here, was to pick the best team of Celts to have appeared in English football in the last 50 years and the best team of other nationalities. From those two, I selected a composite side to meet the final English XI I came up with. It wasn't easy, and I had to take a few liberties here and there. Because the number of available foreigners is not that large, for instance, I have allowed myself the luxury of picking quite a few current players. Anyway, these are the teams and formations I decided on in the end:

CELTS XI

Pat Jennings
(N. Ireland)

Alf Sherwood	John Charles	Paul McGrath	Eddie McCreadie
(Wales)	(Wales)	(Rep. of Ireland)	(Scotland)

George Best	Danny Blanchflower	Dave Mackay	Cliff Jones
(N. Ireland)	(N. Ireland)	(Scotland)	(Wales)

Kenny Dalglish   Denis Law
(Scotland)   (Scotland)

FOREIGNERS XI

Peter Schmeichel
(Denmark)

Dan Petrescu	Ruud Gullit	Philippe Albert	Henning Berg
(Romania)	(Holland)	(Belgium)	(Norway)

Andrei Kanchelskis	Ossie Ardiles	Jan Molby	Bryan Roy
(Russia)	(Argentina)	(Denmark)	(Holland)

Eric Cantona   Jürgen Klinsmann
(France)   (Germany)

COMBINED XI

Jennings

McGrath   Charles   Gullit   McCreadie

Dalglish   Ardiles   Mackay   Best

Klinsmann   Law

Substitutes: Schmeichel, Albert, Blanchflower, Jones, Cantona

As I've said, I was always a big fan of Ted Ditchburn, the Tottenham goalkeeper in the 1950s. I used to watch Spurs as a kid, and I thought he was sensational. So when I was asked to pick an old-time Tottenham team once, I put Ditchburn in it in front of Pat Jennings. But I think I was listening to my heart and not my head. Now that we are looking at a Great Britain team, I think you've got to say that Jennings was the best. His competence on left and right arm was absolutely brilliant, and for a big guy his agility was so quick and sharp. He had an excellent temperament, too, and was great on one-on-ones. I know that from personal experience. After I'd left Tottenham and gone to Queens Park Rangers, we played Spurs. We had quite a good team at QPR then, and I got through twice with only Pat to beat. But he was one of the best I've seen in that situation. He stood up well and you couldn't see any of the goal. He made it so difficult that I missed twice. I'd seen him do it before in training at Spurs, but he was equally calm and effective when the heat was on in a real match. He had the ability to control the situation, and you, without having the ball. That was the mastery in that type of thing. In addition to everything else, he was great on crosses. He'd come and catch them one-handed regularly, not out of flashiness, but because he had big hands and you have a slightly longer reach with one arm than you do with two. He was a magnificent goalkeeper.

Magnificent is a word I'd also use to describe Paul McGrath, although phenomenal might be even better. Every World Cup, the BBC used to make me pick an all-star World Cup team, and I'd always have McGrath in it. I get him in somewhere, even if it was in midfield or at right-back, or wherever. And everyone would say: 'Paul McGrath? You can't be serious.' There's always this feeling that the guy abroad must be better than the home-grown player, and they'll always come up with a foreign alternative. But this man can compete with the best anywhere: he's brilliant. He was certainly one of the main reasons for the Republic of Ireland's success under Jack Charlton. Physically, of course, he's an absolute freak. He's had a bad knee for years, doesn't train, only plays on match-days and seems to be ageless. He's 36 now, but he's been there in Aston Villa's defence doing the same things he's always done. That is to say, reading the play like a clairvoyant, tackling like a tank-trap and distributing the ball like a gifted midfielder.

I felt we had reason to put McGrath in at right-back because he has played there for the Republic of Ireland on occasions. Not only that, but it gives us a chance to select John Charles in central defence. At the time he was playing for Leeds and Juventus in the 1950s and 60s, big John was possibly the best player around. He had a great temperament, never got ruffled. A magnificent centre half, he would get up head and shoulders above everybody on headers and come out majestically with the ball. He was a good passer and a big man who was the personification of style. He could play up front, too, of course. In fact, he did both jobs so well that no one knew what his best position was – centre-half or centre-forward.

This brings us neatly to Ruud Gullit. I remember when I was at Barcelona in the 1980s, Gullit came to the Nou Camp with PSV

Eindhoven. He played at the back, just as he did for Chelsea at the start of the 1995–6 season, and he was hitting 40- or 50-yard passes with such accuracy that he was controlling things from there. Then, about three months later, he returned with Holland, played at centre-forward and scored with a magnificent header. Leo Beenhakker, Real Madrid's coach at the time, came to the game with a view to buying him, and I told him I thought centre-forward was Gullit's best position. But even today, none of the coaches in Holland are sure what his best position is. He can play in midfield, at the back or up front with equal brilliance. That is real versatility.

Versatility is perhaps not the first word many people would associate with Eddie McCreadie, the Chelsea and Scotland left-back in the 1960s, but he was one of the first full-backs to expand the role. We talk now about how the game has changed and how people like Gullit come out from the back, but players didn't do that sort of thing years ago. Full-backs always stayed at the back: that was their defensive duty. So Eddie took people by surprise when he started going forward at Chelsea. With his tremendous pace, he was well-equipped to get up and down the wing; and when he went forward he would put crosses in like a winger and maybe even score a goal. Great in the air and aggressive, he was a good, dynamic defender who could pass the ball well. Eddie was a wonderful full-back, and it was a pleasure to have played in the same team as him.

Ossie Ardiles, I think, was perhaps the first of the foreign players to come to England and hit us with the fever of his native land. I remember going to that first home game of his for Spurs at the beginning of the 1978–9 season, and the ticker-tape was all over White Hart Lane just like it had been in Argentina during the 1978 World Cup finals. Even though Spurs lost 4–1 to Aston Villa that night, it was the beginning of a great time. Ardiles and Ricky Villa were very beneficial for our game in a way that's been continued by Jürgen Klinsmann, Eric Cantona and Ruud Gullit. Ossie's skill was quite outstanding. He seemed so small you'd think the opposition would be able to kick him out of the game, but they just couldn't get near him: it was almost impossible to get the ball off him. He was strong and he screened the ball superbly. He dribbled it on the half-turn and held people off before passing the ball with great skill. Wonderful stuff.

Dave Mackay was another hero of mine. People who say he was only a hard man are talking nonsense. Although he was a great tackler, his skill at playing one-touch football had to be seen to be believed. However awkwardly the ball came to him, he would get it to you accurately all the time. Then, on top of everything else, he had tremendous presence and authority on the field. I remember playing against the Tottenham double-winning side of 1960–1 when I was with Chelsea and thinking: 'Oh, my God, this is a great side and the one I used to support.' I was only 17 and it was about my third game for the first team. Anyway, we were warming up when Tottenham came out. Mackay had the ball above his head, and he shouted to me: 'Better have a touch of it now, son, because you won't get one when the game starts!' And, of course, the telepathic swine was absolutely right. Together with Ardiles, he would make a nicely-balanced and formidable unit in the centre of midfield.

Either side of them, they would have Kenny Dalglish and George Best, which is about as good as it gets. What can you say about Dalglish that is new? You find yourself saying the same things about all the top quality players. That's why they are chosen in a team that represents the best of 50 years. Like Bobby Moore, he may not have had great pace in his legs, but he had great pace in his head. He was very quick in his mind, and he would never give the ball away. His passing and vision and awareness made him very exciting to watch. And, on top of everything else, he was a deadly finisher in all situations.

George Best you could play on the left or the right. He had everything: a devastating change of pace, a change of direction perhaps better than anyone, balance so marvellous that he could be almost falling to the ground before coming back up again. He was reminiscent of Finney in the way the ball seemed part of him. He would swagger and sway either side of it, and you didn't know whether he was going right or left. Normally, you would say so-and-so goes to his right or vice versa, but you just didn't know with George. People forget how hard he worked for his team, too. He would tackle back, those great lay-down tackles sweeping the ball back in, and he'd get up in defensive situations for a header. There are not enough superlatives for George Best, and I'd willingly go along with the claim that he was the best British footballer since the war.

Jürgen Klinsmann, whom I would pair up front with Denis Law, only had one season in English football with Tottenham, but 'better to have loved him and lost, than not to have loved him at all,' as you might say; though I doubt whether Alan Sugar would agree. Klinsmann made such an impact on the English game that, previously derided as a 'diver' by our fans, he did himself and his country no end of good. The intelligence of his attacking play, his appetite for hard work, his deadly finishing and his engaging personality were such that I think he'll always be part of the English game now. It's amazing to think he's gone into the folklore of our football on the strength of just the one season. Those who disagree need only to check who was England's Footballer of the Year in 1995. Every name on that long and distinguished list is part of the game's folklore, Klinsmann's included.

Denis Law was another blond bomber who would look very similar to Klinsmann from a distance. What I liked about Denis was that he was so careful and precise. His movements were always exaggerated, with his arms up. He'd toss his hair and make Italian-like gestures. He'd express his annoyance to teammates with a flick of the wrist or two hands outstretched. Everything was very artistic. For a comparatively little guy his heading was magnificent, as was his finishing in general. I can remember being really excited when I saw Denis play against West Ham in an afternoon game on an icy pitch. It was for Huddersfield, his first club, in an FA Cup replay. The game shouldn't have gone ahead, really, because no one could keep their balance and everyone was slipping over. Everyone except Denis Law, that is. He made the pitch look perfect: he was just waltzing past people. It was an incredible performance. What I also loved about him was his ability to adapt to any kind of game. If it was a proper football match, he was delighted to play football; but if it was a war, he'd have a bit of that as well. There was no hiding with Denis, and he was a real warrior when the circumstances demanded it. Basically, the pitch was his theatre. You got the feeling he was both playing to win and playing to the audience. He knew the fans loved his histrionics, and he set out to charm them as well as play football to the best of his considerable ability. I thought he was magnificent.

The goalkeeping spot among the substitutes gave me a big problem. I was sorely tempted here to find a place for Bert Trautmann, the former German POW who made a name and a career for himself with Manchester City after the war. He was an outstanding example of the way sport can break down barriers. As a youngster growing up in the post-war years, you knew the Germans were the enemy even though you might be only vaguely aware of the things that had happened. Then you've got this affable, likeable bloke everyone talks about, and it's good for the country at that time in particular. In those still dark days, it must have been awfully difficult to feel any affection for Trautmann, to say the least. But he won people over with his talent, which was considerable, and the charm of a gentle giant. In the end, though, I decided to stick with Peter Schmeichel, who has done such a wonderful job since coming to Manchester United. He's been outstanding for his club and his country. I don't know whether we can class him with Pat Jennings and Trautmann in terms of temperament, but his goalkeeping ability is exceptional.

Newcastle's Philippe Albert had only had a couple of seasons at St James' Park when this book was being compiled, and injury meant he hadn't finished his first season there. Even so, I thought the freshness of this Belgian international, not only breaking forward from defence into midfield but often past his front players, was quite amazing. It was something so different and wonderful for our game. A capable defender, he has remarkable skill and ability on the ball.

Relegating Danny Blanchflower to the bench was not the easiest of decisions for me, given the fact that he was another of my idols when I was supporting Tottenham as a kid. If I'm honest, I probably liked Dave Mackay a bit better because he was more down to earth, but Danny really was something special. He waltzed through games so effortlessly he gave you the feeling that, while everyone else was rushing around and tackling, he could play – as Bill Shankly said of Tom Finney – with his overcoat on. He was one of those guys you could never imagine sweating because it was beneath him. His hair, always nice and flat, looked as neat at the end of a game as it had at the start. There was definitely an unruffled air about him.

I used to pride myself on being able to tell a footballer's personality from the way he played. You know, Rodney Marsh would be eccentric and unreliable, while Maurice Norman was steady as a rock. Blanchflower, from my observation, was sophisticated and above it all. Then he would suddenly surprise you with this flashy scissors-kick from the right-half position. It was the one where he would put one leg behind the other and fire a 20-yard pass like an arrow straight out to Terry Medwin on the right wing. He loved to do that, and it made me believe there was something more to his personality than appeared on the surface. He's not just sophisticated, I thought; there's a show-off inside him, a little devil trying to get out.

For the most part, though, he was very controlled, very sophisticated. He played so much above everyone else, you felt he was out of place somehow. It was as though he'd come from Cambridge University, lost his way, been offered a game by Spurs and then been asked to keep playing. The real story, that he'd found his way to Tottenham via Barnsley and Aston Villa, seemed much harder to believe. A very charming and interesting bloke with unlimited opinions, he was not the sort of guy you come across too often in football. I thought he had some fantastic ideas, but I wasn't surprised he didn't do well as manager of Chelsea in the late 1970s. I don't want to sound condescending, but Danny couldn't keep the message simple: he wanted to talk too much.

As a player, though, he was exceptional. He could make the simple pass or the disguised one. He'd hit that ball consistently to Les Allen from right-half to inside-left. He could drop it anywhere at just the right pace. If there was a small gap, he'd punch it through. If there were no defenders in the way, he underhit the pass so you had no problems controlling it. It didn't matter how rough the game was, either, because he seemed to know instinctively where the danger areas were. He didn't hide from trouble, he just had this knack of avoiding it. It was as though he was gliding through a minefield.

Because Cliff Jones is another former Tottenham player, his selection leaves me open to accusations of favouritism; but I thought this little Welsh international was simply excellent as a wide player in that double team of 1960–1. Like George Best, he was a winger who could go both ways and play left side or right side. He'd run with the ball at pace, and defenders couldn't afford to turn. They either got the ball or brought him down. And his heading . . . I always remember playing against West Ham and the ball was sort of coming down towards Bobby Moore at the back post. Bob couldn't have gone to meet it because he'd have been underneath it. So he had to wait; but Cliff had this habit, just as it was nearly on the defender's head – in this case Bobby Moore's – of coming across the front of him and punching it into the far corner with his own head.

Eric Cantona, I think, would have done himself a favour to have been without a lot of the controversy that surrounds him, but there is so much colour in his game. You can understand why the Manchester United fans love him. He's different, he's special and he's what you want in the game. He supplies the fantasy you want. He's able to play deep like Nicky Barmby: he doesn't play right up there. You can see the picture of him sprinting 35 yards to get on the end of a cross with a header, something he does brilliantly. Because he's a big lad, he's intimidating to people. Coming in late, he's much more difficult for defenders to pick up, because they are marking, they are looking at the ball. You see someone 20 or 30 yards away, and you feel comfortable. Martin Peters was great at that. You take your eye off him and you think, 'Oh, he's out there somewhere.' The next thing you know, he's round the back of you or round the front, and he's scoring a goal. Likewise Cantona.

The one thing all great players have in common is that they are prepared to work hard for the team. Anybody who is not a team player is not a great player, in my opinion. If you look at the footballers who are generally regarded as the most talented the game has ever seen, you won't see a shirker among them. Just go through the list – Alfredo di Stefano, Johan Cruyff, Pele, Ferenc Puskas, Bobby Moore, Diego Maradona, Franz Beckenbauer, George Best, Bobby Charlton – and you will know what I mean. Even the Brazilian Romario, who has a reputation for being a bit of a prima donna, behaved impeccably during the finals of the 1994 World Cup according to Carlos Alberto Parreira, the Brazilian coach. No doubt winning the biggest tournament of them all was something Romario really wanted. So he accepted, albeit on a temporary basis perhaps, that you had to be a team player to be successful.

Maradona, I know from personal experience, was very popular with the other players at Barcelona. And I've already cited an example of how highly regarded he was by the other members of Argentina's national team. That's because he was a giver, and not a taker, in the team context. Paul Gascoigne's the same. All Gazza wants is to be one of the boys. Normally, the rest of the players have got a little bit of carefulness about them towards the big star. He gets the best, and so on. But they want Gazza to have it because he only gives it back, anyway. That willingness to give of themselves for the sake of the team usually overrides any jealousy their team-mates might feel towards the star players. Only when someone is getting the best of everything and is not contributing to the team effort do the others feel put out. If the stars are doing the business and scoring goals or stopping them, fine. But if they are not doing that and not working for the team, their colleagues will quickly lose their appetite for friendliness.

I've not had a problem with star players while I've been a manager. Maradona was the biggest name I've had to handle, but that didn't last very long because I made a decision and he had to go. Handling star players is not about the players, but about the manager. He's got to be a star manager. He's got to be good at dealing with people who are short or tall, fat or skinny, angry or quiet. Everything they do, you've got to handle it as fairly as possible. Players like fairness, and if you try to be fair you'll win. If you let someone travel by car when the rest of you have to go by bus – and that sort of thing does happen – then you are making big mistakes. The star player is only part of it: you've got to handle all the other players as well.

Gary Lineker's loss of his goal-scoring touch at Tottenham was a case in point. It wasn't hard to handle Gary because I got on pretty well with him. He couldn't take criticism very well, but I used to give it to him and the others liked it when I did. I didn't do it on purpose, but you could see they felt that was fair. Anyway, he had this very dry spell on goals, and I suspected what the reason was because we'd been together at Barcelona. He'd hardly stopped playing for three or four years. He'd been with the England team when he wasn't at Barcelona and had only had about three weeks break in the summer. In other words, he was knackered.

It was prior to our 1990–1 FA Cup run, and I knew I had to do something about it. So I told the whole squad I was going to do something they might not like. That was to give Gary an eight-day holiday during the season. I think he went to the Canary Islands. I said to the other players: 'I know what you're feeling, but we are all suffering. He's not scoring goals and it's not like him. All I've got to say to you is that when you were on holiday, he was there playing and working. I'm not making any special rules for him, but I've got to solve problems and I want you to accept it.' To be fair, they all accepted it and he came back and never stopped scoring goals. I took a big risk because if he hadn't started scoring again, the other players would have said sarcastically: 'Oh, well done!'

Players will not stand for lazy team-mates if they are not scoring goals. If they are scoring, they'll say: 'OK, fine. I'm getting a bonus if he's getting the goals.' But if, all of a sudden, he's not scored for ten games and he's not doing anything for the team, you've got big problems. This is where the correct handling of players comes in. Not of the star player as such, but of situations like the Lineker one. I should add that, on occasion, I've sent Joe Bloggs on holiday to recuperate from injury as well. You've got to be consistent because, when the star striker isn't scoring goals, Joe Bloggs at left -back is just as important. At times like that, you don't want to give goals away.

So, at the risk of stating the obvious, it's a team game. It's a chain with cogs, and if one cog is broken the chain doesn't go round. If one of our players is not functioning, the team is not working. If we are relying on 25 goals from Gary Lineker and he's got two, it's not working. If our strategy is to get the ball up to the centre-forward so he can knock it back to the third man running and the knock-back is inaccurate, that cog is not working. So, deep down, it's an individual game. An individual game to make a team. The more you think about it, the more important are the individual cogs.

I used to have a running day when I was a club manager. We did everything with the ball except on that particular day – athletics day – which they were terrified of. But I used to make sure no one missed it. They would have to have a bloody good excuse to get out of it. Gary Lineker, never the most enthusiastic of trainers, might miss his football work, but I never let him miss his running work. Those little details are important. Even if he was scoring goals, the other players wouldn't accept it if he wasn't doing his running work. You have to understand that athletics day was sheer torture for them. They didn't want to do it themselves, so why should someone else get out of it? It really highlights the whole problem with one decision. Are you going to let him get away with this or not? Gary did it and he did it well, because he was quite a good runner. But it was a really important decision for me and the team, because you've always got to think how to win over the team.

It's not very often that any personal animosity among team-mates is carried on to the field. Who, if they did not know the truth, would ever have guessed that Denis Law, George Best and Bobby Charlton were not always the best of pals behind the scenes when they were delighting everyone with their brilliance as an attacking trio for Manchester United in the 1960s? The way they combined, you would have thought they were blood brothers. Denis and George were matey enough, but they didn't always see eye-to-eye with Bobby by any means. As a manager, you don't want your players to go out dancing or on holiday together: you want them to produce a winning team. Then we all get the rewards, the stars included. The more you don't want to get on with someone, refuse to pass to them, the more difficult you are going to make it for everybody. God knows, it's hard enough finding someone to pass to without going out of your way to make choices. What every manager has to make clear to his players is that, once they come through those doors for training, they are all members of the same team pushing towards success. So you don't want any of the individual parts stopping that being achieved.

There can be problems, I must admit, when great players are playing regularly with ten team-mates of lesser ability. Johnny Haynes' decision to stay with Fulham, when he was wanted by a number of much bigger clubs, is a case in point. Johnny used to get so frustrated at Craven Cottage because he was such a perfection-ist. Yet when he played for England, with players of his own standard, he wasn't frustrated at all. It was his own fault, really, because he had the opportunity to get away. He preferred to remain with Fulham because it suited his lifestyle. He was a big fish in a small pool.

The other thing – the main thing – all great players have in common is a love of the game. They must have loved it dearly at some stage in their lives to put in the practice that made them great. You don't become great by lying in bed. You become great by being born with the necessary talent and then polishing it to a fine sheen. I think you are blessed with a talent, but what you do with it can become a curse.

You will have noticed by now that none of that group known usually as 'the mavericks' appears in any of my teams of great players. I refer, of course, to the likes of Rodney Marsh, Charlie George, Stan Bowles, Frank Worthington, Tony Currie, Alan

Hudson and Peter Osgood. They were all gifted individuals who gave a lot of pleasure to the fans, and not many people could understand why they were not permanent fixtures in the England team during their careers. Even now, no doubt, many will think it wrong of me not to have included them in my selections. But the reason for omitting them is quite simple: on the whole, I don't believe they were great players.

I would make two or three exceptions to that generalization. Stan Bowles is always put among the mavericks, but I don't think he deserves to be there. Stan was a wonderful player, a good team player liked by his team-mates. There are two kinds of bravery in football. One is tackling and the other is wanting the ball when things are not going well. And Stan would never shirk wanting the ball. The first time he and Gerry Francis played together for Queens Park Rangers, it was as though they had played together all their lives. Their one-twos were marvellous to watch. Stan's weakness was off the field, where he was a compulsive gambler.

I could never understand why Tony Currie was included among the mavericks, either. I thought he was a terrific player – though not as good as Gazza. There was some of Currie in Gazza, but there wasn't enough Gazza in Currie. He had Gazza's strength on the ball, and his ability to keep it, plus lots of other things; but Currie had no idea how to score goals like Gazza. He could put them in from 30 yards, but he wouldn't score them from six. He couldn't head the ball like Gazza, either, or tackle like him. For, despite that self-destructive business with Gary Charles in the 1991 FA Cup final, tackling is one of Paul's strengths.

As for Alan Hudson, he was the best English 18-year-old I'd ever seen. I remember playing against him for QPR in the later stages of the FA Cup at a time when we were going well. There was this teenager directly opposing me, so I thought I'd give him a whack to see what he was made of. But he out-tackled me and out-ran me. He was magnificent. Peter Osgood was another one with terrific ability, but he lost his way, too. They all went through a cranky sort of period at Chelsea when the Kings Road nonsense was at its height in the 1970s. Dave Sexton, their manager, expected more from them and I think a lot of them would admit they weren't as professional in their behaviour off the field as they should have been. They were not on their own. A lot of us were the same. It all got too heady and too out of control. I thought it was particularly sad that Hudson and Osgood didn't make more of themselves. They were wonderful players. It just goes to show how careful those young boys at Ajax have got to be. No one can wait to see how good they will be when they are 25, but steady improvement doesn't necessarily follow. It depends on what happens to your appetite.

I think being a true maverick goes back to your upbringing as a player. I think gifted people end up in that category because the coach lets them get away with too much early in their careers. He does that because he is giving in to success. This outstanding player is winning him matches, so he is more concerned about himself than about the player's future. It would be better if the coach fought him and insisted on more discipline and development in his play. I'm sure some do do that, but the maverick is too strong for them. He wins the argument, but loses his way.

Take the case of Rodney Marsh. When I went to Chelsea, I was lucky. I got there with about 14 other excellent boys. Every day we were competing against each other, stretching each other. We couldn't wait to get into training to play football because we wanted to be better. But Marshie came through at Fulham with a lot of players who weren't as good as him. If he had been brought up in our group, it would have made him a much better player. To be honest, he didn't really stretch himself until he got to Manchester City and was surrounded by players like Colin Bell and Mike Summerbee. He wanted to be one of them and worked very hard to be an athlete like them. It was late in the day, but he saw the appeal and the excitement of what Malcolm Allison and his players were doing.

The trouble with the true mavericks is that they really want to play an individual game. They want to be tennis players or golfers with a football. They want to travel on their own, be on their own, and they find themselves in a team game. It is an individual game in the sense that each player is a cog in a chain. But if one cog doesn't work, the chain doesn't work. You want these guys to fit into the team and give it the benefit of their gifts because they could be the difference between winning and losing. And when that ability is not on tap for one reason or another, the other players want to see the maverick giving something else. They don't mind if he can't perform so long as he fills a hole, tries to make life easier for his team-mates. Then they can still win even when he is not playing well. It's not so much a question of not trusting someone. When you don't trust someone, you are not sure about them. But you know these players have ability, so trust is not quite the right word. A better way to put it is that you can't rely on them. The sad part about it is that it's not their fault, it's the coach's.

The maverick represents a point where the fan and the press on one hand and the professional on the other are at loggerheads. The fan and the press don't seem to understand that the professional, too, wants to see all the clever stuff the maverick can provide. Matthew Le Tissier could be said to come into this category, and don't they think I might have been a lot more popular if I had picked him? We professionals don't just want workaholic players, but we want to win. Now the maverick might help you to win, but he might also help you to lose. The other players will suffer him if he's scoring goals; but when he's not, he's the villain of the piece and, to be fair, he doesn't understand why. It's not just a question of technique. You've got to know what to do with it, how to hurt the opposition.

The players who don't play for England are always the best, if you know what I mean; but one thing I find really annoying is the suggestion that only in England could individuals as talented as those I have mentioned be left out of their national team. That is absolute rubbish. The Brazilians are always complaining the coach has picked the wrong players, and how come Gianluca Vialli and Roberto Baggio were ignored by Italy for Euro '96? Most foreigners, certainly, would have made Attilio Lombardo a regular in the Italian side. Then there was the omission of Eric Cantona and David Ginola from the French team. You could go on and on with examples which completely disprove the theory about England being the only country that spurns its finest talents. In any case, picking a national team is not necessarily about choosing the best 11 players in the country. It's about picking the 11 who fit together best. That was the advice Enzo Bearzot offered Ron Greenwood when Ron took over as England manager in 1977, and it will do for me. Enzo, as you might recall, won the World Cup with Italy in 1982.

I don't want to criticize Le Tissier because he's a nice lad. But since my eventual refusal to pick him for England sparked off a national debate, not to mention outcry, perhaps it is time to offer an explanation. I feel that Matthew, like Rodney Marsh, is just one of those guys who was allowed to develop in the wrong way as a footballer. If I had been at Manchester United, say, I'd have been prepared to take him and work with him every day. But as England coach I hadn't got the time to re-educate players and I did have people like Peter Beardsley and Nick Barmby, who were able to play good football, be effective, score goals, do all the things that are necessary.

I mention Beardsley and Barmby because it's my view that the only position Le Tissier could have played in for England is that of support striker. It's absolute nonsense to say he and Paul Gascoigne were rivals for the same position. Le Tissier couldn't play out wide, he can't play up front and he certainly can't play in midfield in the way Gascoigne does. He can do that job dropping off the main striker, but it's a hard-working position. It's a goal-scoring position where the player has to link with his midfield. It went to Teddy Sheringham in the end, because I think he is a better all-round player than Matthew. Ted scores goals, works back and is very aware of team play. So, weighing everything up, I didn't feel that, with all the competition for that particular position, I had the time to get Le Tissier to do what I wanted him to do.

I was looking for people who recognize there are two sides to the game. You've got to be able to defend as well as attack. As Bobby Charlton has said, playing for England is a slog. That's a very accurate observation, because the better the players you play against, the more difficult it is to get the ball back from the opposition. And you must get it back quickly, or they gain confidence. What I was trying to do was undermine their morale by breaking up their passing movements. So you can't afford to have someone not pulling his weight in that respect. I'm not saying I wanted Matthew to make crashing tackles; I wanted him to fill spaces, I just wanted him to be close to the other players in the team. I think he most likely tried to do that, but it wasn't a habit with him. Under pressure, the last thing you learn is the first thing you forget. The sad thing is that it was not Matthew's fault. That side of the game had not been impressed upon him early enough in his career.

I used to think Jimmy Greaves wasn't as brave outside the penalty area as he was inside it. He was a bit sloppy with his passing outside the box, but everything he did inside was spot-on.

Because he was near goal and there might be a reward for it, he seemed to sharpen up. Likewise, I felt Le Tissier's precision around the box, his passing and all that, was far greater than when he was away from that area. The pass count showed that to be the case for quite a long period before I became England coach.

To be fair, they get enough from him at his club to build a team around him. That's fine, and he's become used to it. You can't blame him for saying: 'I'm doing well my way!' But the higher you go, the less you can afford to do that. We know he can do things other people can't do; but the really great players, the Peles, the Maradonas, the Cruyffs, the Bests, the Charltons, the Laws, were all proficient at both sides of the game. They didn't feel hard work was a dirty word, or two. Don't tell me Darren Anderton, Steve McManaman, Robbie Fowler, Paul Gascoigne, Jamie Redknapp, Alan Shearer, Nicky Barmby and Teddy Sheringham aren't gifted players. They are; but they are prepared to graft as well.

It could be because they play in big teams that make demands on them. You might say Eric Cantona gets a bit of special treatment, but he drops back and does his job, does his work. If you are with a smaller club, and have become a big fish, they rely on you. They need to set their stall out to get the best out of that particular player, which is often his goals and his artistry. But if you are with a big club, and they expect you to win leagues and the pressure's on, you can't do too much of that sort of pampering.

I would love to see Le Tissier at a club like Manchester United or Liverpool, where they would make greater demands on him. I think he could handle them, given time, and perhaps he will prove me wrong. Now that I have left the job, he might be chosen for England and prove he's all that everyone said he would be. I hope so, for his sake. He's still only a young guy, and I wish him well.

Chapter Three

The Manager

A crazy job, an almost impossible job, was the way Ron Greenwood described the manager's role in the developing post-war English game long before Graham Taylor got round to the idea. It came as a bit of a shock, since I had not long been appointed a manager for the first time myself, as successor to Malcolm Allison at Crystal Palace in 1976. I had just bumped into Ron and his grandson at a summer fête to which I had taken my two young daughters. But I listened hard because he was a wise and knowledgeable man whose experience of the business then spanned all the major developments in football since the abolition of the maximum wage in 1961. That was the point at which he had become manager of West Ham, a post he held with distinction for 13 years before making way for John Lyall and stepping upstairs for three years as general manager. Subsequently, of course, his qualities were recognized by his country, somewhat belatedly, when he was asked to fill the England void left by Don Revie's defection to the Middle East. So when Ron Greenwood complained about the increasingly complex nature of the job, you paid attention.

There's a spiral of people in and around the club, he explained, and there in the centre of it all is you, the manager. First of all, you've got your own managerial and coaching staff, which you have to organize and keep under control. Then there is the playing staff: but you are responsible not just for the first team, but the second team and the youth team as well. To get a youth team, you have to attract young players to the club. So that means talking to new boys and their mums and dads, using energies in that direction. Then there are directors to deal with and transfers, in and out, to conduct. You handle the players' contracts, too, and coach the first team. Coach the coaches of the other teams as well, travel thousands of miles looking at players and deal with the media. What this wide variety of situations boils down to is that you are responsible not only for the results of the first team – by which you are judged – but the building of the club. Responsible for both the short term and the long term, in other words.

The basic nature of the job hasn't changed much in the 20 years since Ron and I met at that fête. In most cases, it is still enormously demanding. If there has been a change it has been one of intensity. With the fierceness of the competition increasing all the time, the pressure on the football club manager has grown almost unbearable. The demand for success at every level of the game is now so great that no fewer than 43 clubs – almost half the number in the Premier League and Football League – changed their manager at least once during the 1994-5 season. That staggering figure is a stark reminder of how precarious the profession has become. Yet the sheer impossibility of the job, I believe, is beginning to lead to a lightening of the load, a hiving off of some of the manager's duties to others. Gradually, we are moving towards the continental concept of a division of responsibility between the coach, whose only concern is the preparation of the team, and a general manager, who deals with all other administrative matters. That, I am convinced, is the right way to go.

It's certainly a far cry from what I recall of the manager's job when I first came into the game in 1958 at Chelsea. People like Ted Drake, the manager at Stamford Bridge then, used to go and play golf with each other every afternoon. And when you went to see them in their offices, they'd be practising their putting on the carpet and all that. It was far more relaxed than it is today. That was because wages and transfers were strictly controlled by the regulations and the manager needed to do little negotiating or long-term planning. Since it wasn't uncommon in those days for managers to be signed on ten-year contracts, the future tended to take care of itself. There wasn't much coaching, either, so his responsibilities didn't extend much beyond getting the team together and perhaps conducting the occasional transfer with the secretary of the club. 'Just fizz it [the ball] about a bit,' Johnny Carey, the manager of Everton and Nottingham Forest in the 1960s, used to say by way of pre-match instructions. Marketing the game was certainly no problem: as there weren't too many counter-attractions, you just opened the gates and the crowds poured in. There was no television coverage to speak of, and the only thing to get people interested in the game was the press and, at the cinema, *Pathé News*. But that was enough, because nearly everyone bought a newspaper and went to the pictures.

It had been like that, so far as I can tell, since the resumption of normal service after the Second World War. I'm told Herbert Chapman, who performed wonders with Huddersfield and Arsenal before the war, is considered to be the first of the truly modern managers. From what I've heard of his expertise as tactician, strategist, publicist and all-round genius, I'm quite prepared to believe it. He even persuaded London Transport to rename the nearest Tube station to Highbury after the club! But I think Chapman may have been the exception that proves the rule. So far as I'm concerned, the modern managerial era begins with men like Sir Matt Busby, Bill Nicholson, Bill Shankly and Ron Greenwood about 15 years after the war. That's when the game started to get more professional and became more popular with the media. It wasn't a question of change right across the board all at the same time. There was just a process of evolution in which the manager became the all-important figure at certain clubs. In the 1960s and 70s particularly, it was the manager who ran the show and gave the chairman his orders, so to speak, because he was the only person on the books who knew the game. What has happened now is that the relationship between manager and chairman has come full circle. I think the manager, in lots of cases, is in a weaker position today than he was 50 years ago.

There are two reasons for that. One is the emergence of a new breed of wealthy and ambitious chairmen/owners in the last ten years or so, and the other is the gradual acceptance in this country of the continental idea that the management of a football club should be based on a division of responsibility. The relationship between chairman and manager is of vital importance in any club, and its quality depends to a very large extent on the personality of the chairman. If he, having put a lot of money into the club, is reluctant to let the manager spend it as he wants and demands a say in the purchase of players and other football matters, then there are bound to be problems. If, on the other had, you are a Jack Walker and accept that team-building is the manager's job, the rich benefactor gets his rewards through the success of the team. Even then, the power of enormously wealthy men like Blackburn's Walker, who may not be chairman but still calls the shots, Newcastle's Sir John Hall and Wolverhampton Wanderers' president Sir Jack Hayward can be a burden on even the most charismatic of managers. Kevin Keegan, don't forget, had to walk out of St James' Park to get his own way over strengthening the side not long after he had been appointed manager.

I know domineering chairmen are not exactly a new phenomenon. Burnley's Bob Lord, for instance, was a legendary figure in that respect, almost an ogre at Turf Moor in the 1950s and 60s. But he was, by trade, a butcher in the days when all football club directors were typecast as butchers, bakers and candlestick makers. What that cliché is intended to convey is that, before the property developers and industrial tycoons decided to move into football, the game was run by local businessmen of comparatively modest means. As such, most of them knew very little about professional football and were in no position to dictate to the manager of the club. Some would try, but others would lean heavily on his expertise. The latter was certainly the case with managers like Bill Nicholson at Tottenham and Ron Greenwood at West Ham. Bill ran Spurs. He certainly ran the chairman, as a lot of managers did then. Many chairmen were happy to be run because they didn't know enough about the business. Even so, they would get rid of you if you weren't successful. They had the ultimate say, but they let the manager do his job.

Matt Busby had a slightly different situation to contend with at Manchester United, in that I understand Jimmy Gibson, the first of the three chairmen he served under as manager at Old Trafford, was something of an autocrat and Harold Hardman, the second, a former player who expected his views to be taken into account. Busby came out on top through sheer force of personality, it seems. He stood up to Gibson and eventually developed a good relationship with the awkward, old-fashioned Hardman, who used to say at board meetings: 'Our manager has asked us for advice and we will give it to him [pause] and then he'll please his bloody self!'

Sir Matt is the thread that runs through the history of the period. United's manager from 1945 to 1969, he stayed on at the club first as general manager and then director and president until his death in 1994 at the grand old age of 84. The really impressive thing about Busby's managerial skill is that he sustained the club's success over

24 years, an incredible length of time by any standards. But that sort of lifelong, all-knowing relationship with a club will become increasingly rare as English football moves towards the continental concept of strict demarcation. At most foreign clubs, the coach coaches and the general manager takes care of the contracts and the financial side of transfers. At Ajax Amsterdam, the division of labour is even more pronounced. The club is run by a board of five directors, each with a specific area of responsibility. One man is in charge of technical affairs, someone else is director of youth and the others are responsible for finance, marketing and public relations. That's the way it's moving here, with the chief executives of Premier League clubs gaining more and more responsibility and curtailing the manager's sphere of influence. Or relieving the pressure on him, as I would prefer to think of it.

The English club manager is losing that control of the whole club he used to have, but his power in the dressing-room and on the training pitch remains undiminished. If anything, the latter is probably increasing along with his market value. He's been told to stick to what he's good at and mind his own business. You don't cross that dividing line now unless you become a director or a managing director. You can't have that sort of power any more if you didn't start off with it in the club's structure. Ajax, ironically, are going in the opposite direction. Louis van Gaal, their equivalent of a manager, is increasingly involved in the running of the whole club, and he's got there by being a successful coach. Their grooming process is to learn your trade, learn about the team, be successful, then learn about the club. But as soon as you finish playing in England, you become a manager and have all these responsibilities thrust upon you. So, until now, we've not been given the chance to build up to them as Van Gaal has.

It would have been interesting to see how a young Matt Busby might have dealt with the latest developments in English managerial circles. After all, his success stemmed largely from an ability to know what was going on in every part of the club and how to control it. He was one of those managers who was on as good terms with the tea ladies as he was with his most valuable player. Everyone talks about his understanding, in fact. You could go to him with your problems and he always had time to sort them out. He was a real father-figure. A man blessed with natural warmth and charisma, he had this uncanny ability to act as if he'd known you all his life when you met him for the first time. He was up-to-date with everything.

He also rebuilt United from the ruins of war, quite literally. Old Trafford had been so badly damaged by German bombs that home games had to be played at Manchester City's ground during the early years of Busby's first and only managerial job. It wasn't as though he was handed a ready-made team, either. Returning from army service, he inherited a squad of players that was made up of a handful of veterans and a few untried kids. Yet, by 1952, United had won the FA Cup in what is considered to be one of the finest of all finals (beating Blackpool 4-2 in 1948) and had claimed the League Championship for the first time in the post-war period.

It was then that Busby began to put into practice the plan he had had up his sleeve all along. From the start, he and his right-hand man Jimmy Murphy worked hard to attract gifted youngsters to Old Trafford from all over the British Isles. I think United must have been just about the first club to run a youth policy on such a grand scale, and their foresight was rewarded with the emergence of the legendary Busby Babes during the 1950s. A brilliant team made up largely of home-bred youngsters, they won the title twice in succession, in 1956 and 1957, before eight of them were killed in the 1958 Munich air disaster.

Busby himself was lucky to escape from the crash with his life, of course. Yet, once he had recovered his health, he and Murphy built another great side around Bobby Charlton, Denis Law and George Best and achieved a life's ambition by winning the European cup in 1968. It was the first time an English club had won the premier European club competition and it was fitting that Busby, who had rightly defied the Football League to take United into Europe in 1956 and pave the way for others, should have been the man to break our luck.

He was, I think we've got to say, the best of all the great managers there have been in English football in the last 50 years. Considering everything he went through in his life and the influence he had on his club and the game, he stands head and shoulders above everyone else. He had the Midas touch for the whole thing. He could motivate with the best of them and he knew the game inside out. He also insisted on the highest standards in the sort of players he had at his club and in the sort of football they played. It was a skilful, adventurous style of play, which was good for the English game.

He must have had a good relationship with Louis Edwards, the last of the three chairmen he served under and an ally on the board long before the death of Harold Hardman in 1965: that will have been important. In fact, I think we've got to acknowledge the part Louis Edwards, father of United's present chairman and chief executive, Martin Edwards, played in the club's success in the 1960s. They fell out towards the end, and Louis died in disgrace after revelations about corruption in his meat empire, but there's no denying the effectiveness of the partnership when they were friends and allies driving United forward.

If there was a blemish on Sir Matt's record it had to be the loss to the game of George Best, who retired at only 26 after a series of well-documented failures to turn up for training, matches and appointments. As much as George speaks highly of him and loved him, Busby never really won the battle between them, did he? A lot of people criticized him for his handling of Best but, as I've said already, I always believed that George grew into too big a star for the city of Manchester to handle and ought to have gone to a London club. Or to Italy. Why George was never transferred to one of the big Italian clubs has always baffled me. After all, he came into the United first team not too long after Jimmy Greaves and Denis Law had been signed by AC Milan and Torino respectively. Perhaps their failure to settle there put him off.

Anyway, you got the feeling George's superstardom was over and above anything Busby had had to handle before. You felt that if anyone could have handled it, he could – but he didn't. Maybe the problem was simply insoluble. Sir Matt always insisted that he tried everything from persuasion to punishment in his efforts to keep George on the straight and narrow, but he realized Best, the first British footballer to become a national sex symbol, was subject to psychological pressures unknown previously in English football. Drink wasn't the problem with George in the beginning. It was the girls. But finding the girls took him into places where he drank. Then that started getting a hold of him. He was unreliable so far as training was concerned because he just couldn't cope with burning the candle at both ends. His lifestyle caught up with him in the end.

Like Sir Matt, Bill Shankly had that wonderful gift of making you feel important the first time he met you. Shanks was really brilliant at it. You'd never met him before, but he'd know your first name even though you'd only just got into your club's first team. He was another father-figure in many ways. The Liverpool players didn't go to him with their problems like United's did with Busby, they went there to listen to him and his stories. They just wanted to be around him all the time because it made you feel good to be in his company. I remember sending Shanks a copy of *They Used to Play on Grass*, and the next time I met him he said: 'Terry! Jesus Christ, son, you're the H. G. Wells of football!' He was so funny because he was deadly serious at the same time. He didn't tell jokes: he just offered a stronger version of ideas than most other people. 'Football isn't a matter of life and death – it's more important than that,' was the classic example of his hyperbole and huge love of the game. Out of that strange mixture came a great team spirit. If you ever saw hero-worship from the players and the fans, it was never bigger than that for Sir Matt and Shanks. I think you had a situation where the players didn't want to leave Liverpool because of the affection Shankly inspired. They would feel they had lost something if they left. A footballer's career is a short one, and he wants to enjoy what he is doing. So he is ready to sweat blood for this guy and this club. Bill Shankly was the epitome of that.

Again, like Busby at United, Shanks' greatest achievement at Liverpool was to lay down a pattern. When he arrived in 1959, Liverpool were a big club who had gone to seed. Through sheer force of personality, he brought the whole place alive again, gave everyone a new sense of purpose and unity. He also insisted on the passing game which has been Liverpool's trademark ever since, and he introduced new training methods that made them just about the fittest team in the land. Last, but not least, Shankly established the club's reputation for buying nothing but the best in players. Once Bill had left Anfield so unexpectedly in 1974, after 15 years as manager, Bob Paisley just took over a going concern: nothing shifted. I think a sure sign of good management is that it doesn't collapse when you go. You can't guarantee it for ever, but it's all done and set and ready for your successor.

Paisley has never quite had the praise he deserves for his part in restoring Liverpool to the top flight of English football in 1962 and making them its dominant force and standard bearer at home and abroad in the 1970s and 80s. I had always suspected he might have been the brains of the outfit, quietly plotting and planning behind the scenes while Bill was showing he had few equals as leader, motivator, communicator and general driving force; but I am told that Bob was very much the number two until, reluctantly, he was compelled to take over the reins following Bill's premature retirement. It was only when Shankly went that Paisley emerged as someone with his own concept of how the game should be played. Just how effective that concept was can be judged by the remarkable haul of six League Championships and three European Cup wins, plus several other glittering odds and ends, in his nine years as manager. It is an extraordinary record of achievement that may never be surpassed.

A quiet, unassuming guy with a strong character and a good sense of humour, Bob was unquestionably one of English football's outstanding managers. In the eyes of the public he may have been the lesser half of a very successful partnership with Bill Shankly, but people like Alan Hansen still quote him on programmes like *Match of the Day*. So there's obviously tremendous respect among former Liverpool players for his knowledge. Don't forget, either, that he had to make the difficult transition from being the buffer between the players and the manager to being the manager. It's a skilful business because you've got to bring the information back to the manager, but do it such a way that it doesn't look as though you are carrying tales and losing the confidence of the players. In his favour, of course, was the fact that he had back-room staff like Joe Fagan, Ronnie Moran and Roy Evans to back him up. They knew the background and how to sort people out.

Although Paisley didn't want the job at first and tried to persuade Shankly to stay, he was probably fortunate, in the managerial sense, that Shanks did not hang around at Anfield after retiring. Busby remained at Old Trafford in one capacity or another for 25 more years, during which time his reputation was a big, intimidating shadow over the managers coming in to succeed him. But United were just trying to repay Sir Matt for what he'd done for the club. After all, he'd not only put them on the map, but made them a household name across the world. So was their decision to keep him on any worse than Liverpool's to let Shankly drift away? I understand Shanks' family wanted it to be a clean break, but those of us who saw him moping about unhappily elsewhere afterwards will always wonder whether he wasn't treated a bit shabbily by the club he transformed into one of the modern game's greatest. I've always thought it was unfair that men like Shankly, who had dedicated their lives to a club and done so much to make it rich and successful, were not treated with more respect and rewarded more handsomely when their reign was over. Instead of clubs thinking they might give them a little job lurking in corridors or going scouting, they should be handing them a package of shares to show they still belong and to give them something to pass down to their children and grandchildren. That said, I ought to add that Liverpool made Paisley a director after he had stepped down as manager. So perhaps they did learn something from the Shankly experience.

Bobby Robson could have stayed as long as he liked at Ipswich in the end, but that would have seemed an unlikely prospect when he first went to Portman Road in 1969. He even had to have fist fights with certain players to assert his authority. Having been sacked by Fulham, he'd gone to Ipswich, a fairly unfashionable club not doing particularly well, as an unsuccessful manager. They'd had success under Alf Ramsey, won the League for the only time in their history, in fact, but it was all going downhill until Bobby arrived. He turned it round with good players. They had a back four of George Burley, Terry Butcher, Russell Osman and Mick Mills, who were all internationals. Then there were people like Eric Gates, Paul Mariner, Alan Brazil, Kevin Beattie and John Wark, who were all internationals in the making. What a player that Beattie was! He might have been another Duncan Edwards if he'd managed to steer clear of injury. And what about Wark? He got 30-odd goals one season from the deep midfield position. That's never been equalled. They used to hit the front two, Mariner and Trevor Whymark, early in those days; but when Bobby brought in those two marvellous Dutchmen, Arnold Muhren and Frans Thijssen, it all settled down and they played some lovely football.

They were a very good side, yet they never actually won the championship. They won the FA Cup and the UEFA Cup under Robson, but they were twice pipped for the First Division title, first by Aston Villa then by Liverpool, in 1981 and 1982. So, in assessing Bobby, people will hold it against him that he didn't win the English championship. But no one can take away the fact that he had a really good team at Ipswich for a long period of time. He did well as manager of England, too, taking them to the quarter-finals of the 1986 World Cup and, memorably, the semi-finals of the next one; but he came in for such a slating along the way, all he'd achieved beforehand seemed to get forgotten. Far too much attention was paid to the tabloids' hysterical reaction to his setbacks on the field and their muck-raking over his private life. It was as though people were saying 'How can we make him a great manager if he's made a fool of himself?' But he didn't , really. I thought he stuck at it well with England. He was in the job for eight years, and that's a hell of a long time to be manager of the national team with all its unique stresses and strains.

Alf Ramsey, Ipswich's first managerial gift to the nation, was in the hot seat for even longer, of course. He occupied it for a dozen years, 1962-74, although the heat wasn't quite as intense then as it became later. I always rated him very highly as a manager, and not just because we are both Dagenham boys: in fact, I don't know him very well personally. He did a good job at Ipswich, where, in 1961-2, he won the League Championship for the only time in the club's history with a squad of decidedly moderate ability. That achievement alone is testimony to both his tactical know-how and powers of motivation, but he also made some good decisions at the very highest level.

When Don Revie took over from Ramsey as manager of England in 1974, success seemed assured. Here was the most successful English club manager of his day, albeit not the most charismatic, reaching the pinnacle of his profession. Yet his disappointing record as England's manager served only to wipe out the magnitude of his achievements with Leeds. In the 13 years between 1961, when he became manager at Elland Road, and 1974, the Yorkshire club won the League Championship twice and were runners-up on no fewer than five occasions. They also won the FA Cup, the Football League Cup and the old European Fairs Cup (precursor of the UEFA Cup) twice. Even so, all Revie will be remembered for by a lot of people is the unforgivable sin of breaking his contract in 1977 and going off to a well-paid job in the United Arab Emirates when England were struggling unsuccessfully to qualify for the finals of the 1978 World Cup.

At Leeds, Revie had been very similar to Matt Busby. He was responsible for everything – saying hello to the washroom ladies, having a cup of tea with everyone, giving the groundsman a Scotch after the game, all that stuff. In general, he enveloped the whole club. But he's got to be regarded as a great team builder as well, because he produced a great club side. I think you would have to say that professionalism was his strong suit, the essence of his leadership. It would be wrong to claim that Revie tried to copy Busby, but I do believe he tried to have at Leeds the all-round control of a club that Sir Matt enjoyed at United. I'd guess that was simply the way Busby lived his life: it wasn't planned. But you got the feeling with Revie that, in his case, it was a calculated operation, that he organized and knew everything that was going on. The effect was the same, though they went about it in different ways.

Ron Greenwood, who succeeded Revie in the England job, was an excellent manager and an exceptionally good teacher. He was not in the least insecure, either. He proved that by bringing John Lyall on board at West Ham and making him his right-hand man with a view to succeeding him eventually as manager. A lot of people don't like doing that: they get frightened that the number two might take over too easily. But Ron was thinking positively and acting in the best interests of the club. As I said earlier, a good test of management is if it all carries on after you've gone. You've not been dictatorial, you've been a democrat and it's not suffered through you leaving. You've been the leader of the band rather than a one-man band. When that one-man band, that dictator, goes, the whole thing collapses. That's why it's dangerous even if the man concerned is good at his job.

As for Ron's skill as a teacher, he produced three great world-class players for West Ham and England in Bobby Moore, Geoff Hurst and Martin Peters. As youngsters, they weren't actually world-class individuals; but Ron made a great contribution to their development. They were always exceptionally good players, but he taught them things and brought them on. Fortunately, they were intelligent enough to pick it all up. That's where Alf Ramsey was clever. He took that nucleus of world-class players and realized how valuable it could be. I think Ron, without knowing it, did a lot to help Alf win the World Cup.

I've always been impressed by Ron, his knowledge, his generosity, his humility. He's the sort of guy you are pleased to know. He was very authoritative on his subject, almost an academic in some ways. I believe his nickname among the football writers was 'the bishop,' and I can see why. He was a sort of throwback to Walter Winterbottom's scholarly days as England manager in the early years after the war and different from the usual football breed. For one thing, he used to hold sherry parties for the press after West Ham's home games. At them, Ron would conduct lively tactical discussions and invite everyone to contribute. It was probably his way of trying to make the football writers understand the tactical changes that were taking place in the game. Certainly, the press guys who used to attend those post-match 'parties' at Upton Park still talk about them with affection.

Ron's generosity showed in things like giving Bill Nicholson a scouting job at West Ham when Bill fell out for a while with the love of his life, Tottenham Hotspur, after he had been replaced as manager in 1974. Nicholson was Spurs through and through. If you were a Tottenham player, he was on your side and he wouldn't let you down. He had the sort of integrity that Alf Ramsey had. Eddie Baily, his number two, was the complete opposite of Bill in many ways. Whereas Bill was a dour Yorkshireman who never talked about anything but football, Eddie was your typical chirpy cockney with an opinion about everything. I loved Bill for his seriousness, but I often wondered whether there was a completely different side to his personality. That was largely because his wife, Darkie, was a real character. A very down-to-earth, independent lady, she used to ride her bike to the shops rather than take the car. So, deep down, he might have been attracted to lively people. After all, Eddie was an Alf Garnett type of character, effing and blinding all over the place. In fact Bill had to do a lot of repair work after Eddie had slaughtered players by telling them they were no good. They were real opposites, those two.

Even so, they produced a wonderful side in the one that did the double in 1960-1. Bill's strengths were his dedication and his straightforwardness. His shyness stopped him being a great motivator, I think, although he was a different proposition when he lost his temper. I struggled when I first went to Spurs in 1966. In fact, I didn't have a great time overall, although we were always in the top four in the League and won the FA Cup in 1967. But Bill Nick would never have you in and tell you what you were doing wrong. I thought that was a bit strange. He would give team talks, but do nothing on an individual basis. He might just have felt it was up to me to get myself right as I was a fairly experienced player. Perhaps that was because he was used to dealing with self-sufficient people like Danny Blanchflower and Dave Mackay.

Although Bill was not a tactical wizard, he was a good team selector. He knew what pieces he wanted in his team and he would go out and get them. There's a nice story about him going to Wales to sign Mel Charles, but the deal fell through because Charles wanted to join the Arsenal or was in hospital or something. Then, on the journey home, somebody tipped Bill off about this talented player up in Scotland. So he went up there instead, saw him play and signed him on the spot. That player was Dave Mackay.

Nicholson and Baily weren't quite a partnership, because it was always one of Eddie's moans that he had to do as he was told; but he was important to Bill. Eddie did all the work with the players, really, in my time at Tottenham. I think Bill used to get the track-suit on a few years earlier, but he would be in his office attending to that side of the job. Down the road at the Arsenal, on the other hand, Bertie Mee and Don Howe were a genuine managerial partnership of the sort that has succeeded spectacularly in the last 50 years of English football.

The Arsenal players used to swear by Don Howe. They reckon his organization is what got them through to win the double in 1970-1. Don concentrated solely on team matters. I think Bertie picked the team in the beginning, but then it became Don's responsibility with Bertie having a strong involvement in selection. Bertie won respect by imposing a code of discipline and making sure everyone in the club behaved as correctly as an Arsenal person should. He could be quite a tough little fellow, Bertie. He had quite a handful with some of the guys who were there then, people like Eddie Kelly, Peter Storey, Frank McLintock and George Graham, but they all had to do as they were told. George was a different character as a player, and he didn't really change when he became Arsenal's manager – he just put on a different face around the club when he was a bit depressed. Outside the marble halls, he was the same fun-loving guy he had always been. I couldn't help smiling when people called him a disciplinarian. 'Disciplinarian?' I'd say to him. 'Don't make me laugh!'

Don Howe, of course, went off to West Bromwich Albion and tried to repeat the success he'd enjoyed at Highbury; but it didn't work because he had a different type of player there. It's interesting, in fact, to look at the people who are successful at one club, but not at another. Now why is that? I always believe that if you can do the manager's job it's like riding a bike. If you can do it, you can do it. OK, it might take a bit longer because you start off with worse players or have less money, but you get there in the end. Anyway, I think Don had a group of seasoned players at West Brom who were not ideally suited to what he wanted to do. Instead of breaking himself in gently, or doing what he had to do gently, I think it was a case of 'I've proved myself: I've just done the double! My way is right.' There was a battle on between them, and he never really got it going at The Hawthorns.

What has to be remembered is that Don had been idolized by those young players he had at Highbury. They loved his coaching, couldn't get enough of it. They wanted to learn more all the time about what else there was in the game. Then he took his strategy to West Brom, where they had had quite a lot of success doing just the opposite. If people have been successful, they think their way is right. But there are many ways to be right. I don't know whether Don was unbending, but he got the backlash of what Albion had been doing under their previous manager, Alan Ashman. Don wanted to get into the coaching and the hard work, and perhaps there was no middle road. Sometimes you have to do a deal to get the players' confidence. You let them have their six-a-sides today on condition they do the work you want tomorrow.

How successful a manager is at another club usually depends on what material he's got and how good he is at changing. If you took over a really good team, you would expect to improve it and do well the following season. I was in that position at Barcelona. When I went to Tottenham, on the other hand, the club was in terrible shape. So you know you need three years to get it right, and I'd like to think Spurs were in good condition when I left. Normally, you go to a club because they've had a bad time. So you have to change your style initially to suit the players who are there. The first step is to get them feeling good about themselves again. Even the best managers can have problems when they change clubs. Alex Ferguson is an outstanding example. Manchester United won nothing in the first three years after his move from Aberdeen, and they might have let him go if they could have afforded to pay up his contract. They were not particularly well off

in the late 1980s, believe it or not, but Alex's spectacularly successful record since 1990 has helped change all that.

Like Don Howe, Malcolm Allison found it difficult to be as successful alone as he had been in his outstanding partnership with
Joe Mercer at Manchester City in the late 1960s. Together they
were formidable: apart they did nothing. When Malcolm went to
Crystal Palace in 1973, he just couldn't get it right. But he worked
out for himself where he had gone wrong. When he appointed me
coach at Palace, he made an observation I've remembered ever
since. I'd started by doing the basics with the players, and Malcolm
said it reminded him of himself at the beginning of his eight-year
spell at Maine Road. He left City with a very good team; but
instead of starting at Selhurst Park as he had at Maine Road, he
started as he had ended there. In other words, he began at Palace
by asking the players to do things that were perhaps too complicated for them. He'd gone straight into coaching ideas he'd been
working on with players who'd been with him for several years.
Heeding what Malcolm said, I decided that wherever I went, I'd
try to start with the basics and build it up from there.

Malcolm, one of the game's great thinkers, got it absolutely right
as a coach at Maine Road, of course. The wonderful side he and Joe
put together was one of the most difficult to play against in the old
First Division, I found. They had some good players and Malcolm
worked out the fitness regime and tactics to perfection. They used
to play in a shape that was not unlike the old WM formation of the
pre-war and immediate post-war years. (For those not familiar
with the expression, it was called the WM formation because you
could make the letters W and M by drawing lines between the
positions of the players. But more of that later.) They certainly
used two wide players, Mike Summerbee and Tony Coleman, and
one striker, Francis Lee, which may strike a tactical chord here and
there. Then Neill Young and Colin Bell would come from deep to
join the attack. Their system was not dissimilar to Ajax's now.
They had three at the back, Tony Brook, Tommy Booth and Glyn
Pardoe, and four in midfield. Of that quartet, Young and Bell were
the attackers and Mick Doyle and Alan Oakes did the defending.
In fact, Doyle would drop back alongside the centre-half when
necessary. It worked, too, as they proved by winning the League
Championship in 1968, the FA Cup in 1969, and the League Cup
and the European Cup-Winners' Cup in 1970.

It is perfectly true that Joe was a big restraining influence on Malcolm. They had their rows, which any partners do, but I think they were very close. They were both volatile characters, but they liked each other. Malcolm is not a guy who holds grudges, anyway. He gets things off his chest and then he's fine. Joe's trick was to act as a buffer between Malcolm and the directors and keep the relationship nice and sweet. I don't know if Joe managed to restrain Malcolm's taste for the good life as well, but I should think the bills for cigars and champagne must have been astronomical! Malcolm was larger than life and a very funny guy. He was also shrewd enough to recognize that Joe, while not really a coach as such, had leadership qualities in terms of charisma.

Another reason the partnership worked was that Joe used to have a lot of time off. Malcolm reckons the manager of any football club should have one or two 'thinking' days off a week; but, being young and enthusiastic then, he did all the coaching and training himself. Joe, meanwhile, would attend the matches and they'd chat about it afterwards. Then he'd go off for three or four days. It kept him lively, Malcolm said, because he was getting a bit older. He might have Sunday, Monday and Tuesday off, then come back on the Wednesday, or even the Thursday; but he'd always come back with a couple of good points to make. Sometimes, when you are as involved as Malcolm was with the training and all the other day-to-day duties, you can't see the wood for the trees. Joe, however, would retreat from the hurly-burly of the football world and sit on the beach or play golf. Then he'd come back with one or two fresh ideas.

I had a good run with Malcolm when he was the manager at Palace and I was the coach. Although we were a team in the old Third Division, we got to the semi-final of the FA Cup. We beat Leeds and Sunderland away, neither of whom had lost at home for two years, and we beat Chelsea at Stamford Bridge. It was a great run, that, and he was great fun to be with. He only had one lung because he'd contracted tuberculosis at the age of 28, I think it was. I used to say to him: 'You're a hell of a man with one lung. I don't know what you'd be like with two!' One of his problems was that he was always so extreme in his judgment of a player. He'd work with someone and see something in him that reminded him of Colin Bell, for example. Then, in next to no time, he'd be saying that this player is as good as Colin Bell, maybe better. Usually, the similarity was only slight and nowhere near the real thing. He used to go over the top a bit and get everyone wound up in it. In the end, they'd all believe he was absolutely correct.

Malcolm was certainly good for the press. He enjoyed the company of journalists, but he made himself a sacrificial lamb in some ways. I'm thinking particularly of the time he got himself the sack from Palace in 1976 when he allowed that nude model from the men's magazines, Fiona Richmond, into the players' bath at Selhurst Park. I was in the bath at the time and left it like a rocket because I smelled trouble. Malcolm said on television later that he never knew I was so quick. Like a rat up a drainpipe was the way I think he described my departure. But Malcolm, of course, followed Fiona Richmond into the bath. Then, all of a sudden, there's a photographer and Malcolm hasn't considered the players. He just didn't think in those situations. I went mad with him, absolutely berserk. I said: 'You've got married boys in there. They are really going to get it in the neck.' To which he replied: 'I'm sorry, I didn't mean it.' And he didn't; but he didn't think things through, either. Even so, they were good days.

Perhaps the classic managerial partnership, in terms of evenness, was the one between Brian Clough and Peter Taylor. They were like Mutt and Jeff, those two. One would come in and go berserk and knock a player flat verbally. Then, to make sure he didn't lose his confidence completely, in would come the other one and say something like: 'He doesn't mean what he said. What he means is this. He's got a point when he says you've got to do this, that or the other, but you're really great at doing that other thing.' The player is built back up again, but he knows he's been told where he's going wrong. Usually it was Clough who got into them and Taylor who repaired the damage and built them up. But they were so evenly matched, they'd sometimes do it the other way round. Between them, they were the absolute masters of man-management.

Clough was a good team selector, two. He always played in the same way, with two wide players and two strikers. As time went on, one of the strikers, his son Nigel, came off and played deeper. But they always had two 'engines' in the middle of the park, two players capable of getting up and down the field for 90 minutes, and a big centre-half to win the headers. Cloughie would say to the big centre-half: 'Look, you can't pass the ball; so you head it down to a midfield player, he'll pass it, the winger will cross it and a striker will knock it in the net.' It was all simple, common sense stuff.

Their success was built on a contain-and-counter strategy, too. They gave Dave Mackay's career an Indian summer as a central defender at Derby, of course, and I think it was he who pointed out that Clough's teams were brought up on the 'clean-sheet philosophy'. That is to say, the number one priority was not to concede a goal. People go on about the good football Derby and Nottingham Forest played under Clough and Taylor, but they could be very defensive, especially away from home. Even so, their achievements were outstanding by any standards considering they managed two clubs of relatively modest size. It was a very good Derby side that won the League Championship in 1972, but they equalled that at Forest and then surpassed it with two European Cup triumphs.

Although people like Kenny Dalglish, Alex Ferguson and George Graham have won more silverware than most, it is difficult to evaluate current managers for precisely the same reason as it is to pronounce current players great. Dalglish, Ferguson and Graham all have the potential to be considered great in the future, but their careers are not yet over and things could happen which would enlarge or diminish their reputations. They might have several years of bad results that could affect their successful images. In George's case, too, it's a matter of restoring his reputation after his dismissal by Arsenal and the one-year ban imposed on him by the Football Association for accepting an 'unsolicited gift' of £450,000 from Rune Hauge, the Norwegian agent, for helping him to sell players to English clubs.

Almost certainly, clubs will be falling over themselves to employ George once his ban is completed, and what happened to him may be regarded in the future as just a hiccup along the way. That hardly seems possible at the moment while the moral outrage is still understandably strong; but if he won two more League Championships with someone, people would say he might have had a problem halfway through his career but he came back and got over it. In fact, just like his hero, Herbert Chapman, who was banned for administrative irregularities while manager of Leeds City. What George did was not the norm for him, but I'm not trying to excuse him. I was shocked, I have to admit, because I didn't think he would have done a thing like that. But he's a good friend of mine and always will be. And once he's served his sentence, should he be serving it for the rest of his life? I don't think so.

Everyone seems to think English football is riddled with corruption, but that's not been my experience of the game. There's always been talk about two or three managers who were on the fiddle, but nothing has ever been proved about them. And, for the umpteenth time, I want to deny categorically the allegation that I once said a certain manager liked a 'bung'. In fact, I cannot recall ever having used the word. When I was a player, too, I can honestly say I never came across any funny business at first hand. I was as shocked as anyone when the match-fixing scandal involving three (old) First Division players, Tony Kay, Peter Swan and David 'Bronco' Layne, was revealed in the early 1960s. Their involvement was probably a reflection of the low rates of pay professional footballers were still getting then, but I just couldn't see how any player could reduce himself to throwing a match. You have to have a strange sort of mind to do that. You are betraying the whole of your life, betraying your country, your family and yourself. You've worked all your life to win games, so how can you possibly throw them? I just don't understand. I could rob a bank before I could so something like that.

There's another category of great managers altogether. I'm thinking of those people who do magnificent jobs with comparatively limited resources but are unlikely to win certain things because they don't work for one of the bigger and more powerful clubs. Nottingham Forest's Frank Clark is the first name that springs to mind. At the time of writing, Frank is continuing the success he'd had in 1994-5, when Forest finished third in the Premier League after gaining promotion. If he can keep doing that, Frank could become a truly great manager, a manager's manager if you like. That sort of manager I regard as outstanding. So far, you've got to say, he's proved a terrific successor to Brian Clough at the City Ground. Jim Smith's another of these unsung heroes, because he's done a good job at a succession of unfashionable clubs. Dave Stringer and Mike Walker did extremely well at Norwich, too. Likewise Mark McGhee at Reading and, now, Alan Curbishley at Charlton. Then there's a whole string of managers who have succeeded in making Wimbledon successful against all the odds. Perhaps managing director Sam Hammam, as the constant factor there, really deserves the credit.

In this context, I think, the essence of greatness is leadership. That can come in many forms, as we have seen. Sir Matt was this father-figure, a giving person who made sure the players were looked after and got everything they wanted. Then you've got Alf Ramsey, who was slightly aloof from the players but commanded total respect from them. Shankly was this huge personality who generated amusement and seriousness in equal parts. But what it added up to in every case was leadership.

Patience and tolerance are other qualities you need to make a good manager. They are very important because the press and the public want success tomorrow. You know you can get there, but you also know you can't do it tomorrow. So you've got to go along steadily. I've always said that all I can hope for at the end of any year with a football team is improvement. If you can get some improvement every year, which I tried for at Tottenham, I think you'll get there in the end. It may be slower if you haven't got as much money as other clubs, so you've got to do something to even things up. You've got to get success through good organization that knits the team together.

Honesty with your players is another essential requirement. I really believe you cannot retain their respect over a period of time if you are dishonest with them. That will come through: they'll find you out. You can fool all of the people some of the time, etc., but it won't last. You also need a willingness to understand your players. You've got to be prepared to listen to their problems and help them out, not just say you've got other things to do. If you can rid them of their problems, you give them a clear mind to concentrate on the game.

Personality, too, is an important ingredient in the identikit of a successful manager. You've got to have a warmth towards the players, so that they can enjoy being part of the club. If a manager can create the right sort of atmosphere, it makes players want to come in for training and want to stay at the club when they might have had a slightly better offer from someone else. It also helps you get over bad results if there's a firmness in the club, a determination to stick together: you'll come through that storm and get back on track again.

Football knowledge is fairly essential, of course, but it's not enough just to have played the game professionally. The good manager has to have a teaching knowledge of the game. You must be able to improve your players. Technically, you can improve them with practice. Tactically, you can improve them by developing their knowledge of the game. Personality or pace you can't improve, but you can do something about those first two. It's very important that you give them a plan where they are in no doubt about what they are supposed to be doing in the team. Norway under Egil Olsen are quite a good example of that. They've worked to a tactical pattern they all understand.

All those things amount to the sort of leadership qualities demonstrated by the Busbys, Shanklys, Paisleys, Nicholsons, Greenwoods, Revies, Robsons, and Cloughs of this world. Man-management and knowing your players: that's how you get the most out of them. Money is the be-all and end-all for some players, whereas others just want a pat on the back. Then there are others again who need the carrot and the stick. The trick is to know what's required to get the best out of them all so they can do in your team what they do best. What you try to do is give them a clear mind to perform at maximum ability and draw them together as a unit.

Outstanding ability as a player is certainly no guarantee of success as a manager. On the face of it, one of the most surprising things about English football in the last 50 years has been how few of the truly great players have gone on to become great managers. But that's probably because some of them never had to think about playing football: they just did it. I'm thinking particularly of people like Jimmy Greaves, George Best and Denis Law, although Bobby Charlton and Bobby Moore have to come into it as well. Jimmy, George and Denis didn't even try it, and the two Bobbys didn't make it. Bobby Charlton had every chance at Preston in the old Second Division 20-odd years ago, but I'm not sure Bobby Moore got an even break. The big disappointment for him was when he was going to take over as manager of Watford in 1977. It looked to be all signed and sealed until Elton John suddenly changed his mind and went for Graham Taylor instead. And the rest, as they say, is history.

Bobby Moore was a thinker, though, and a good talker on the game. I believe he could have become a good manager at the right club. He ended up in charge of Southend in the old Fourth Division for a couple of years in the 1980s, but that was too little too late. I gave him his first job with the youth team at Crystal

Palace. The same applies to Frank McLintock and George Graham – fellows I felt should have been in the game and weren't. Sometimes, people are frightened of big personalities like them. Anyway, I think Bobby would have made a very good manager. He was very organized in his own life and also knew what he wanted on the field; but he may have needed someone alongside him who had a tough streak.

There's no reason, of course, why simply having been a professional footballer should qualify anyone to cope with the complexities of the modern manager's job. OK, he's a former player and he knows something about how the game should be played and how to handle players. But can he take care of the press, radio and TV? And can he deal with directors, contracts, transfers, the police and all the other elements in the spiral we were talking about earlier? A lot of them haven't got any coaching qualifications these days, either. Because the top players are so well paid, most of them have never bothered to go on coaching courses. But they can get over that deficiency because they have been in and around football for most of their lives. Bryan Robson, Ray Wilkins and Gerry Francis are proof of that. You get some managers coming through because they are bright and smart and pick things up well.

It may seem contradictory, then, to say we don't need training courses for would-be managers. But I'm making a distinction here between managers and coaches. That sort of course is unnecessary now because the multi-purpose manager, as we have known him in English football, is gradually disappearing. He is being replaced by the coach, pure and simple, and the only practical requirement is for coaching courses. They are going to be upgraded so that English coaches can qualify for the UEFA certificate or licence that will be required to hold down a coaching (manager's) job anywhere in Europe. You might need management skills with the players as well, plus a knowledge of sports medicine and so on, to acquire an all-round grasp of the physical and mental aspects of the game.

I believe we are now entering the era of the coach. As he gets better at the job, he will become more influential if only because there are so few genuinely good ones. Top coaches, the guys who really know what they are doing, will become as highly prized as quality players. AC Milan's Fabio Capello and Ajax's Louis van Gaal have been hugely successful, but there are not too many of them around. Louis says that even in Holland the quality of coaches is not good enough. You'd have thought that if they had got it right anywhere, it would have been in that country; but they haven't. Louis is not saying Dutch coaches as a whole are not good enough. Some are very good, but there are very few of them.

The importance of the coach will grow because of what he can bring to successful teams through his strategy. If someone like Louis van Gaal can actually influence his team to win games at the very highest level of European competition, he's got to be more valuable than any one player. Yet you look at the salary differentials now in this country and you see a different story. At one time, when the players started to earn good money, the strong managers would insist that no player earned more than he did. Now, though, some players are getting £15,000-£20,000, or more, a week and clubs are prepared to pay the leading managers only a third or a quarter of that.

That can't be right. The top player might be injured for six months of the year, but the manager's still there influencing his team. It amazes me that clubs will pay big money for the big players, but not the big manager. In Spain and Italy, people like Johan Cruyff, the coach at Barcelona, and Arrigo Sacchi, who coaches the Italian national team, are on annual contracts of £1 million plus, which puts them on a par with the players or just above. Players in England are close to that now, but the top managers are still back on £250,000-£300,000. I don't think anyone outside the game will feel too sorry for them, because what the most successful ones earn is still a massive amount of money. Nonetheless, I think they are entitled to argue that barristers, for instance, would not be accused of being greedy for demanding a proper rate for the job. Basically, it's a question of market forces and high pay for a high-risk job. He's a pawn in the game a lot of the time, I think, the coach/manager. He's tossed to the wolves to save everybody else's skin.

The high turnover in managers is the main reason clubs want to pay them as little as possible. They are reluctant to give them too much for too long because they've got to recompense them for all that if they sack them. What will happen is that managers' wages will rise, but the clubs will be prepared to employ them only on short-term contracts. It will become more sophisticated, as it is abroad. Giovanni Trapattoni's short stay at Bayern Munich is a case in point. With four or five months of his contract still to go, he knew he was returning to Italy at the end of the 1994-5 season. Bayern were quite happy with that until the team suddenly started to become successful. But that's the job put on a proper level. It's simply a question of working and being as successful as you can. At least Trapattoni made nonsense of the claim that if managers know they are going to leave a club they will stop trying. That's ridiculous, because any manager or coach worth his salt will not stop doing his job properly because his contract is nearing its end. You want to leave with a good reputation and not look a failure.

I certainly think it's wrong to leave before your contract is up, as Brian Little and Mark McGhee did at Leicester. I think McGhee is right when he says the managers of English clubs are now jobbing professionals who go from club to club doing the best they can in each case. Even so, it's not right to leave in the middle of a contract, in the middle of a season when a club has hopes of winning promotion. You are playing around with people's dreams then. Financial compensation is one answer, but it doesn't make the move less unethical. You are saying it's all right to go somewhere else if they pay the money; but it's not really if you are still under contract. As a manager, I would never argue with any player who wanted to go at the end of his contract because that was his time to negotiate a good deal for himself. But heaven help him if he messed me about during the contract.

What does annoy me are the newspaper pieces asking 'Whatever happened to loyalty?' when a manager leaves before the end of his contract to join another club for a bigger salary or better prospects. Journalists, of course, never move from one paper to another before their contracts are up. The truth is that loyalty is a rare commodity in football these days. The clubs, for instance, want to sack you and not pay what they owe on your contract. Then they get upset when you leave of your own accord. Loyalty has to work both ways, otherwise you will never get a solution to the problem.

A solution is needed urgently because, as his heavyweight duties of old are slimmed down to little more than pure coaching and the pressure on him to succeed intensifies, the English football manager will move from club to club far more frequently than before. So you have got to have a rule that is fair to both the club and the manager. If he's sacked, he's got to be paid up immediately. People say the smaller clubs can't afford it, but we keep gearing the game to the bottom end of the market. That can't be right. There should be an agreement about compensation before a manager leaves, be it of his own choosing or not. Otherwise it's only guilt and public relations considerations that make clubs pay sacked managers what they are owed. If a manager is moving from one club to another during his contract, compensation should be agreed amicably between the clubs. Then the club who are losing out might be able to buy a good player with the money. Which helps you realize just how much more important than a good player a good manager is.

Chapter Four

The Chairman

For the most part, the history of the English football club chairman is a sorry tale of power without responsibility. Since the Second World War, the chairman and his board of directors have been perfectly happy to accept all the glory that goes with success, but much less willing to shoulder any of the blame when things go wrong. That, in their eyes, is the responsibility of the manager. He is the expendable one who always pays with his job, not them. But that doesn't seem fair to me. After all, they are the people who appointed him in the first place. So why should they escape scot-free every time? Especially in cases where their faulty judgment is clearly as much to blame as anything else for failure.

It doesn't happen on the Continent: or at least it doesn't happen at Barcelona, where I was the coach from 1984 to 1987. There, the president – the equivalent of our chairman – is subject to an election every four years. It means he is answerable to the fans, who vote in the elections as members of the club, and he can be unseated if they are not satisfied with the club's record during his period of office. If he is clever, the president can use the system to his own advantage. Josep-Luis Nuñez, the Barcelona president when I was there, had served two years of his four-year term when we won the Spanish League title for the first time in 11 years. So he immediately called another presidential election and got himself voted in for another four years, making it six in all.

But at least Barcelona fans have a say in who runs their club, a right the supporters of English clubs ought to be given as well. I know many fans here are shareholders of the club they support, and can express their feelings at the annual general meeting, but their shareholdings are usually so small that they cannot vote anyone in or out of office. Their only alternative, if they feel strongly that the current chairman and board are not acting in the best interests of the club, is to stage demonstrations at matches and call for the resignations of the people involved. It has worked in some cases, notably that of Peter Swales at Manchester City, and failed in others, as we saw for a long time during the period Robert Chase was under fire at Norwich City (though all the criticism from the fans seemed to get even to him in the end). Generally speaking, however, such internal strife has got to be counter-productive. It cannot possibly help the team to concentrate when the crowd is calling for the chairman and/or the board to go.

That is the most relevant consideration because the team is – or should be – sacrosanct at any football club. I make no apologies for repeating that the game is the product of the team, and the team is all-important. So although the game belongs to the fans, they shouldn't have the right to interfere with the team directly. What they should have is the power to say who runs the club and, by extension, the team. Some, no doubt, will argue that I am advocating mob rule; but I have rather more faith in the average football fan than that. He or she has shown, through their existing supporters' clubs, that they are quite capable of behaving responsibly.

It would be a step in the right direction, therefore, if all English professional clubs ceased to be cosy little private operations and became democratic institutions along the same lines as Barcelona. Since it would mean replacing the age-old limited company structures with membership schemes, I realize the transformation could not be accomplished without considerable difficulty. But I think it is worth making the effort. While there is no such thing as the perfect system for running a football club, I believe membership schemes and elected officials are preferable to unelected boards of directors.

I stick to that view despite the fact that there have been big changes in Spain since I left nine years ago. Barcelona are now one of only three First Division clubs who have been permitted to retain their membership structure; and the other two, Real Madrid and Athletic Bilbao, are thinking of becoming public companies like the rest of the leading Spanish clubs. The change was forced on the others by the government two years ago because the finances of so many clubs were being handled irresponsibly by elected presidents, who could walk out without being under any legal obligation for the huge deficits they had run up. Valencia suffered severely in that way, while Real Madrid's debts were £62 million and rising in late 1995. Such mismanagement does not necessarily prove my theory wrong. All it proves is that the Spanish system was blighted by too many irresponsible individuals and did not have enough safeguards built into it.

Barcelona cling firmly and proudly to their old status because they enjoy the massive wealth that comes from more than 100,000 members paying a basic £90 a year each for the privilege, and because they are run on a tight budget by my old friend Josep-Luis Nuñez. At the time of writing, the Barcelona president is still in the job 17 years after first being elected, so he must be doing something right. The Catalans are known as the Scots of Spain because of their carefulness with money, and Nuñez has become famous for his refusal to pay outrageous wages or transfer fees. That policy did not always please coach Johan Cruyff, I'm told, but it does keep Barcelona in the black.

At the other end of the spectrum is Jesus Gil, the flamboyant, autocratic president of Atletico Madrid, who hires and fires coaches at the drop of a hat. He can do what he likes because he is wealthy and the majority shareholder. It is difficult to criticize Gil's quixotic approach to club policy, since Atletico won the Spanish League in 1995-6 under Raddy Antic, the former Yugoslav international and Luton midfielder. Nevertheless, I much prefer the situation at Deportivo La Coruna, where the change to a limited company saw the stock bought by 14,000 shareholders. That way, the fans can continue to have a real say in the running of the club. It would be nice to see the influence spread as evenly in our football now that clubs, increasingly, are coming under the domination of a chairman so wealthy and powerful that he is little short of their owner.

I think the situation becomes more difficult when there's an owner. We've seen the problems they've had in America with the baseball strike over the owners' attempt to cap the players' pay. No one won that. The owners didn't win, the players didn't win and the fans lost, too. But the real problem here, as I see it, is that the clubs should not become reliant on the wealth of one man. Contrary to football's received wisdom, money can buy success. A little money can't, but a lot of it can if you spend it right. AC Milan have proved that, and so have Blackburn Rovers to a lesser extent. So it's fine while your Silvio Berlusconi or Jack Walker sticks around. But what happens if he decides to withdraw his money for one reason or another? It's going to be a huge disappointment for the fans if the whole thing suddenly collapses like a house of cards.

Something insidious and unhealthy develops when a club is too dependent on a wealthy benefactor. The rich guy thinks you are after his money. He begins to think the manager only speaks to him when he wants to buy someone. That's why it is absolutely essential to get the club's budget sorted out from the very beginning. Then both the chairman and the manager know the rules of the game they are playing.

It's much healthier, it seems to me, if a club can be put on a sound financial footing in one way or another and then become self-generating through an extensive membership scheme. That way, the fans have a say in the running of the club and the whole operation is not at the mercy of the whims of just one man or the self-interest of a self-perpetuating board of directors. Ideally, you want to be in a position where you don't have to rely on people who can put money into the club. Apart from anything else, there is the chance you are inviting in people who may know nothing about football, and care less.

Occasionally they are footballing guys who have made a lot of money; but the publicity English football can offer now is also a powerful attraction to anyone looking to raise his profile. Even if you're worth £100 or £200 million, the best you can expect in the posh papers is a little photo in the business section. But if you become chairman of a well-known football club . . . well, hold the back page! It's a wonderful opportunity for a bit of self-projection and ego-massaging. In other ways, too, it's very seductive to be the chairman of a professional football club these days. I hear people saying it's a tough job, but they don't want to leave when things are going badly because they will lose face. They vow they will get out only when they have got things right. But once they have got them right, they cannot let go. All of a sudden, they love it and there's no way they will give up.

As we have seen in the tug-of-war between Ken Bates and Matthew Harding at Chelsea, and my own dispute with Alan Sugar at Spurs, the danger when a wealthy man takes over, or tries to take over, a football club is that there will be too much pulling in too many different directions. First he decides to put money in, but then he begins to worry about losing it. When the other directors say they think it's right to buy some player or another, he starts saying, 'It's all right for you, but it's my money. Are you going to put your money in?' Then when he raises the money and buys the player the manager wants, the player doesn't play well straight away. So now there's an undercurrent of ill-feeling between the chairman and the manager. The chairman has already put the manager on the spot by shooting his mouth off about what he's got to spend. Years ago, you didn't tell the world what money you had because you didn't want to up the ante. But the modern chairman wants to prove he has put money in, wants to tell you what it is and wants everyone to think he's wonderful. In reality, he's fallen into his own trap because the new signing is going to be more expensive than he ought to be.

If your hopes and dreams for a football club are to be governed by someone who will, or will not, put his money in and doesn't really care whether he's there or not – because he's in the job for other reasons – the fans are going to say, hell, he'll be ruling the roost no matter what happens and what we think will count for less than ever. As with a lot of other things, the fans have no voice because of our history: that's the way it's always been. Most of the professional clubs may have been founded as communal enterprises, but they were soon taken over and turned into private clubs by local businessmen and professional people.

I've no doubt many of them became directors with the most honourable of motives and intentions. I'm equally certain, however, that the chance to raise your profile in the local community, make yourself a bit of a celebrity at the golf club or whatever, was a relevant factor, and still is. I know Alan Sugar was always telling me his mates didn't reckon Spurs had a good youth team. Simply being chairman has always imposed a sense of responsibility, however. Since you have to live in the town or area where your club plays, you are going to want to do the right thing. As I've said, ego usually plays a big part in the situation, and you will want to keep your name intact at the golf club, or wherever you socialize. It doesn't always work, of course. Even as the Premier League clubs were signing the much-touted *Chairmen's Charter*, designed to regulate their behaviour towards each other, Sugar was having to apologize to David Dein, Arsenal's vice-chairman, because he had been quoted as ridiculing Tottenham's north London neighbours and rivals in the papers for buying Dennis

Bergkamp. What it all comes down to in the end, whatever the structure of the club, is the personality of the chairman. Now the manager's onerous responsibilities are being whittled away to something more manageable, the chairman is taking over from him as the most important figure in the club. So it's more vital than ever that the chairman and the manager are singing from the same song-sheet, so to speak. That relationship is the key to a club's success . . . or its failure. Inevitably, there will be clashes. The manager thinks he knows the job inside out, because it's something he's been doing all his life, but the powerful, wealthy chairman does not like being told what to do. It is something that has to be smoothed out from day one. You've got to get your lines of communication right and decide how to get over your problems. The one thing the two of them have in common is that they both want success. They possibly want to go about it in different ways, but their goal is the same. It is absolutely vital, therefore, that they agree on a clear-cut, long-term policy for their club.

Not only that, but it's up to the manager to make the chairman understand he's not really part of the team, even though he may own the club. The owner must realize he is not one of the team, not the main product. The players and the technical and medical staff are the team. Every club needs a structure of communications that recognizes that the team is at the centre of everything. In fact, there should be a sort of credo pinned up in the boardroom, the manager's office and the dressing-room which reads as follows:

1. The game is the sport of the players.
2. The players and the technical and medical staff are the team.
3. The game is a product of the team.
4. The game belongs to the fans.
5. No outsider should interfere with the team.
6. Outsiders (i.e. the fans and the media) have to communicate with the team to improve the game.

If it wasn't for the chairman they might not be there; but he's got to be wise enough to accept he can get his satisfaction out of seeing the team do well. If, on the other hand, a chairman says, 'To hell with all that. I want to be the one who tells everyone what to do', that's the end of it. You can't implement a structure the top man doesn't want. But if the chairman and manager can agree, it's the beginning of a sound structure that will survive even the stormiest weather.

Liverpool have been proving that for a long time now. They've had Peter Robinson, their chief executive, sorting out contracts and looking after the administrative side of the game for years. Although Bill Shankly was called a manager, he was more of a team manager – somewhere between a manager and a coach. So Liverpool were ahead of the game. It wasn't just the way they played that made them so dominant in English football for 25 years; the way they structured things off the field gave their managers the best possible canvas on which to paint. I understand Liverpool have a kind of three-man sub-board consisting of the chairman, the chief executive and the manager. That makes sense because it enables them to take quick decisions. Not only that, but the late Sir John Smith, chairman during most of the club's great years, and his successor, David Moores, have both understood that it's the chairman's function to provide leadership without telling everyone else how to do their jobs. No doubt Peter Robinson helped them grasp that essential fact. In the game, it's common knowledge how influential Robinson has been, but it's not so well-known to the outside world. He was able to clear the way for Shankly, Bob Paisley, Joe Fagan, Kenny Dalglish, Graeme Souness and, now, Roy Evans to do their work. And that's what clubs abroad have been doing for years, of course.

Ajax, one of the outstanding examples of how a football club should be run, have a structure and a policy designed to get the best out of footballers from the age of eight right through to the pinnacle of the game. They are not subject to the whims of someone who might want to put money in one minute, then change his mind the next. Or want to run the whole show himself. They have a 96-year-old constitution designed to ensure the club is administered properly by that five-man committee I was talking about earlier. The 650 members of the club – all of them current or former players and officials, who pay between £65 and £140 a year for the privilege – elect 23 of their number to choose the five-man board and see to it they carry out their duties in the best interests of Ajax. The five-man board, in turn, appoint what we would call the manager, the youth coach, the commercial manager and the chief executive. The checks and balances are deliberate, because the intention always was that no one man should have too much power. Yet, despite not having a wealthy benefactor, Ajax have contributed £8 million to the building of a new, £100 million stadium in conjunction with the local authority and the state. That is real money, and the funding is all in place. The fans may have no direct involvement in the decision-making, but they know their club is in the hands of people who are Ajax through-and-through. And once they choose their administrative and coaching staff, they don't interfere. You've got to let the players play and the coaches coach. Then, with any luck, the coach's short-term plan becomes long-term.

It could all go horribly wrong if complacency were to set in, but I can't see that happening. The thing I like about Ajax is that the tail doesn't wag the dog: just the opposite, in fact. It looks like they've got everything in perspective; they know what they can afford. Any club's got to be disciplined if it is to succeed: there's a need to make rules in a thoroughly professional way. You've got to agree on a budget, for instance, and use some clever thinking to make sure you stay within it. While it's necessary to keep the squad up to strength in case of injuries, it's important to spend money sensibly on new players. What worries me about clubs like Blackburn, who have been revitalized by the wealth of one man and have comparatively modest support at the turnstiles, is what happens if Jack Walker pulls the plug on his money all of a sudden. Would they be capable of financing themselves then? I seriously doubt it.

We keep seeing the financial warning signs in English football, but we don't seem to take any notice of them. What the clubs are doing is paying too much in transfer fees and wages and going outside their budgets because the pressure is on them to compete with someone who is richer. Real Madrid did the same thing, and look what happened to them. You can spend a lot of money for about five years, but then you'll go bust. The only lasting way to compete is to stay within your budget, no matter how great the pressure to exceed it. The board of directors must set a limit and tell the manager that, if he wants to strengthen his squad, he's only got X amount of money to spend. Anything beyond that he will have to generate by selling players. Then you go and make it clear to your shareholders and your fans that you are not being mean, you are simply making sure the club can survive financially.

What all of England's leading clubs should be aiming for in ten years' time is not only to stay at the top of the tree, but to be self-financing. To achieve that, you'd need a lot of support through the turnstiles, plenty of television and sponsorship revenue and a lot of money from your youth scheme. I'm talking, in the latter case, of the kind of profit Tottenham made on Nicky Barmby, who cost them only a £20 signing-on fee, when they sold him to Middlesbrough for £5.25 million. Similarly, Ajax sold Clarence Seedorf to Sampdoria for £4.5 million then replaced him for nothing with Edgar Davids, who came through the youth scheme and is just as good, if not better. That's where big money can be made. Ajax are so good at it that they finished the 1994-5 season with a profit of £25 million. A lot of it came from winning the European Cup, I know, but a substantial amount was generated in the transfer market. That is going to be harder to do post-Bosman; though I cannot see Ajax failing to protect their investment in young players.

Staying within budgets and producing good players is where the talented coach proves his value. If you have only so much money to spend on new players, it helps if you've got someone who can get the best out of the existing squad. Not so long ago, club chairmen tended to believe coaches were ten-a-penny. 'We'll get another geezer,' said Alan Sugar when I was forced out at Tottenham. But they are beginning to realize the 'geezer' is quite important. He's actually going to knit it all together, so maybe he ought to earn similar money to the players. Perhaps a club can't afford the top players, but they might be able to afford the best coach. It's about priorities, it's about doing the job more skilfully. Johan Cruyff is a case in point. The president of Barcelona most likely detested him, but he appreciated his value because they've had a lot of coaches there and Cruyff had proved himself the best at doing a very difficult job. Otherwise, he wouldn't have stayed at the Nou Camp for the comparatively long period of seven years.

Most chairmen want it both ways. They don't want to pay top money and they don't want complete freedom of contract. But the implications of the Bosman case are something to be worked at, not something to be frightened of. With UEFA and the individual national associations mounting a vigorous campaign against complete freedom of contract, I seemed to be alone in thinking it could actually benefit English football. Graham Kelly, the FA's chief executive, has been recommending the English transfer system, with its independent tribunal, as the basis for a compromise agreement. But why should we be messing about what that kind of thing? Compromise, I've always believed, is a good way of making two people unhappy. Without question, it should be a simple matter of the player fulfilling his contract, saying cheerio and leaving his club to curse their bad luck, if that is what it is. If you want him so much with a year or two left, you give him a bigger contract. And if it means paying him more, you sell another player to cover the cost.

Trying to insist on some form of compensation for a player who is out of contract is unfair and simply prolonging the agony. You are still restricting the player's basic right to move freely to another job, there's no guarantee his old club and his new one will agree on a fee, and it's not certain anyone would want to pay the fee imposed by the independent tribunal. Anyway, why should a player serve out his contract and still have to rely on someone coming to an agreement before he can do what every other employee in the European Community does without hindrance and change jobs? Don't tell me football is a special case. Provided it is still possible to claim a fee for a player who is transferred while still under contract, I don't see what the problem is. Apart from anything else, it is now against European Community law to want a fee for a player who has finished his contract. You might want to rob a bank because it would make you wealthy, but that's against the law, too, I'm afraid.

Nor am I swayed by the arguments that complete freedom of contract would force many clubs to go part-time and abandon their youth schemes. It seems to me that going part-time is a good idea, not a bad one, for the 72 Football League Clubs. With a lucrative new television deal in the bag, this is the ideal moment for them to draw up new budgets, get their houses in order and accept that part-time football is inevitable for most people outside the Premier League. The danger is that the clubs from the lower divisions will see their new, £25 million-a-year deal with Sky only as something that will keep them alive a little while longer as full-time operations. Instead, they should regard it as a heaven-sent opportunity to introduce long-overdue economic and structural reforms. With more money coming in, and the players on part-time pay, they can work out budgets that will really ensure survival. Think it through. You are not paying the players more because your income has increased, but paying them less.

Obviously, the change-over from full-time to part-time would not be painless for the players. But they'd accept it, however reluctantly, because there are only so many clubs prepared to employ them and they are not going to be getting offers from the likes of Arsenal. That may sound callous, but I prefer to regard it as being realistic because I believe most footballers in the First, Second and Third Divisions of the Nationwide (Football) League would actually be better off financially playing their football on a part-time basis. Take Barnet Football Club as an example. I'm told their players get £300 a week at the moment. But £300 is not only insufficient to provide for a player's future when he retires from the game, it's not enough for him to survive on now if he's got a wife and family. So his football ability has been a liability to him in a way.

If, on the other hand, you tell the player you'll pay him £250 for coming in only three days or nights a week, you do two things. You reduce the club's wage bill by £50 a player per week – a saving of £1,000 if there are 20 on the staff – and you make it possible for the players to take a job outside the game. Now I know jobs are not that easy to come by in the present labour market, but it is difficult to believe footballers could not find something that would take their combined earnings above the £300, say, they were getting from just playing football. Perhaps taxi-driving is the answer. I understand you can make as much as £500-£600 a week from driving a mini-cab. So then the £250 for playing football part-time becomes a bonus.

Gordon Taylor, the chief executive of the Professional Footballers' Association, won't agree with me, I know. In fact, I've argued with him for years about this. He wants to keep all his 4,000 members happy by keeping them in full-time employment, and that's understandable. But I believe you'd actually be doing those in the lower divisions a favour by letting them go part-time. The reality, in most cases, is that we are giving the fellow who wants to be a top footballer false hope. He loves the idea of earning a living as a full-time player, but he's lazy or lacks the ability or temperament for it. Then, when he finishes lower down the scale, he's hardly got a penny to his name. He's now got to start again, find a job and start catching up on people who, in their early 30s, are reaching their peak in that particular occupation. In two, three or four years' time, I believe, part-time football with be the norm in the Nationwide League.

The initial change-over will be the only problem, and Gordon has to be strong enough to carry it through. Since the PFA have so many members and must try to represent them all equally, something like Bosman puts the union in a difficult position. The verdict could make the lower divisions of English football redundant as full-time professionals; but if the PFA try too hard to cater for them, they risk stopping the top end of the game, the end where the excellence is, from progressing.

It certainly doesn't follow that part-time football inevitably means poorer football. Look at some of the Scandinavians if you don't believe me. Sweden and Norway have done pretty well at club and international level for a bunch of part-timers. We should be particularly aware of that by now, considering Sweden's Gothenburg and Trelleborgs have embarrassed Manchester United and Blackburn respectively in recent European competitions. And Norway, if you recall, were one of the teams who stopped England qualifying for the 1994 World Cup finals. I know most of the Norwegian national side are full-time professionals now, many of them playing for clubs over here in English football, but they have graduated to that from more modest beginnings at home. Whatever the reason, parental guidance or sheer common sense, they find themselves a job or a profession outside football from the very start. Then, if they are talented enough to be signed by a big, full-time club somewhere, they put their other occupation on hold until their playing days are over. That's the sort of sensible arrangement we should be looking to introduce here.

As for the claim that complete freedom of contract would discourage clubs from running youth schemes, I can see that some might be put off by the prospect of losing their best youngsters to other clubs after they had spent a lot of time and money grooming them. But that possibility exists now, and all that's really required to avert it is some imaginative thinking about the length of contracts and so on. Big clubs using smaller clubs as nurseries is another solution worth a try. West Ham or Tottenham might have Leyton Orient, for example. The big club bolsters the smaller one with finance, and I can't see anything wrong with that. The Premier League clubs should do a deal with those in the Nationwide League and guarantee to put a percentage of the television income into the nursery clubs. The big clubs might want to send their youth players to the nursery club, or clubs. You might want more than one, and have them in different parts of the country like the schools of excellence. The more you spread them out, the more chance you've got of unearthing talent.

That kind of nursery system might stop big clubs losing late developers, as Manchester United did with David Platt, and help reduce the high wastage rate among young players. United wouldn't have lost Platt if Crewe, the club they let him go to, had been their nursery. You know Platt is going to be a good player, but he's too small and a bit frail at 18. So you loan him to the nursery club because he's getting a bit restless. There, he acquires experience, gets paid and makes progress under the umbrella of the big club. Then, bingo, at 21 he's ready physically and mentally to return to the big time. The player doesn't feel as though he's been tossed to a lower club with his tail between his legs, but he has been taught a lesson. He's been pushed back down the ladder a bit, so is he going to make it back? He's got two years to do it and it's up to him. I think that's sometimes the motivation young players need around the time they start meeting girls and going to the pub. They go one way or the other: that's why we lose so many players at that age.

To be fair, some top executives have already absorbed the implications of the Bosman case and thought the situation through. Sam Hammam, Wimbledon's managing director and owner, is one of them. He's been thinking about it for a long time, as he made clear when he said: 'We have known about Bosman for years. So we took care of contracts. The senior players are on long-term contracts, average players on average contracts, and those players we can do without are on short-term contracts. We have sold very well and we are cash rich at the moment. So if the transfer law changed we would become predators.' If he's attacking the problem, he might get a steal on those who are still hoping the whole thing might go away or are trying to sweep it under the carpet. At a club like Wimbledon, where gate receipts are small, Sam's got to examine all the ways he can to keep in touch with the big boys. He's worked out that the big boys can still have only so many players, so the same principles of scouting and recruiting good players still apply. A series of managers have had success at Wimbledon, and you get the impression Sam has played a big part in it all. I think he works things out and he's prepared for everything. In short, he is one of the outstanding executives in the game.

The sort of chairman I like most is the solid, supportive guy who stays in the background. Liverpool's David Moores is an excellent example. I think he's terrific. I find him so approachable and so nice, but I bet a lot of people in the south don't even know his name. David, a member of the family who own the Littlewoods pools, stores and mail-order empire, loves his team and is really into his football. I sat with him watching two of Liverpool's pre-season games in Germany last year, and he never took his eyes off the pitch. You know his club are always going to be successful because he will let his people do their work without interfering; and I'd like to think they've got a healthy respect for him. His power comes through the satisfaction of knowing he's helped to deliver a successful product by allowing the technicians to do what they are good at. He may be up front for the pictures when things are going well, but he's also up there when they are not so good.

Jim Gregory was another chairman of that type. When I was in trouble as the manager at QPR in the early 1980s, he was at my side; and if I was winning, he'd push me into the spotlight because he got a different kind of satisfaction from success. I don't know if he ever actually did this, but he was entitled to look at that smashing little Loftus Road ground and say it wouldn't be there if it wasn't for him. We all played our part – Frank McLintock, me, Rodney Marsh, Stan Bowles and Gerry Francis – along the way, but it was mainly down to him. The power and the glory: I really do believe chairmen can't have them both. It's when they try to that they get themselves in trouble.

I know Jim had his critics and could be a very tough man, but I found him wonderful to work with. Maybe I was just lucky I got the job when I did. Before I arrived, apparently, he used to go into the dressing room and have the players up in the lounge, the sort of things that create problems at a club. In fact, he'd had lots of problems and lots of managers. So when I got there, he put the back of his hand under his chin and said: 'I'm up to here with that managerial nonsense: you get on with it.' It was great having that degree of independence, but I always showed him respect and always told him what I was doing. We'd having meetings three times a week and I used to look forward to seeing him. At six o'clock, after talking business for about four hours, he'd get a bottle of champagne out and we'd relax. We had our discussions and disagreements, but I don't think we ever really fell out. What always impressed me was his gift for lateral thinking, something I like to think I got from him. There would seem to be no way out of a particular problem until Jim suggested turning it around or upside down. Then, hey presto, there was the solution. He was actually a good judge of football, too. He loved his football. In fact, Jim Gregory was just about the perfect role model for a chairman in my opinion.

In addition to everything else, he used to spend a lot of his own money on QPR. That links him with the new breed of chairmen in a way, because there's no doubt they have put an awful lot of finance into the game. You can say this, that and the other about them – and there's no doubt they love the limelight and what goes with it – but the one thing you can't accuse them of being is money-grabbers. I'd be more suspicious of the chairmen of 40 years ago, when there were 80,000 people coming through the gates and they couldn't pay players more than £20 a week. You wonder where all the money went then. In those days, of course, there was an awful lot of mystery about directors as well as about players. Today, everything is in the open and you feel you almost know them because they are on television so much. They are getting more and more high-profile, and they love it. The publicity also helps their businesses, of course.

I just wish they were a bit more knowledgeable about the actual game of football and a bit more interested in it. As chief executive at Tottenham, I was involved from the very beginning in the meetings leading up to the formation of the Premier League in 1992; and what struck me most was how the chairmen switched off if I, almost the only football person there, raised a football issue, such as a winter break, a transfer 'window' or an Under-21 league. I felt they were really against me because they weren't sure where they stood on football issues, were uncomfortable with them. They only came alive when the television issue, commercial aspects, things they were familiar with, were on the agenda. It certainly worries me that there is only one person – Jimmy Hill – with a true professional football background on the FA council, which is about 90-strong and runs English football.

One reason we find it difficult to make progress in English football is that the chairmen, the people in charge, are unsure about football issues and don't want to make mistakes. It's not because they don't want to improve matters: it's because they are not sure how they should be improved. But then they should get reports from their managers so that they can come to a meeting with a view on football issues. If you don't consult the managers, you are not going to get very far very quickly with the Premier League.

What I'm not suggesting is that we necessarily need more ex-footballers as chairmen. Having played the game does not automatically qualify you to run a football club. Franny Lee, for example, was an England international, but he never went through the managing and coaching and organizing of a club. His administrative experience was gained in the waste-paper business and horse-racing. I hope he does well at Manchester City because he's a character and he's put his money where his mouth is. So good luck to him: I think he'll need it.

Ron Greenwood, on the other hand, was a real football person and he's lost to the game. Now I think Ron would have made a good chairman. He'd understand the multitude of problems a manager faces, whereas others would not. I'm thinking of guys like Mike Channon and Emlyn Hughes. They were good players but are too ready to shout their mouths off about the way the game is conducted without having the experience, really, to back it up. Channon has never coached or picked a team in League football and Hughes had just the one stab at it when he was manager of Rotherham. Even the Alan Hansens and Gary Linekers have to be regarded with suspicion. They've got a view, are entitled to their opinion and are experts on playing the game because they were top-class footballers. But they've never picked a team, never pinned a team-sheet on the wall. If they had, they wouldn't say some of the things they do on television. I think they are way off beam at times. I notice Ian St John is more cagey than Jimmy Greaves and understands the problems better. I have done both jobs and know which is easier. Johnny Giles is a good judge. He thinks his opinions through in his column in the *Daily Express*.

Most chairmen, in my experience, find it extremely difficult to resist interfering in the running of the team. That is especially true of the millionaires who have come into the game over the last ten years or so. It was certainly true of Irving Scholar, the young property developer who brought me back to Tottenham as manager at the end of 1987. He would always interfere, not only in my area of responsibility but right across the board. When I first got there, the merchandising guy told me to be careful of the chairman. 'He'll let you do all the hard work,' he said, 'but when it comes to having your photograph taken, he wants to be there in the front.' One of the reasons for Irving's interference, I think, was that he loved Tottenham so much: he was an absolute Spurs nut and wanted to be involved in everything. He was also a charmer. I would imagine that, as a little boy, he charmed his grandmother and his aunties and always got whatever he wanted. He tried the same thing with me, but it didn't work too well.

Alan Sugar is the exact opposite of Scholar. He doesn't bother too much about the niceties of social intercourse. Where he is like Scholar is in wanting to be in charge of everything. In his business dealings, Sugar is the man who makes the decisions about how his money is spent. But here he is in football, going to put up £5-6 million, and the guy who actually decides where the money goes is not him, but the manager. That must kill these chairmen/owners. It's the one thing they will never really come to terms with. Even Jack Walker, a hands-off chairman for so long, has been trying to have a say in who his club buys. It was his idea, I believe, for Blackburn to offer Southampton £10 million for Matthew Le Tissier. With things going badly, he wanted to be the saviour, the local hero, again. Ray Harford and Kenny Dalglish preferred Lars Bohinen, however, and pulled off a masterstroke by signing the Norwegian international midfielder at a much cheaper price.

From what I have read in the papers, Newcastle's Sir John Hall reckons it is the new breed of wealthy, dynamic chairmen like himself who are driving the game forward at the moment. Priming the pump, I think he calls it. But it is the Premier League, and the fat television contracts it has attracted, which has pushed us on. The new chairmen cannot claim the credit for launching the Premier League, either, because most of them were not in power or in a position to influence events when it came into being in 1992-3. Newcastle, for instance, were still in the First Division then.

The prime movers were Martin Edwards (Manchester United), David Dein (Arsenal), Irving Scholar (Tottenham), Peter Robinson (Liverpool), Philip Carter (Everton) and, last but not least, the Football Association themselves. Without the FA's support, the idea would never have got off the ground because FIFA and UEFA would have withheld recognition of any league not sanctioned by the domestic governing body.

Where the above-mentioned clubs failed was over the TV

contract. They wanted to do a deal with ITV but were outvoted. That was largely because of Sugar's successful and well-documented intervention in the discussions on Sky's behalf. Ironically, he made his move when I was called away from the meeting to deal with what looked to be a hitch in Paul Gasgoigne's transfer to Lazio. So, to the extent that he was instrumental in persuading the Premier League clubs to accept the joint Sky-BBC TV bid of £304 million over five years, Sugar could be said to have driven the game forward. Yet the new league would hardly have been impoverished if they had gone for ITV's £262 million instead. In other words, the Premier League would have made a lot of money from television with or without Alan Sugar.

As for the Premier League itself, I think a lot of people have been surprised by its success, myself included. I was one of those who thought it would simply be the same old First Division under another name. But it has streamlined the structure, made money available to clubs to update their playing staffs and brought in the best from abroad. What the TV companies have done, in effect, is invest their money in the clubs to make the coverage of the game more attractive. So they have really invested in their own company, haven't they?

Nevertheless, some of the clubs have made good use of their new-found wealth. Sir John Hall, in particular, is doing a very impressive job of upgrading Newcastle. He is in a hotbed of football there, and making the most of it. One reason for Sir John's success is that he has done his homework. He's been on a fact-finding trip round Europe and he's copying the best of what he found there. I know he wants to copy Barcelona's multi-sport facilities because he asked me about them. That's why he's branched out into rugby, I suppose. Then it will be basketball teams and members' clubs, where your season ticket gives you access to facilities like a swimming pool and gymnasium as well as the football. Except your season ticket will cost a lot more.

Manchester United were a big club before the Premier League came along and they were very strong financially before the TV contracts brought so much money into the game. If you are a big club, it sweeps you along with it: it doesn't need driving. Arsenal are well organized, too, and have made good progress. Tottenham are so close to being there as well. They only need a bit more of a push because they have got the players to make them successful.

So, in advocating a change-over to a more democratic way of choosing club chairmen, I'm not calling for a bloody revolution. I don't want to see the good ones swept out of office just for the sake of it. If these guys are the men in possession, they should be put up for re-election with everyone else. Then it would be up to the people with the votes to recognize the worth of the candidates. If they decide Martin Edwards at Manchester United, say, or Dave Richards at Sheffield Wednesday has been doing a good job, give them another four years. But if others have been behaving badly in the job, vote them out of office. Only then will it be possible to hold the chairmen of English football clubs truly accountable for their decisions and actions.

Chapter Five

Great Teams

What does the average football fan want more from his or her team – results or attractive play? I'd be very surprised if he or she didn't say both. But what if you could choose only one of those alternatives? Would it be the ability to win things or the capacity to play with style, intelligence and imagination? I suppose it depends to a large extent on the traditions of the club you support. Speaking as a lifelong Tottenham supporter, I'd like a couple of years of winning the League any way we could, because it's 35 years now since we last did it. But I wouldn't want that for ever. I'd settle then for a couple of years when we finished second or third playing lovely football. Spurs, of course, have a reputation for providing entertainment and it comes very high on the fans' list of priorities. Arsenal, on the other hand, have always been more about winning than entertaining. But you can see lots of good things in a team that's won 3-1 away from home through sound organization, as Arsenal often have throughout the post-war period.

Results come first, I think, because you are dealing with human beings and some can't see things as clearly as others. They won't believe you when you tell them their team is playing well even though it's losing. But if the team is playing badly and winning, which is possible, the fans and the directors have got confidence. They look at that league table every morning, and you are up there. From that point, you can start refining the way the team plays and changing it slowly. Even Wimbledon have done that in the last couple of seasons: Joe Kinnear has actually had them playing good football. But it came off the back of organization. You can't do it the other way round. If you are going to complete a painting properly, you've got to get the base on first, then the

97

decoration. That's the only order you can do it in. Winning is not necessarily synonymous with organization, because it depends how good your team is. The Manchester United of Law, Best and Charlton didn't have to be that organized because those three just happened to be extravagantly talented. But the more organized you are, the better your chances of winning something.

I make the distinction between winning and entertaining because it is undoubtedly a combination of the two that bestows true greatness on a football team. It is the ideal most coaches and managers have striven for in the past 50 years, and it is a blend that is very difficult to achieve. Take the finalists in the 1994 World Cup, Brazil and Italy, and their respective coaches, Carlos Alberto Parreira and Arrigo Sacchi. There they are, the two most successful members of their profession in the world at that moment, and they are booed when they come to the final because their teams don't entertain. And if you can't enjoy appearing in a World Cup final, what's the point of doing the job? But they were men who were prepared to take it on the chin in support of their view that you cannot afford to give goals away first. It's harder than ever now to get goals in international football because defences are so much better organized. So if you are going to give them away, you are going to have twice the problem.

Brazil won on penalties after what I found a tactically fascinating, 120-minute goalless draw; and I didn't notice too many of their fans complaining afterwards as they did the samba in the streets of Pasedena and Los Angeles. All that mattered to them then was that their team had regained their rightful place as world champions after an agonizing wait of 24 years. Which is precisely what Parreira set out to achieve, of course. And the best way of doing that, he decided, was to replace some of Brazil's traditional flamboyance with a spot of good organization. It was a brave move because, with the fantastic 1970 team as their benchmark, the Brazilian fans had come to regard success with style as their birthright.

The performance of that 1970 side, Pele, Tostao, Gerson and company, was the best I've ever seen throughout the duration of a World Cup tournament. But no one else had the talent they had; and no one had any organization to counter it, either. Then, as the years went by, everyone else started to become more and more organized and the skill factor was gradually nullified. So Brazil didn't win any more. They kept going with their flamboyance and they satisfied the public, but only up to a point. Parreira decided, therefore, that if Brazil's superior skills were to count, they had to match the organization of their opponents.

Getting the balance right between winning and entertaining has become increasingly difficult to resolve because the importance of winning has grown greater and greater with the passage of time. It is especially difficult in England, where the competition in League football is fiercer and deeper than anywhere else in the world. We may not have the best League, technically speaking; but nowhere is it tougher to win a high proportion of your matches and carry off the championship. At least that's how it used to be: very little to choose between the teams in the top division and no such thing as an easy match against anyone. Nowadays, I'm afraid, we have grown more like most of the continental leagues, where only a handful of clubs have a realistic chance of winning the title and the others just make up the numbers.

But that is a fairly recent development. In the main, the greatest teams of the period have had to prove their durability as much as anything else. With 22 clubs in it for most of the time, the top division of English football has usually been bigger than those elsewhere. Therefore, it has provided a longer and harder test than most of the fitness, skill, nerve, morale and leadership required to win things. That test has been made even more severe by the authorities' refusal to copy the sensible example of other northern European nations and have a winter break. So the top English footballer not only has to ply his trade in a wide range of climatic conditions, but is provided with no respite from what has been rightly called the nine-month slog of an English season. Yet, despite all those handicaps, some teams have succeeded brilliantly in providing both success and entertainment over that gruelling course.

While selecting those I thought outstanding in that respect, it occurred to me it might amuse, stimulate or even provoke to list them in some kind of order of merit. So the evaluation that follows of the outstanding dozen teams of the last 50 years is what you might call the premier league to end all premier leagues. In my opinion, that is. It's difficult to compare like with like, because the quality, intensity and volume of English football has changed so much over the 50 years in question. All one can do is evaluate teams in their own historical context. With that in mind, here is my top 12:

1 Liverpool (1981–4)
2 Manchester United (1955–8)
3 Tottenham Hotspur (1960–3)
4 Leeds United (1964–74)
5 Manchester City (1965–71)
6 Everton (1984–7)
7 Nottingham Forest (1977–80)
8 Arsenal (1988–91)
9 Derby (1971–5)
10 Wolverhampton Wanderers (1953–5)
11 Aston Villa (1980–3)
12 Ipswich (1978–82)

The first and most important criterion was that they must have won the League Championship at least once. I then ignored my own restriction immediately to include the marvellous Ipswich team Bobby Robson put together in the late 1970s and early 80s. Since they twice finished second, to Aston Villa in 1980–1 and Liverpool the following season, and won the UEFA Cup to boot, I don't feel any apologies are required for stretching a point to accommodate them.

If you look round that team of Cooper; Burley, Osman, Butcher, Mills; Thijssen, Wark, Gates, Muhren; Mariner, Brazil, you'll find a very strong outfit indeed. Paul Cooper apart, they were all internationals. No disrespect to Cooper, but I could never understand why Bobby Robson didn't go out and buy a better goalkeeper. Someone like Peter Shilton might have made all the difference. Russell Osman and Terry Butcher were England Under-21 internationals when I was coaching the team, so I saw for myself that they were exceptionally good players. So were Paul Mariner, Alan Brazil and Eric Gates, who played in the 'hole' behind the other two. Then there was the incredible, abnormal goal-scoring of John Wark. The season Ipswich won the UEFA Cup, 1980–1, Wark finished up with a total of 36 goals in all competitions. And he was the *holding* midfield player! I know a lot of those goals came from the penalty spot, but no one could deny the Scotsman's skill at arriving late in the penalty area to meet crosses. He's just got the knack. Wherever Wark's been in his long career, he's scored goals.

But it was the introduction of the two skilful Dutchmen, Frans Thijssen and Arnold Muhren, that really set the team alight. By putting them either side of Wark in midfield, Bobby added a liberal dash of flair to the solid, typically British qualities of good players and good competitors like Mick Mills, Butcher, Osman and Mariner. It was an early example of how talented continental imports could improve the local product; and, even now, it's difficult to believe that Ipswich side didn't win the League. They were certainly super to watch.

So were the three teams at the top of this table. There was so little to choose between their quality, I had the greatest difficulty in separating them. In the end, the Liverpool side of 1981–4 (Grobbelaar; Neal, Lawrenson, Hansen, Alan Kennedy; Lee, McDermott (Whelan), Souness, Ray Kennedy; Dalglish, Rush) got my vote by the narrowest of margins over the Busby Babes of Manchester United and Tottenham's double-winning side of the early 1960s. But that was only part of the problem. First, you had to decide which was the best of the four great sides Liverpool produced in the 26 years between 1964 and 1990 and the three that emerged from Old Trafford between 1948 and 1964. In Liverpool's case it came down to a straight choice between the 1981–4 team and the one Kenny Dalglish built in 1987–8, halfway through his six years as manager at Anfield. The latter, the side that beat Nottingham Forest 5-0 and moved no less a judge than Tom Finney to describe their display as the best he had ever seen from an English club side, had John Barnes, Peter Beardsley, Ray Houghton, John Aldridge and, following his return from Juventus, Ian Rush, as its stars.

When it came to Manchester United, it was a question of deciding whether the Busby Babes were better than both the magnificent first side Matt Busby built from nothing after the war and the one, graced by Denis Law, George Best and Bobby Charlton, that finally realized, in 1968, his driving ambition of winning the European Cup. A lack of first-hand knowledge about the 1946–52 team (Johnny Carey, Allenby Chilton, Jack Rowley and company) probably affected my judgment, but I narrowed it down to the Babes v. Law, Best and Charlton; not an easy decision by any means. I went for the Babes (Gregg; Foulkes, Byrne; Colman, Jones, Edwards; Berry, Whelan, Taylor, Violett, Pegg (Charlton)) because they had real talent in more positions than their distinguished successors. You wouldn't find three individuals in one team who were better than Law, Best and Charlton, but their outstanding ability was all concentrated at the sharp end. I'm afraid we have to accept there were other areas of the side (Stepney; Brennan, Foulkes, Stiles (Sadler), Dunne; Best, Crerand, Charlton, Aston; Herd (Kidd), Law) that weren't quite as strong as the Babes' or Liverpool's.

Ultimately, I suppose, that Liverpool team of the early 1980s edged out the Babes largely because they won more. Remarkably, they carried off both the League Championship and the League Cup in each of the three seasons they prospered. Then, in the final season, they added the European Cup for good measure. Against that, the Babes could offer only two consecutive League titles and a few near-misses in the FA Cup and European Cup. The sad thing is that, because of the Munich air disaster in 1958, we don't know how that youthful Manchester United team would have developed. The signs were that they could have become the best English club side ever. But we don't know and never will know: it's one of those unfortunate, tragic situations. Quite possibly, the Babes *were* the best side we have ever seen, but we didn't see enough of them to be sure. The record books, on the other hand, show Liverpool were the best, and that's good enough for me.

Besides, any team lucky enough to include Kenny Dalglish, Graeme Souness, Ian Rush, Alan Hansen and Mark Lawrenson must be counted exceptional. Perhaps Dalglish, Souness and Rush were not quite in the Law, Best and Charlton class as individuals or an attacking force, but they were only a fraction away from it. As for Hansen and Lawrenson, it was almost worth the admission fee just to see them operate together as a central defensive partnership. Hansen's reading of the play and coolness under fire were second to none, while Lawrenson's wonderful mobility, clean tackling and general awareness made him the perfect foil for his tall, upright Scottish partner. Unusually, too, both were capable of carrying the ball comfortably out of defence and putting it to good use in attack. Hansen, in particular, would step out from the back like a continental defender and make unexpected forward runs that were invaluable to Liverpool when they were having trouble breaking down defensive opponents. If he had done it more often, and in a more forthright way, he would have been even more effective.

It is only fair that Liverpool should be hailed as the best of the best, because they have won more trophies and produced more good sides than any other club in the history of English football. In the years between 1964 and 1990, which were their greatest, they won the title 13 times and finished out of the top five only once. They also won the European Cup four times, still a record for an English club, and the UEFA Cup twice. There was, too, the little matter of four wins in both the FA Cup and the Football League Cup. It is a staggering record of achievement that will probably never be surpassed. No other club, certainly, has set such consistently high standards at home or represented English football abroad with such sustained distinction.

What made it all the more impressive was the way Liverpool managed to sustain their success over such a long period. They used to be famed, of course, for their ability to renew their teams as they went along, so that one just blended into another seamlessly and a very beneficial continuity was established. The same policy was pursued at managerial level, with Bob Paisley succeeding Bill Shankly, Joe Fagan taking over from Bob and then Kenny Dalglish replacing Joe, the appointments always being made from within. It was a strong, durable structure that produced nothing but good until Kenny shocked us all in 1991 by suddenly deciding the pressure was too great and walking away from the job. It seemed a good idea in theory to lure Graeme Souness, one of Liverpool's most distinguished former players, away from Glasgow Rangers and back to Anfield as Dalglish's replacement, but it did not work out in practice. However, learning from their mistakes has always been one of the club's strengths. So, following Souness's departure in 1994, they wasted no time in returning to their old policy and promoting Roy Evans – like Paisley and Fagan a product of Liverpool's famous boot-room think-tank – from within.

Currently in the process of re-establishing old habits, Roy seems to be on the way towards building yet another of the club's outstanding sides. They have had four of them already although, as I said earlier, they blended into each other so well it was not always easy to tell where one ended and the next began. Perhaps the easiest way to define them is through their striking partnerships. First you had Roger Hunt and Ian St John followed by John Toshack and Kevin Keegan. Then there was Rush and Dalglish followed by Aldridge or Rush and Peter Beardsley. Roy had a few problems choosing two from three, in the form of the veteran Rush, local sharpshooter Robbie Fowler and expensive signing Stan Collymore, until an injury to Rush allowed Fowler and Collymore to establish a formidable understanding. So formidable that Liverpool felt able to offer Rush a free transfer at the end of the 1995–6 season. Roy broke the existing British transfer record by paying Nottingham Forest £8.5 million for Collymore, but that should surprise no one. Liverpool have always been the biggest spenders in English football, yet they have never been labelled as such for some strange reason.

Whether the team were coached properly is something of a moot point. I say that only because Liverpool have never liked the word 'coaching'. Even now, Roy insists they don't coach their players, just 'organize' them. But it beats me what the difference is. If there is one it must be very subtle, because once you start 'organizing' a team, you are coaching it. I think it's just splitting hairs. What Ronnie Moran, their long-serving coach, would do in training is stand behind the players and shout something like, 'Come up, up, up!' Then the players would all push up, and he'd say, 'Go to him, go to him! Don't run across there, don't run across there!' This was happening day-in, day-out, but when you spoke to Liverpool players, they said they didn't do any coaching at the club. Everyone thought they must be covering up and trying not to give away any secrets, but then you realized the players really didn't think they were doing any work of that kind.

If you notice, whenever a Liverpool player is asked to define the secret of the club's success, he says there is no secret. I put the same question to Phil Neal once when I was the England Under-21 coach, but it was obvious from his reaction that he didn't think they were doing anything out of the ordinary. But they *were* doing something, all right. It was team planning and picking the right players to fit what they wanted to do, which was to push up from the back, use the goalkeeper as a sweeper, and make the pitch as big as possible when they had the ball and as small as possible when the opposition were in possession. The Dutch have put a lot of thought into altering the dimensions of a football pitch through the alignment of their players, but no more so than Liverpool. Just try to recall how many players have flourished after leaving Anfield. Offhand, Kevin Keegan is about the only one I can think of: the careers of most of them seem to dip when they move on. Perhaps it's because they don't know what to take with them. If so,

Liverpool's approach to coaching and tactics – sorry, organizing – is even cleverer than we thought.

Strong characters are an essential ingredient for any team aspiring to greatness. The outstanding Liverpool side had at least three, in Dalglish, Souness and Hansen, while the Babes were blessed with Roger Byrne, Bill Foulkes and Duncan Edwards. Better still, the two strongest characters in Tottenham Hotspur's double-winning side of the early 1960s, Danny Blanchflower and Dave Mackay, were in the all-important belly of the team. It helped that they were also among the most talented players. That side read as follows, in the 2–3–5 lay-out popular at the time: Brown; Baker, Henry; Blanchflower, Norman, Mackay; Jones, White, Smith, Allen, Dyson. They probably had fewer stars than the great sides produced by Manchester United, Liverpool and Leeds, but they were a very difficult team to play against because they were so quick-moving and passed the ball so accurately. No doubt their style of play could be traced back to the fact that the manager, Bill Nicholson, had been a member of the club's other great side, Arthur Rowe's 'push-and-run' team, a decade earlier.

John White, the Scottish international inside forward who was killed so tragically by lightning on the golf course, was particularly difficult to play against, I found. The truth is that John wasn't actually appreciated at the time. It was only after his death that people realized how good he was. He used to get some stick from the crowd because he was a bit lightweight physically, but he was actually a terrific player. Because of his light build, he'd lay the ball off very early so you couldn't go in and hit him. Like Tommy Harmer, the lightweight who preceded him in Spurs' midfield, John had gone before you got there. He never seemed to stop running, and trying to stay with him was unbelievably difficult. He'd wear you down just by running and running. When you put John White together with the cool, calculating Blanchflower and the buccaneering Mackay you have one of the greatest midfields ever. The wingers were Cliff Jones on the right and Terry Dyson on the left. You had a worker, a real forager, on one side, and a talented one, Jones, on the other. Cliff, as I hope I made clear in the chapter on great players, was one of my all-time favourites because of his searing pace, limitless bravery and wonderful heading ability. The wingers' job was mainly to provide a service for the strikers – Bobby Smith and Les Allen, two guys who couldn't make it at

Chelsea. They certainly made it at Tottenham, the clever, cagey Allen playing round the big, battering-ram centre-forward that Smith was. A lot of people assume Jimmy Greaves was a member of the double-winning side, but he wasn't signed from AC Milan until the start of the following season. Les Allen was the man who had to make way for him, and the experience left its mark on Les. He was a team player, and it's said the loss of his place to Greaves, a goal-scoring specialist, was the reason he encouraged his son, Clive Allen, to be as single-minded as possible anywhere near goal when he, too, became a leading striker.

It wasn't easy to score against that Spurs team. Peter Baker and Ron Henry, two strong full-backs, flanked a tall, commanding centre-half in Maurice Norman. Because Norman was so good in the air, it didn't matter too much that the goalkeeper, Bill Brown, wasn't great on crosses. He made up for that weakness by being a great goal-line saver. They weren't all internationals by any means. Baker and Dyson didn't win any caps at all, and Henry only played the once for England. You just had all these pieces of the puzzle that fitted together. It was the blend, the mixture of players, that made it so successful; and it worked to perfection. That, of course, was down to the skill of the manager, Bill Nicholson.

The formula did not work for as long as Don Revie's at Leeds, though. Tottenham won the FA Cup again and the European Cup-Winners' Cup in the couple of seasons after they had done the double, but that was just about the extent of their successful run. Leeds, on the other hand, came very close to dominating English football totally in the ten years between 1964 and 1974. Close, but not close enough. Although they were champions twice in that decade, they finished as runners-up on no fewer than five occasions. Similarly, they won the FA Cup once and lost three other finals. European football offered little respite from the bridesmaid syndrome, either. Two wins in the Fairs Cup, later to become the UEFA Cup, were balanced by defeats in the finals of the European Cup and Cup-Winners' Cup.

It was a classic case, really, of not resolving soon enough the problem of organization and entertainment I was talking about at the start of this chapter. Leeds were a wonderful passing team, and it was a great pity Don didn't let them off the leash a bit earlier. I know John Giles agrees with that, because he often had debates, discussions and arguments with Revie about it. Don had a very 'safety-first' approach to the job, but the sheer quality of his team simply demanded to be expressed in the end. The decision was virtually taken out of his hands, so to speak. Had it happened earlier, they might have won more trophies. It would have been easier, too, for new players to come into the side and perhaps create the sort of continuity that developed at Liverpool for 25 years. But it wasn't to be. There was just that one era, and then it was over.

Remarkably, the team changed very little over those ten years once the side that lost to Liverpool in the 1965 FA Cup final had been rebuilt. In its most recognizable form it read: Sprake; Reaney, Charlton, Hunter, Cooper; Lorimer, Bremner, Giles, Gray; Jones, Clarke. David Harvey eventually replaced the accident-prone Gary Sprake in goal, and Paul Madeley, Trevor Cherry and Terry Yorath had forced their way into contention by the time Revie left in 1974 to manage England. But that was about it. Some of the key figures, like Norman Hunter, Billy Bremner and Giles, played right through the whole period.

As a team, they had a lot of good passers of the ball. Terry Cooper could play from the back, and so could Hunter despite his hard-man image. Jack Charlton was a bit upright, but he knew his limitations and would give the ball to the nearest white shirt. Paul Reaney was similar to Charlton, but the rest of them all had outstanding qualities. Eddie Gray, for instance, could go by defenders with ease and provide the sort of crosses that produce goals. On the other flank, Peter Lorimer was possibly the hardest hitter of the ball we've seen in English football. He could score goals from huge distances. Last, but not least, there was the drive, aggression and extraordinary passing ability of the central midfield players, Bremner and Giles. For two small guys, what they put into Leeds' play was quite something.

Malcolm Allison and Joe Mercer's Manchester City were different again: very different, in fact. They introduced mobility and movement before its time, and they used a sort of WM formation at a stage, the late 1960s, when it was being replaced by 4–3–3 and 4–4–2. The WM formation was the system of play used by most English teams before the Second World War and for quite a few years after it. It was called WM because the positioning of the players was such that, if you joined up the dots, as it were, you created the letters W and M. Below is an example of what I mean, using the old positional terminology rather than dots:

Goalkeeper

Right-back   Centre-half   Left-back

Right-half   Left-half

Inside-right   Inside-left

Outside-right   Centre-forward   Outside-left

Thus, that City side used to line up as follows:

Dowd

Book   Booth   Pardoe

Doyle   Oakes

Bell   Young

Summerbee   Lee   Coleman

At the time, as I say, City were bucking the tactical trend by rely-ing on what had become an old-fashioned system. But that was Malcolm and his unusual thinking for you. He was ahead of his time, because it is very like the system used now by Ajax, the European and world club champions. The only real difference is that, in Ajax's system, the two full-backs play much closer to the centre-half to help deal with opposing strikers and to stop the other team exploiting the spaces between the three defenders. The classic way of destroying the WM defence was to hit long balls inside the full-backs. Johnny Haynes, the Fulham and England inside-forward, was the expert at that. He and his kind became such a threat that coaches moved one of the wing-halves back alongside the centre-half to plug the gaps and create what has become the familiar back-four. You now have a 4–3–3 formation, which can be converted to 4–4–2 by pushing one of the inside-for-wards up to play alongside the centre-forward and withdrawing the two wingers to slightly deeper positions.

Before 4–3–3, there was 4–2–4. That was the system popularized by the Brazilians when they won the World Cups of 1958 and 1962. Brazil chose it partly because the 'third-back' (i.e. two full-backs plus a centre-half) game was foreign to them, and partly because they had, in Didi and Zito, two players capable of dominating the midfield on their own. They had full-backs who played like wingers, too. They've still got them now – Roberto Carlos on the left and Jorginho on the other side.

The appeal of 4–2–4 diminished in this country when teams realized you could outnumber the opposition in the most important area of the pitch, midfield, by playing an extra man there. I remember vividly playing for Tottenham against Arsenal on a red-hot day early in the season during the late 1960s. Most of us were playing 4–2–4 then, but Arsenal had three in the middle of the park. It gave us a real problem because it was so hard to get the ball. So we, and everybody else, brought someone back. Then somebody else brought another one back, giving four against three. The next step was to bring a striker back, so you had five in midfield. The whole idea, of course, is to have your players in the area or areas where the ball is going to be most often.

Graham Taylor's Watford were a bit of a throwback, tactically, while he was manager at Vicarage Road between 1977 and 1987, but not in the way you might think. Basically, they played 4–2–4 because they transferred the ball from the back to the front very quickly and everyone had to push up to get the knockdowns. If, on the other hand, you are going to play through the team, you've got to have a lot of players where the ball's going to be, i.e. the middle of the park. Otherwise, the two strikers will be isolated. That kind of isolation is one of the things that's wrong with Arsenal's present system, in my opinion. They use three at the back, but find it difficult to play the ball out of defence because the two central midfield players operate too close together. Dennis Bergkamp is the playmaker they want to get the ball to, but the defence can't do that as often as they would like because other players are in the way. So they are forced to lump it upfield.

What it all boils down to is trying to get some sort of advantage over the opposition. In any team sport, tactics must play an important part. The trouble is that, since the last war, a lot of the best English teams would say: 'Oh, tactics are nothing. Coaching coaches the good play out of the game.' It was that kind of blinkered attitude which enabled the rest of the world to come and look at us, take what was good from our game and improve on it.

At any rate, the WM formation worked so well for the Manchester City of Allison and Mercer that they won the League Championship, the FA Cup, the League Cup and the European Cup-Winners' Cup between 1967 and 1970. It worked, I think, because there was a good mixture of strong characters, such as Mike Doyle and Tony Book, and outstanding players such as Colin Bell, Francis Lee, Neil Young, Mike Summerbee and Tony Coleman, some of whom were also strong characters. The most outstanding of them, for me, was Bell. Like John White of Tottenham, he was a wonderful athlete, very difficult to stay with and not given his due at the time. Perhaps it was because this great talent didn't manage to reproduce his club form at international level for England as he would have liked. But there's no doubt that his heading, ball skills and passing were all very good indeed.

Bell, in fact, was one of the few players we've had in this country who could do everything. People might say he didn't have the ability of a Rodney Marsh or a Tony Currie, but they would be wrong. He was a long-distance runner, he could tackle, he could head the ball, he could shoot, he could pass, he could beat people. In many ways, Bell was similar to Johan Cruyff in his own day and to the Dutch players Edgar Davids and Clarence Seedorf today. If you look at our players over the years, a lot of them are one-dimensional. They are great defenders, great dribblers, great goal-scorers, great passers, but not many of them have been able to do all those things. They are always clever players who didn't want to work, workers who had no cleverness. So the all-round qualities of Colin Bell really set him apart.

He was such a thoroughly modern footballer, he would not have been out of place nearly 20 years later in the fine Everton team with which manager Howard Kendall threatened to break the steely grip neighbours Liverpool had taken on English football. At the time of the Heysel Stadium disaster in May 1985, Everton had deposed Liverpool as English champions and were preparing to show what they could do in the European Cup the following season. Sadly, it was not to be. They were deprived of their reward by the banning of English clubs from European football as punishment for the lethal misbehaviour of Liverpool fans at the European Cup final in Brussels. It's not difficult to imagine how frustrated Everton must have felt, since they had qualified for Europe twice over by winning the European Cup-Winners' Cup, tool. They reacted remarkably well to the disappointment, nearly doing the double the following season and winning the title again the season after that. But the continuation of the European ban is thought to have been one of the reasons a disillusioned Kendall left Goodison Park in 1987 and went to Spain to coach Athletic Bilbao.

Kendall was already an Everton folk-hero before he started filling the club's trophy cabinet as their manager. You've only to say 'Kendall, Ball and Harvey' and the eyes of any Everton fan will light up with pleasure at the memory of a very special midfield trio. Kendall, Alan Ball and Colin Harvey were the heart and soul of the Harry Catterick side that won the League Championship in 1969–70. It was a very good team which also included England internationals Brian Labone, Ray Wilson and Joe Royle; but it was not as good as the side Kendall produced during his first spell as Everton's manager, in my opinion. Overall, the balance of that team and the quality of the individuals in it were not as impressive as those of the side that ought to have become a dominant force at home and abroad in the latter part of the 1980s.

The team that won the title in 1984–5, Southall; Stevens, Mountfield, Ratcliffe, Van den Hauwe; Steven, Bracewell, Reid, Sheedy; Sharp, Gray, had remarkable all-round strength and balance. Everyone but Derek Mountfield was a senior international, or about to become one, and there was hardly a weakness anywhere. Perhaps the excellence of the team's balance was best illustrated by the sight of Trevor Steven, a wonderful player, tucked in a little on the right wing and Kevin Sheedy going out wide on the other. Graeme Sharp and Andy Gray were two outstanding strikers who worked together well despite being a bit similar in style. Gray, I thought, was a better player than he is a pundit, though he's pretty good at that, too. With Graeme and Andy there, they had to play it to feet or head because those two didn't have the pace for the ball over the top of the defence.

All that changed the following season, when Everton bought Gary Lineker from Leicester and paired him with Sharp. Gary was really quick in those days, and his exceptional pace was soon being exploited by Sharp's flick-ons or Sheedy's first-time balls over the top. The change of style very nearly won Everton the League Championship and the FA Cup, but Kendall, steeped in the club's 'School of Science' traditions, wasn't happy about the directness of

111

his team's play. So when I, as Barcelona's coach, offered Everton £2.2 million for Gary only a year later, Howard was quite prepared to let me have him. He then proved a bit of a point by reverting to the team's previous, more studied style of play and winning the title again the following season. By then, Adrian Heath had replaced Lineker in attack and two new signings, Dave Watson and Paul Power, had come into the defence.

Changes of style were not something that ever happened to teams managed by Brian Clough. Throughout his productive years in charge of Derby and Nottingham Forest, Cloughie built sides that were essentially counter-attacking units. Although Brian's teams have always been admired for the quality of their passing game, and rightly so, it has sometimes been overlooked how defensive they were. Dave Mackay enjoyed an Indian summer as a central defender at Derby before succeeding Clough as manager in controversial circumstances, and it was he who revealed the simple truth that the great man's teams were imbued with the 'clean-sheet' philosophy. In other words, the first priority was to stop the other team scoring.

I can remember Nottingham Forest always going to Liverpool and getting good results, basically because they had talented foot-ballers playing defensively. It wasn't really a defensive strategy. The Forest players would put themselves in areas to stop you play-ing; but when they got the ball they had attacking players in their defensive set-up, not defensive players in a defensive set-up. They just put enough bodies in there, and if they got them to work hard enough they could play out and give you problems when they won possession. Here, then, is a prime example of what I was say-ing when I was talking earlier about organization and entertain-ment. Clough realized, as do all great managers, that you cannot entertain, or win, unless you get organized first. It has to happen that way round: no other sequence is possible.

Tactically, Derby and Forest were very similar. They had the same basic pattern. There would be four players close together at the back, one midfielder holding and grafting and one breaking forward, one winger tucked in but the other right against the touch line. In the Derby team, it was John McGovern tucked in and Alan Hinton out wide: in the Forest side, Martin O'Neill and John Robertson. Then you had two strikers working off each other non-stop: John O'Hare and Kevin Hector for Derby and Gary Birtles and Tony Woodcock for Forest. Both teams had Brian Clough written all over them, but there's nothing wrong with that. I don't know whether it was by design or not, but Clough's Derby played a more attacking game than his Forest. That was probably because they had a lot of good attacking players. Central defenders like Roy McFarland and Colin Todd, for example, could come out into midfield and put you under pressure. Derby would win by fours and fives because they were such an attacking threat.

Forest were the more successful side overall, but Clough spent much longer at the City Ground (18 years) than he did at the Baseball Ground (six years). Curiously, though, Clough won the League Championship only the once with Forest (1977–8), as he had with Derby (1971–2). The bulk of his success came through the League Cup, which Forest claimed four times, and the European Cup, which they won twice in consecutive seasons (1978–9, 1979–80). Quite clearly, Forest were more of a cup side than anything else. Which makes it all the stranger that the oldest prize of them all, the FA Cup, should have eluded Cloughie right to the end of his long and colourful career.

There were certain similarities between the teams of Brian Clough and George Graham in that both men believed fervently in the value of a strong defence. From his arrival at Highbury in 1986 until 1991, George was content for Arsenal to play through the midfield. In fact, they were playing really well at the time I came back from Barcelona in 1987 to manage Tottenham. We were all over the place, and they'd had a terrific year with all the youngsters who had come through. Players like Tony Adams, David Rocastle, Michael Thomas and Paul Merson, who had been brought on by Don Howe while he was manager before George. It was one of the most exciting Arsenal sides I've seen. We played them in a Makita Tournament, as I arrived at White Hart Lane for my first pre-season, and they beat us 5–0.

It was a good, solid team that developed into an outstanding side over the next few years as Arsenal won the League Championship twice in three seasons (1988–9 and 1990-1). David Seaman, Lee Dixon, Nigel Winterburn and Steve Bould were bought to supplement Adams and provide a defensive backbone that was still going strong last season, 1995–6; but the midfield was the really exciting part of the team. There was Rocastle, so clever, so sharp, so quick; Thomas, who would get from box to box making great runs and worrying the life out of you, yet able to do his share of tackling and get stuck in; Paul Davis, a very skilful player and great passer of the ball; and Brian Marwood, who wasn't at Highbury for very long but arrived at exactly the right time. Going into a team like that brought out all his good qualities as a winger. Then, up front, there were two really accomplished footballers in Merson and Alan Smith. I thought that team had everything: they were a team for all seasons.

They were definitely more exciting than the Arsenal side that did the double in 1970–1. That was an excellent team, too, but their triumph was based principally on solid teamwork. The back-four gave very little away, even though they had two reasonably small centre-backs in Frank McLintock and Peter Simpson. Tactically shrewd, those two kept getting up to the 18-yard line so quickly that you couldn't get near the goal to outjump them. McLintock and Simpson were very strong and intelligent footballers, but the team as a whole was a bit stereotyped. It didn't have the charisma that George's team of the late 1980s and early 90s had to go with the teamwork.

Sadly, George's purple patch didn't last long. Rocastle and Thomas were transferred and Davis lost his first-team place as Arsenal's dour image of old was allowed to reassert itself. To be honest, I don't think George would ever change: he'd always want his team to be a bit solid, with two six-footers in defence and two in attack, and grind out results. It's strange that a guy who was so skilful as a player should want to play that way, but there's no accounting for that sort of thing is there? No doubt he would reply by pointing to the cup double – FA and League – Arsenal achieved in 1992–3 and the good teams they beat to win the European Cup-Winners' Cup the following season. But it's not my idea of how the game should be played.

George didn't want a boring team, he wanted a successful one. He just felt that, by entertaining too much, he was giving himself less chance of winning. He thought there would be more chance of being inconsistent, I think. But he should have gone on from there. There are similarities between George's Arsenal and Egil Olsen's Norway. Olsen did well to devise a new strategy and get his country to the 1994 World Cup finals; but that's as far as it went. Playing against Italy, who were down to ten men, Norway did not change their ultra-cautious tactics. So they gave the advantage back to the Italians. They went a goal down, and still they didn't change it. They were so indoctrinated with Olsen's brainwashing about how to play that they couldn't go on from there.

If the Arsenal of Graham's later years at Highbury typified the directness that crept back into English football during its banishment from Europe, the Wolverhampton Wanderers team of the 1950s were the outstanding exponents of how it used to be played. The difference is largely one of precision. Today, it's a question of getting the ball forward early, usually to a big striker, then battling untidily for the knock-downs or flick-ons. But in Wolves' era, the ball was hit long with a specific purpose, usually to find the wingers with a pass inside the opposing full-back. Released behind the defence, the wingers would then shoot at goal or play the ball across it for the centre-forward or attacking inside-forward to finish off.

Stan Cullis's formidable team thrived on those straightforward tactics because they had two quick and dangerous wingers in Johnny Hancocks and Jimmy Mullen, an inside-forward in Peter Broadbent who could drop 30- and 40-yard passes on to a postage stamp, and a succession of strikers – Jesse Pye, Dennis Wilshaw, Roy Swinbourne and Jimmy Murray – who were deadly in front of goal. I have to confess to a vested interest here, because Tottenham were not the only team I supported as a boy. Wolves were my other favourites; and the very fact that I, a young Londoner, should have been attracted to a side from the Midlands shows what a powerful influence they must have exerted at the time.

It's little wonder, really. The team that won the League Championship in 1953–4 – which my elders assure me was the best of the three slightly different ones with which Cullis won the title three times and the FA Cup twice between 1948 and 1960 – also thrilled and reassured the nation with their exploits against a succession of top-ranked European clubs at Molineux. Between November 1954 and November 1955, Wolves beat Moscow Spartak (as they were known then) 4–0, Honved 3–2 and Moscow Dynamo 2–1 in a series of televised challenge matches (this was before the advent of the European competitions). All those results were important, but none more so than the victory over the Hungarian side, Honved. Since their opponents fielded six of the Hungarian national team who had destroyed England 6–3 at Wembley only a year earlier, Wolves' triumph was seen as both revenge for that humiliation and proof that the supposed superiority of English football might not be at an end, after all. For the record, that all-conquering Wolves side was: Williams; Short, Pritchard; Slater, Shorthouse, Wright; Hancocks, Broadbent, Swinbourne, Wilshaw, Mullen.

There was something of Arsenal's dourness and Wolves' directness about the Aston Villa side that won the League Championship in 1980–1 and the European Cup the following season. Tony Barton was actually in charge when they became champions of Europe by beating Bayern Munich 1–0 in Rotterdam; but the team was really the creation of Ron Saunders, whose no-nonsense methods had previously won Norwich promotion to the old First Division of the Football League. If you are an Aston Villa supporter, you will always love that side for what they did; but they qualify for my premier league on their record alone. Their actual football has been likened critically to Arsenal's, and I have to say it wasn't my cup of tea.

If you are a player, a member of the management team or a director from that period, you'll probably be a bit upset by such criticism. No doubt you'll be saying, 'Well, we must have been doing something right!' And that Villa team did do a lot right, of course. Peter Withe and Gary Shaw were a good attacking combination, for instance. I liked Shaw a lot, and it was a great shame he got the bad knee injury that finished his career so early. I think he could have gone on to be a player of real stature. He played with Adrian Heath and all those other promising lads in the England Under-21 team I coached, and I was convinced he was going to become a star. Apart from that, all I can say is that they had an uncompromising back-four in Kenny Swain, Ken McNaught, Allan Evans and Gary Williams, and a good goalkeeper in either Jimmy Rimmer or Nigel Spink. Gordon Cowans supplied what little subtlety there was in midfield and Tony Morley troubled defenders with his pace on the wing. But there was not a lot else to commend that team.

It certainly distresses me to have to put Bobby Robson's attractive Ipswich side below them, but Ipswich are only there on sufferance because they failed the acid test of winning a League Championship. Ron Greenwood's West Ham (1963–5) and Dave Sexton's Chelsea (1969–71) were other entertaining sides I was tempted to include, but like Ipswich they were more successful in European

116

football than in their domestic league. Apologies, too, to all the Portsmouth fans who revere the Jimmy Scoular–Jimmy Dickinson side that won the title two seasons running in 1948–9 and 1949–50. I'm told they were a very good team, but I simply didn't have enough first-hand knowledge to evaluate them in this context.

I think what all my top dozen teams have in common is that they have played their football with great passion. They have also had a lot of outstanding individual players. If you look down that list of mine, all the teams in the top six had extremely good individuals working hard for the side. They all worked their socks off. In fact, you name me a truly great player who didn't do that for his team. When you think of Law, Best and Charlton, for instance, you don't think of shirkers exactly, do you? Forest, Arsenal and Derby had some terrific players, but I don't think they were quite as good as Souness, Rush and Dalglish; Byrne, Edwards and Colman; Blanchflower, Mackay, Jones and White; or Giles, Bremner, Gray and Clarke. Hence, they finished lower down my league.

Something else that strikes me about these teams is the fact that most of them used a 4-4-2 formation. Manchester United, Tottenham, Manchester City and Wolves, all WM sides, were the only ones who didn't play that way. The fondness for 4–4–2 is understandable because it is probably the most serviceable formation of all in a league as physically taxing as ours. It's interesting that several teams went for two full-backs and three central defenders last season (1995–6), because we've never had a team who played that way and were successful. Generally speaking, the most successful teams of the last 50 years are those who have played four at the back. Maybe that's only because they nearly always played against 4–4–2 formations, and things will change now that formations are changing.

I think it's a very good thing for English football that so many clubs are experimenting with three at the back. It means that if you play an orthodox back-four, you've got to do something different with it. You've got to get your full-backs bombing on or you want your central defence coming out and making another man in midfield. Or, you've got to say: this is how we play now; we've got an extra midfield man. I think teams are starting to do that. They will develop it and get better at it, and that's when we will start catching up on everyone else.

In the end, I believe, it all comes down to good organization, tactics, coaching, call it what you will. And that means having a knowledgeable, skilful manager or coach in charge. Ajax, AC Milan and Brazil, the three most successful teams in European and world football during the past five years, all have one thing in common: they are heavily into tactical organization. That's because, at the highest level, you win nothing without discipline. In the past, if you had players who were a little bit better than the opposition's, you would win. Then the opposition started to negate the difference in talent with tactics, and they began to get results. Now, even the top teams have to get organized. Otherwise, they are going to lose the advantage of having better players.

Tactics, as Ajax, AC Milan and Brazil have shown, can be a beautifully creative thing as well as a negative influence. All of those outstanding sides have proved beyond doubt that it is possible to strike a balance between organization and entertainment. Normally, it's hard to persuade your talented players to to be organized or to work awfully hard, because they've had success doing it their way. But that is what Ajax have done. They get their talented players to do the donkey work as well. All of them have to do a pretty hefty team job. Because Ajax shape their players' thinking from an early age, it is accepted without question that being a talented individual doesn't give you the right to a free ride. What Pele called 'the beautiful game' is the ideal most of us are striving for, I'd like to think; but it begins with sound organization, good discipline and sheer hard work. Those are football's three steps to heaven.

Chapter Six

The Media, the Agent and the Fan

Football is a simple game, so they say. And so it is, but only up to a point. It's getting more and more complex all the time on the field as tactics become increasingly sophisticated; and it's been a really tangled business off it for a long time now. Ever since television began to establish itself as king of the media jungle in the early 1960s, in fact. That was a real turning-point in the relationship between football, the fan and the people whose job it is to report the game to the public. On the most obvious level, television brought an immediacy and an intimacy to the relationship that had not been there before. All of a sudden, football was being projected straight into the living-room, and the football fan became so familiar with his heroes he felt he knew them personally. Gone were the days when he or she had to wait for the great players to come to town. Now they could sit at home and see them all on *Match of the Day*.

But the arrival, and rapid dominance, of television had other, less obvious effects. One of them was the pressure, direct and indirect, it began to exert on newspapers. Virtually unchallenged previously as the main channel of communication between football and its public, the papers felt they could no longer sell just on match reports and official announcements from the clubs. Something stronger and more stimulating was required, something even TV could not reveal. Television's coverage of football, I believe, ushered in the age of the back page 'exclusive'. Fairly tame at first, the competition for football 'scoops' grew fiercer as players' wages and transfer fees escalated in the wake of the abolition of the maximum wage in 1961 and the destruction of the retain and transfer system two years later.

At the same time, newspaper circulation figures were shrinking

119

– largely because of TV's popularity – at a rate which sent several of them to the wall. So that battle for survival helped to make the competition for sensational football stories even more cut-throat. Today, the whole business is seriously out of control; but more of that later.

Football reporters had their noses put out of joint in another way during the 1960s and 1970s. Needing help to deal with their own growing affluence and the game's increasing complexity off the field, footballers began to employ agents to look after their affairs. In the relatively simple days before that, the football reporter with good contacts had often acted as a go-between when a transfer was being arranged. The reporter would be grafting in the background to help the club or the player, and to get a story into the bargain. So he lost one of his functions when having an agent became the norm, and it's hardly surprising that the agent became the enemy in the eyes of some reporters. Others, though, quickly realized the agent could be a valuable source of the 'scoops' they were looking for and made sure they contacted him on a regular basis for exclusive information from or about his clients.

The person this system is supposed to benefit in the long run is the fan. He really wants to know about his team, he is bursting for information about it. He wants to be the man in the pub with all the answers when he's having a drink with his mates. The more information he can get, the more knowledgeable he can look. Everybody wants to be somebody; everybody wants to be important; everybody wants to have that little edge over somebody else. When I was a school-kid, I used to go and watch Tottenham. You didn't really get much then about the players because there was no television. So, at school on a Monday morning, I was almost as big a star as the players because I'd actually been to the game on the Saturday and could tell the other kids all about it. Even now, the fans can't go up to Gerry Francis or Bruce Rioch and ask them about the team. There are just too many of them to make it feasible. There's got to be an agency between the fan and the club, and that is why I feel the press and television have a tremendous responsibility. The fan can only make judgments on the basis of the information he is offered, so it's essential the information is as accurate as possible.

For the most part, television cannot be faulted on that score. I have my own reservations about *Panorama*, after the two wildly inaccurate programmes they did on me, but TV's presentation of the game itself is pretty good. Having said that, I do have to admit they don't like you to say there are any bad matches if you are a pundit. They don't actually ask you to tell a lie, but they do ask you to play the bad stuff down, and stick with the good points. I always remember the first World Cup game I commented on. I said it had replaced Mogadon, the sleeping tablet. It was a quip that had been used before, but they didn't like it at all. So I told them I couldn't say anything other than what I saw in a game. Unless I do that, I said, the viewers are not going to take us seriously. The people out there are not fools. We are actually talking to people who have been brought up watching football and they know it's a disappointing match. You can say it was a success tactically, but its entertainment value was awful. They'll go along with that. Which takes me back to England's game in Norway last year . . . but that's another story.

Although Sky have got some pretty good people making a pretty good effort to do it already, I think they've got to become tougher, punchier and more to the point in their coverage of football. Television is a wonderful vehicle because everyone's seen the game and they have their own opinions about it. So if it's a poor game, you've got to say it's a poor game. But you've also got to explain why it was a poor game; and if there was anything good in it, you've got to point that out as well. If it's all done properly, it can be fascinating. It's particularly satisfying to get a discussion going. Arguments, disagreements: that's what people like to watch at home. When I'm on television, I always like to think the viewer is shouting at us on the screen. Normally, everyone agrees with each other and it's all very jolly. That's why it was popular when Jimmy Hill and I disagreed vehemently with each other. That's what the viewers want to hear. They don't want to be patronized.

Overall, certainly, the medium has been beneficial for English football. It has pumped millions of pounds into the game, especially since the old BBC-ITV cartel was broken in 1988. What happened there was that Greg Dyke, then head of ITV Sport, cleverly outmanoeuvred his rivals, who included BSB, the satellite company that was swallowed up by Sky, to scoop the exclusive rights to Football League matches. That broke the cartel, which had kept television fees artificially low, and opened the financial floodgates so far as football was concerned. As Alex Fynn and Lynton Guest put it in their analysis of the modern game, *Out of Time – Why Football Isn't Working*: 'Before 1988, English football received less than £5 million per season from television. After 1988 the figure rose to over £20 million with every prospect that even this sum could be bettered in the future.'

Just how much it could be bettered was shown by the £305 million, five-year deal the Premier League did with Sky and BBC TV in 1992. The injection of £60 million a year was largely responsible for the economic success of the League, the old First Division of the Football League in a new, breakaway guise. Now they have done a new, five-year deal worth £180 million a season from 1997–8, and it's not likely to stop there. As chief executive of Tottenham, I agreed with everything that was done in 1992. I like the idea of a football channel, I liked it right from the beginning. There's a lot of air-time to fill, and you get programmes on there you wouldn't get on terrestrial television. It's an astonishingly good arrangement for football in that the game gets very well paid for lots of free publicity. Contrary to popular opinion, I thought it would enhance gates, which I think it has. Aggregate attendances rose in 1994–5 for the ninth consecutive season, the first time it had happened since the war, even though the game is televised these days more often than ever before.

The ideal in television coverage, I think, would be a sort of terrestrial Sky, if that isn't a contradiction in terms. I am one of the traditionalists who believe the big national sporting events should be made available on television to the whole nation, regardless of whether people can afford to pay for it or not. It's good in some ways that the two terrestrial channels, ITV and BBC, have retained the England games and the FA Cup, because they should be seen by a wider audience than Sky can offer. I can understand the principle of people having to pay extra to see films and other things not immediately available on terrestrial TV, but when it's got something to do with your national team – football, cricket or whatever – I don't think a satellite company should have the sole right to it. But that's what they've cashed in on, of course. They are squeezing people to pay out, virtually compelling them to buy their dishes.

The $64,000 question now is where the relationship between football and television goes from here. The game has to be very careful about the future, I think, because it's not just a question of money, but of control. As things stand, we have gone into the relationship without thinking things through. The clubs are so dazzled by all that money on offer that they think they are in wonderland. They are getting greedy, too. If someone says another channel will give them £100,000 more, they say let's have that one. Instead of just grabbing at the money like that, they should be standing back a little and thinking perhaps it might be better if they took a bit less from someone who would allow them some control over the way the game is covered.

If you are not careful, the TV people will have a microphone up your nose or inside your left armpit. They'll be in the dressing-room and jumping in the bath with you. Football clubs have to have some control over this situation: they've got to retain some dignity. When it comes to television, we should be looking at America to see how the relationship between the medium and sport has developed there. Theirs is the biggest television coverage of sport in the world. So we should examine it minutely, take it apart, to see where the hidden dangers are likely to be in 10–15 years' time.

One danger already sticking out like a sore thumb is that the money from television might suddenly dry up. Let's face it, Sky have not been so generous to English football out of the goodness of their hearts. They know football sells the dishes and attracts the subscribers they need to pay their way. That's why they are so willing to hand over these massive sums to the clubs. But what happens when Sky have sold all the dishes, got all the subscribers, they need? It's most unlikely they would walk away from football completely, but there's every chance they would want to pay a lot less for the TV rights. In other words, the clubs could suffer in the same way as if a major benefactor like Jack Walker or Sir Jack Hayward suddenly decided to withdraw his investment.

The trick, I think, is not to jump into bed with just one television company, but to spread your favours around a lot of them. Trevor Phillips, the FA's former commercial director, was working along the right lines with the multi-company package he tried to sell to the Football League. Each company is then fearful of dropping out because the others will profit from their departure. But if you put all your eggs in one basket with one company and they withdraw, the whole of your budget is threatened, the whole of your existence is threatened. Sir John Hall, the Newcastle chairman, has confessed that his club is becoming increasingly reliant on TV money because, in an area of high unemployment like Tyneside, he cannot afford to increase his admission prices too much. When you are committed to buying the best players and paying the biggest wages, that's not a healthy position to be in. In this context, I've felt for a long while that something unhealthy was getting bigger and bigger. Apart from anything else, it puts the TV company in question into an incredibly strong bargaining position when the contract negotiations come round again.

All in all, I think television is very good for the game provided we can anticipate the dangers it represents. Ideally, we should have someone in charge of the contract negotiations who has the vision to foresee what is likely to happen in the next 20 years! Someone who won't allow the clubs to get carried away by the immediate impact of a big offer. Someone who understands that the game has still got to be able to control television. Because if we don't control it, it will control us - that's for sure. They are already setting the agenda by dictating who plays where and when, and it's going to get worse if we are not careful. The big test will come when television's digital revolution is complete and each club can have its own channel, if it wants it. Will they all sell their souls to TV then, or will those who can afford to put up their admission prices be a bit more choosy?

In the long run, I feel, television will cover football so well and so comprehensively that attendances could be seriously affected. It may get to the stage where people find it inconvenient to leave their homes to go to the game in the rain, and try to park the car, unless the facilities are absolutely superb. But even if they move the grounds to more convenient sites outside the big cities, as they have in America and Spain, I don't think improved facilities will be enough to entice the football fan of the future out of his armchair. What will happen, I'm convinced, is that they will end up giving tickets away for the stadium, as they do for television chatshows. They may even have to go a step further than that and pay people to attend. The clubs will raise revenue through a pay-per-view system at home, but they will have to give tickets away for the game to ensure there is an atmosphere in the stadium. Everyone will conduct their affairs from home in the end, I believe, and not just because television offers an easy and convenient link with the outside world. Society could become so violent eventually that people will be afraid to go over the doorstep.

Talking of violence, I think television has done football a service on and off the field by fixing the game with its all-seeing eye. It's true that the presence of the cameras puts the players and referees under greater pressure than ever, but that's not necessarily a bad thing so far as the players are concerned. If people think they can get away with something, it's only human nature that they will try to do it. So when there was no television, and certainly no video evidence, players could get away with a lot when the referee wasn't looking. Arsenal's Paul Davis tried that when he punched Southampton's Glenn Cockerill off the ball in 1988 and broke his jaw; but Davis couldn't escape the camera's gaze and ended up getting banned for nine games. That was the most famous case of a footballer being found out by television and should have acted as a warning to everyone else. I think it has, to a large extent, although you are not going to eliminate violent behaviour completely simply because the TV cameras are everywhere these days. Eric Cantona is living proof of that. Off the field, of course, the introduction of closed-circuit television has been one of the police's most potent weapons in the successful war against hooliganism. By training their cameras on the crowd, the officers at a match are able to pinpoint any trouble-makers and remove them from the ground.

What you see is what you get from television, but newspapers are a different matter entirely. Interpretation is the name of the game there, and as you might expect after my hounding by more than one section of the press, I think it has gone far beyond the bounds of acceptability in some cases. I can't pretend I wasn't completely forewarned, because I'd noticed a complete change in certain of the English tabloids while I was Barcelona's coach in the 1980s. That, if you recall, was when the *Sun* and the *Daily Mirror* began to get stuck into poor old Bobby Robson. Anyway, every night at 8 o'clock I used to go to the Princess Sofia Hotel, just up the road from the Nou Camp stadium, for a beer. On the way in, I'd buy five or six of the English morning papers from the kiosk outside the hotel. I'd get a couple of the serious ones, a couple of the middle-of-the-road ones and a couple of the 'genned-up' ones. A real cross-section, in other words.

What struck me as amazing was how reckless the popular tabloids had become. They had always been critical, and a lot of us in the game couldn't handle that too well. But now you just saw naked aggression and a lack of truth in certain areas. You knew, years ago, that reporters would always come back to you to check a story. Now they don't because they are afraid you will knock it down. They'd rather run with it, true or false. Rumour has it that the motto in Rupert Murdoch's newspaper empire is 'We don't want heroes: we want fallen heroes'. One of my big bugbears is the way newspapers set out to make people like Paul Gascoigne look a complete mug. I know only too well that he can be his own worst enemy; but the papers go over the top about him and other players and, all of sudden, the kids haven't got any heroes at all. They've got no one to emulate, nothing to aim for and, the way things are going, no playing fields to play in. So they sit on the kerb smoking a cigarette. Whether it's sport or politics we are talking about, we haven't got a short-term plan or long-term vision. That's the problem: we don't want to look beyond next week.

But how do you convince the newspapers of that? On the face of it, they are doing good business because there are people out there who want to read that kind of trash. The papers concerned are not providing the fans with the right kind of information, though, and it's even more worrying because they keep going on about immorality and greedy football clubs and trying to claim the moral high ground. Yet the bottom line in all this is that the newspapers' main concern is money – that is to say, the size of their circulation. I remember Patrick Collins writing a piece in the *Mail on Sunday* complaining that all Tottenham Hotspur was about was sponsorship. There was a sponsor's lounge here, a sponsor's name there, a sponsor wherever you looked, he said. But if you look in his newspaper, it's full of advertising. Sponsorship is support with money, but so is advertising. So what was he talking about? That kind of attitude is just pompous and hypocritical.

It's all a question of pressure. When I was in Barcelona, you could afford to dismiss the excesses of the tabloids as hysterical nonsense. But now the middle-of-the-road newspapers are doing it; and that, in turn, puts pressure on the broad sheets. It's not unlike my profession, where we have to resist the temptation to use the long-ball game, the easy way out. The people I feel sorry for are the youngsters coming into journalism now. Without doubt, those in their 20s working for the national tabloids can't write stories the way they want. Their sports editors say 'No. We want that and that.' But there's got to be a line drawn somewhere.

There's got to be a sense of responsibility, there's got to be truth, there's got to be honesty. OK, we understand poetic licence: a little bit of colour and so on. But the whole business has gone off its trolley. The motto now, I think, is 'What can we get away with?'

Sadly, one of the consequences of this development is a worsening of the relationship between footballers and journalists. We used to mix quite closely when I was a player, but there's not the same degree of trust any more. It's a problem area because the press have become the enemy in lots of ways. Footballers and reporters still socialize, but in my day we did everything together, especially when we were on tour. Ken Jones, once football correspondent of the *Daily Mirror* and the *Sunday Mirror*, and Brian James, formerly football correspondent of the *Daily Mail*, have known me since I was 15. They'd be in the bar of the hotel we were staying in, and we'd spend a couple of hours with them. It was not so much a question of having a drink as of getting to know each other even better. I have to admit I enjoy the company of journalists, because they are mostly bright and lively people, and it saddens me that the development of newspapers has made it increasingly difficult to keep that sort of relationship going.

Newspapers were put under pressure when television came in and the public was able to get a very direct view of what was going on without having to do any work. By that I mean the football fan didn't have to read the paper any more to get information about his club. Reading is hard work for a lot of people. You can see that reflected in the tabloids, where they have gone in for short, sharp paragraphs to make it as simple as possible to understand. Now they even have love stories in cartoon fashion. Led by the *Sun*, the tabloids decided the only way to compete with TV was to become more entertaining. That's fair enough, except the truth often got lost in the jazzing-up process. I understand that the credo of one famous Fleet Street sports editor was 'Don't spoil a good story for the sake of the facts!' He said it tongue-in-cheek, but the suggestion that it wouldn't do any harm to stretch a point here or there was clear enough.

Sensationalism became the order of the day, and gradually began to infect the middle-of-the-road papers and even the broadsheets, which still by and large do their best to cover the game objectively and responsibly. In turn, too, it put pressure back on television. Programmes like *Panorama*, which were part of our heritage, have gradually become tabloid in style. Once upon a time, if *Panorama* said something you believed it without question; but not any more in my case.

You look at these things more closely when you are under the sort of attack I've experienced from the media. If someone else had been the target for the *Daily Mirror*'s 'exclusives', I'd probably have said: 'Oh, I see Harry Harris is writing about Joe Bloggs. It's a load of rubbish!' You don't look into it too closely because it's once removed from you. But when it's hitting *you*, you question why they are doing it. *Panorama*, for instance, realized they had made a mistake in their first programme about me. Then they did a second one which tarnished me more. It made people think, 'Bloody hell, there must be something dodgy about this fellow!' It's nothing but character assassination.

As for the stream of stories in the *Mirror* alleging business malpractice by me, they were just rehashing old and tired allegations. You'd think at some stage the Press Complaints Commission would have said enough's enough. I don't want to moan to the PCC – though I have. I complained to them about 142 articles in all. They should have their own standards and be proactive, not reactive. What would be their attitude to murder, I wonder, or wife-battering or rape? Would it be all right if no one actually complained about it? The PCC is supposed to be a stronger body than the old Press Council, isn't it? It's supposed to mean something now. Well, we'll find out if that's true, won't we? So far, my only consolation has been that I've been getting letters from people sympathizing with me and saying they've cancelled the *Daily Mirror*. I think it got to the stage where the paper's campaign against me was having the opposite effect to the one they intended. Instead of getting me out of the England job, it made people want me to stay.

It's always a big talking point, the press and the England job, and I think it's got to be discussed here. I've resisted the temptation in two previous books, my autobiography and *Venables' England*, to discuss my critics in the media, but so many people have asked me about it that I think I have to say something. My reply would be that, being a high-profile person in a high-profile profession, you have to learn to live with criticism. Normally, however, you will find that even the people who hit you hardest are prepared to praise you if you do something good. It is when they are not prepared to do that, and maintain a vicious and malicious attitude towards whatever you do, that you realize there has to be something more to it. And there have been only four journalists who did that consistently over a long period of time in my case.

They were Harry Harris of the *Daily Mirror*, Mihir Bose of the *Daily Telegraph*, Patrick Collins of the *Mail on Sunday* and Richard Littlejohn of the *Daily Mail*. Harris and Bose are two of a kind, in that neither really likes football in my opinion, and both tried to discredit me with a series of so-called exposés in their newspapers. Both, certainly, seemed to have an unusual degree of access to documents pertaining to my period of office at Tottenham. After I left, they often knew about things before I did.

There are such similarities between Harris and Bose, in fact, that I don't think it can be any coincidence that they are both close friends of Irving Scholar, the former chairman of Tottenham, from whom Sugar and I bought the club. Harris was one of only three guests at Irving's wedding, while Bose wrote his autobiography. I got on all right with Irving because he loved his football. He loved his club, too, until he lost it. Then he became very bitter indeed and blamed me. But it doesn't matter how much you love your club: if you owe £16 million and it's about to crash into the ground you have to go.

It does not seem to me to be without significance that the guests on the *Daily Mirror* table at one of the annual dinners of the Football Writers' Association in recent years have included Alan Sugar and Kate Hoey, the Labour MP. Hoey, who did some work for Tottenham when Scholar was chairman, used the protection of Parliamentary privilege to imply that I was deeply involved in the allegations of corruption being investigated by a special team from the Premier League. Unfortunately, she did not have the courage to repeat her claims outside the House of Commons.

Collins and Littlejohn come into a different category again. They are big-name columnists who seemed to decide, on the basis of their observations of me from a distance, that I was some kind of cockney wide-boy. They don't know me personally, yet felt entitled to suggest I was not to be trusted because I ran a Kensington dining club (drinking club was their preferred description) and kept friends they felt were undesirable. Eric Hall, the 'monster, monster' football agent, was one. Great fun was had, too, with the altercation Dennis Wise got into with a taxi-driver after coming out of my club, Scribes.

So far as I can recall, and I've thought hard about it, I have never given Collins or Littlejohn any reason to attack me as strongly as they have. The only reason I could think of at first was that I presented an easy target for a couple of hacks on the make. That applied particularly to Littlejohn, who was seeking to establish himself on the *Daily Mail* after making a name for himself on the London *Evening Standard* and then the *Sun*.

Which reminds me that he crucified Mark McGhee for leaving Leicester to take over as manager of Wolves while still under contract and has accused me, snidely, of knowing when to leave a job. Yet he does not seem averse himself to moving about to advance his career, or breaking a contract to do it – something I have never done. From enquiries I have made, it appears Littlejohn left the *Evening Standard* in the middle of a long contract. Then he moved to the *Mail* while his three-year contract with the *Sun* was still in force. Yet he has the cheek to criticize other people for what he perceives as disloyalty. I did not agree with what McGhee did, but it was the height of hypocrisy for someone like Littlejohn to take him to task for it. Apparently, his excuse for leaving the *Sun* was that he was ambitious and had always wanted to work for the *Mail*. So that's all right then! He even reminded the *Sun* that they had 'poached' him from the *Standard*. What a lovely fellow he is.

Whether Littlejohn has managed to establish himself satisfactorily after his latest career move, only his new employers would know. As the unanimously critical readers' letters printed by the *Mail* indicated quite clearly, Littlejohn misjudged the mood of the nation completely during Euro '96. He would not admit as much, of course, and tried defiantly to justify himself. All he succeeded in doing, though, was to make himself look even more prejudiced, pompous and wrong than before. How could any credible voice of the people seriously suggest there were England fans who wanted England to lose? And if I am supposed to be a fraud as a coach, as he described me with his usual perception and unrivalled knowledge of the game, I don't know what that makes him. Actually I do, but the laws of libel and obscenity prevent me from spelling it out.

The strange thing is that, two days after I had been forced out at Tottenham, Littlejohn wrote a piece in the *Standard* that was very pro-me. Since then, however, he seems to have done a complete about-turn and become very antagonistic towards me.

As for Collins, I fancy he was influenced by some very questionable people at the time I was buying Scribes. His persistent criticism of me, I believe, had little to do with Tottenham. It stemmed from a different type of camp altogether. Collins seems to have a disdain for football in general and looks out of place talking about the subject. You can see it's too sweaty for him: he'd be more at home with cricket or rugby. Even then, you feel he would prefer polo or croquet. It's right that people should improve themselves; but when they start trying to behave like someone they are not, it sticks in my throat. I certainly cannot forgive him for the derision with which he treated me and the England players for most of the two and a half years I was in charge. Not only that, but he actually lied on television about the relationship between us. Appearing on the Sky programme, *Hold the Back Page*, last season, and asked whether he had ever spoken to me, Collins claimed we had discussed football matters on the telephone. All I can think is that he must have been talking to someone else, because I have no recollection whatsoever of having received a call from him or having made one to him.

In fact, one of the things about Harris, Bose and Collins that irritated me most when they were on the football-writing circuit was that they rarely attended my press conferences. And when they did, it was unusual for them to risk asking a question in front of a lot of other journalists. In the end, I made a joke about it when Harris at last plucked up the courage to say something during Euro '96. 'Hello,' I said. 'After two and a half years without a word from you, I was beginning to think you were a ventriloquist's dummy! ' Collins, meanwhile, would sit somewhere at the back, well out of harm's way. I have to say I would have had a lot more respect for all of them if they had met me head-on and confronted me on issues where they felt I was in the wrong.

Cheque-book journalism was another controversial consequence of the tabloid circulation war. Whereas football reporters had previously relied simply on good contacts to get their stories, buying 'exclusives' became common practice in the 1970s and 80s as the competition hotted up between the two biggest-selling tabloids, i.e. the *Sun* and the *Mirror*. It's a practice peculiar to this country, I think. At least, I know Spanish football writers don't pay for their stories: they get them through building up friendly relationships with people in the game. I think that's a good thing, because if a player or a manager says he doesn't like somebody, it's because he really doesn't and not because he's being paid just to say it.

I have to say, though, I don't think there's too much wrong with paying people for an accurate inside story. We all get involved in that, and if I'm offered £5,000 for something I was going to reveal anyway, I don't see the point of turning it down. If you are actually selling newspapers by attaching your name to a story, you should be paid for it just as all journalists are for doing the same thing. But it's a dangerous area, and you are better off not doing it. What happens is that people say things that are untrue simply to get some money. This is the beginning of the errors and the recklessness that give tabloid newspapers a bad name. I've been paid for doing articles, and it gets to the stage where you have to say you are not prepared to slag somebody off. If your reputation gets big enough, the papers don't mind soft words as long as they've got your name over the top. There's a big difference, in terms of morality, between a football personality who is paid under contract for doing a regular column for a newspaper and someone who is prepared to say he stole the gems simply because he's going to get £15,000 for the story.

British players and their agents have been criticized for asking to be paid for articles, but you can hardly blame them when the tabloids have already set a precedent. If all the papers were unwilling to pay, the players and the agents wouldn't ask. Some agents have been taken to task for adopting the short-term view and demanding money for everything their clients do. Others have been praised for being more far-sighted and calculating that every favourable free piece written about their clients increases their value in other ways. I suppose, in the end, it depends on who your clients are. Whoever the player is, though, he definitely needs an agent.

As I said earlier, I played when there was a maximum wage of £20 a week and you had a contract. When you finished that contract, you had to sign on again even though the money you were offered might not have been as good. It was very, very unfair, but that was the name of the game at the time. Then the market became freer; but what you got offered you took, basically. If you

132

actually said, 'Well, no, I want a bit more', you were being outrageous. The clubs would say, 'What's going on? It's mutiny!' I'd never ever have thought of asking for a new contract while my old one was still in force. If I'd signed it, that was it. It's embarrassing to think about it now, but the players were getting a very raw deal then.

Now, the people at the top of their trade are becoming younger all the time. But at 20 a player doesn't know what he is worth. So he's got to have a representative, whatever you call him – solicitor, father, accountant. I know I am flying in the face of FA regulations, but I make no bones about it: agents are an absolutely necessary part of modern football. If you've got somebody looking after your affairs like that, it keeps them off your list of worries. It's better, too, if contractual affairs are conducted by the managing director rather than the manager. That stops the sort of friction we saw last season (1995–6) at Nottingham Forest between Frank Clark and Ian Woan. If the manager and the player are not directly involved in contract talks, and know it's being sorted out by somebody else, there are no distractions. You are taking pressure off the people who are having to work together day in, day out on the training ground.

The tendency to condemn agents as a breed is ludicrous. You are going to get good agents and bad agents, just as you are going to get good footballers and bad footballers, good journalists and bad journalists. What is essential is that agents are governed by workable and enforceable rules. When I say that, I don't mean rules determining who can be an agent. All this FIFA business about compelling agents to deposit a £100,000 bond to secure a licence is nonsense. I don't think you can make it stick. Lars Bohinen's transfer from Nottingham Forest to Blackburn was a case in point. Rune Hauge was involved, but not directly. To get round his suspension by FIFA, he was on the other end of the phone waiting for his representative at the transfer talks to ring him. That is the sort of nonsense you can get into if you cannot make your rules stand up.

What I would say about agents, in short, is that you, as a player, should have whoever you want negotiating for you. What he's not allowed to do is embezzle money. If there's proof of that, he gets punished. What's needed is a code of conduct which is monitored very simply and very stringently. With that kind of controlling mechanism in place, football should learn to accept agents in the same way that showbusiness has. If you don't have an agent in that game, you aren't any good. The same applies to writers like John le Carré, or anyone else with talent you want to talk about. So why should footballers be any different when they are commanding an audience of millions and earning money to compare with the best?

The unscrupulous agent's biggest 'crime', of course, is that the money he siphons off from transfer deals most likely comes from the poor old English fan. It is difficult to tell, with revenue arriving from so many different sources these days, exactly which part of a club's income is used to buy players. The fact remains, though, that the ordinary fan still supplies a major part of it. The millions poured into the game by television, advertising and sponsorship mean the person who pays for the privilege of watching his favourite club at first hand is no longer its biggest sponsor. Even so, the revenue he or she supplies remains so considerable that it cannot be taken lightly.

Until quite recently, most clubs simply took that kind of solid financial support for granted. The majority of English football grounds were bleak, uncomfortable, unsafe places that had hardly changed since the war. Catering and toilet facilities could best be described as minimal and, as was proved by the Bradford City fire in 1985 and the Hillsborough crowd disaster four years later, the general and continuing disregard for the well-being of the spectator had a potentially fatal aspect to it. Fifty-five people died and another 210 were injured when a fire burned down a stand at Bradford's Valley Parade ground in five minutes on the last day of the 1984–5 season. An enquiry by Mr Justice Popplewell found that the fire had been caused by the accidental lighting of inflammable debris allowed to accumulate beneath the floorboards of a wooden stand. The Hillsborough disaster, which took place at the start of the 1989 FA Cup semi-final between Liverpool and Nottingham Forest, claimed an even greater number of lives. The final toll there was 95 dead and 170 injured as a result of serious overcrowding among the Liverpool supporters at the smaller, Leppings Lane end of the ground. Although Lord Justice Taylor, in his inquiry, put most of the blame on a failure of police control, he was also critical of football club management for its own failure to improve spectator conditions and safety.

The Taylor Report, the final version of which was released in

January 1990, proved a real watershed in the history of English football. Its most dramatic recommendation was that all First (now Premier League) and Second (now First) Division clubs should have all-seater stadiums by August 1994, and that clubs in the two lower divisions of the Football League ought to follow suit by August 1999. As a result of the government backing the report received, most of the country's professional football grounds were either given a major face-lift or, as in the cases of Middlesbrough, Millwall and Huddersfield, for example, abandoned in favour of a purpose-built, state-of-the art structure on a completely new site. Suddenly, for just about the first time in living memory, the safety and comfort of the football supporter became a primary consideration in the game's development.

It came at a price in more ways than one, though. While the massive cost of upgrading the stadiums was offset to some extent by grants from the Football Trust, the charitable body funded by the football pool companies, and underwritten by the huge increase in television income, admission prices had to go up appreciably. And with the emphasis now on catering for the season-ticket holder and the corporate client in his luxurious executive box, a process of gentrification got under way. All of a sudden, the game was being designed to suit the needs and tastes of the middle-class rather than those of the working-class, who had traditionally been the backbone of every club's support. The football fan has become a different person in the past five years, and will change even more in the next five. The working man in the flat cap, if we can call him that, still goes to football; but he is being driven out by the powerful forces bringing in more luxurious and more costly accommodation for the supporters. In the end, I think, the working man will have to settle for watching his club on television at home or in the pub with his mates. That would be a great shame, but perhaps his time will come again when they are giving away free tickets to ensure there is a crowd at a match. To get one even then, I fear, it could be a matter of who you know.

In the meantime, I'd like to think that, if clubs are going to make a killing on executive boxes and the best seats in the house, they would set aside an area where the admission prices are lower. I agree that the first priority is to increase standards for the people with money. They should get what they want and they are entitled to that. They've got their boxes and their corporate entertainment and so forth. But you've still got to involve the man in the flat cap.

They do that at Barcelona. There are cheaper areas behind the goals, 'box noise' as they call them, where the fans can show their support with their flags and their rattles and so on. It's essential to the game. It's cheering your heroes and providing an inspiring atmosphere for them. I also believe clubs should drop their prices for certain games – the least attractive ones, the ones you know are not going to attract a full house. The danger in the gentrification process is that English football crowds will be drained of all passion. When Barcelona's Nou Camp stadium was filled with 120,000 people, the atmosphere was wonderful. But it was so big that there was no atmosphere when the crowd was 60,000–70,000, even though it looked quite full. It always reminded me of being at the theatre. There were rounds of polite applause in appreciation of good play, but it wasn't quite what it was meant to be.

Gentrification is not without its benefits, however. One thing it has helped to do is drive out the hooligan. Without wishing to sound snobbish or be disloyal to my own working-class background, the increase in admission prices is likely to exclude the sort of people who were giving English football a bad name. I am talking about the young men, mostly working-class, who terrorized football grounds, railway trains, cross-channel ferries and towns and cities throughout England and Europe with their violence from the late 1960s until the disaster at the Heysel Stadium in 1985, and the one at Hillsborough four years later, prompted a rethink and a change of mood. Heysel was a turning-point because English clubs were banned indefinitely from Europe after a charge by Liverpool fans at their Juventus rivals before the European Cup final in Brussels had left 39 dead and 454 injured. The ban was lifted after five years, but the shock of exclusion from the mainstream of European football created a new determination to solve the hooligan problem. Hillsborough played its part because the high death toll there was partly attributable to the 'safety' fences that had been erected at English grounds to stop the hooligans encroaching on the pitch. All they did, in that particular case, was to cut off all hope of escape for those being crushed against them. From that moment on, the fences came down and English football set out to create a climate in which they would not be necessary.

It has not been easy, if only because of the profound changes which have taken place in English society during the past 30 years.

136

The breakdown of family life and the declining influence of religion, I believe, were largely responsible for the hooligan phenomenon. If you examine the reasons why the fan of today goes to football, I think you'll find comradeship is high on the list. The thug certainly feels his family is more in there among the football crowd than it is at home. Families are breaking up, religion is breaking up and so is the sense of discipline and self-worth they could impart. The scarf has been replaced by the shirt, which is the fan's new religion. Tottenham or Arsenal are his new religion. He's comfortable only when he goes and meets his mates in the pub. Before, it used to be just a question of having a good day out with your mates and loving the football that was at journey's end. But now its 'We have a fight and we are together'. Tribalism, as several people have pointed out, plays a big part in hooliganism. Insecurity and a need to feel wanted also come into it – Now I'm a star: I'm a leader! At last they belong somewhere. Notoriety is another attraction, given the amount of coverage the hooligans used to get from the media.

Having lived in Spain for some time, I wish our family life could be as solid as theirs still is and ours used to be. At the risk of being branded an old reactionary, I also wish we had some form of national service like them. Having been given good values by their family, young Spanish men have to go into the army for a year at 18, just at that point in their lives when they could go into trouble or away from it. So far as I can see, the experience reinforces their sense of right and wrong, strengthens their conscience and gives them a maturity they might not otherwise have had. People like Nayim, the midfielder I brought to Spurs from Barcelona at the same time as Gary Lineker, are wonderful young men. And that is because of their upbringing. You don't see too many cases of rape out there. When I was living in Catalonia, it was all petty crime, like stealing car radios and handbags. But not hitting old ladies over the head.

Two years, the period of national service we used to have in Britain until the late 1950s, is too long. Reduce it to nine months, or even six, if you like. Most countries still have some form of it, and I think not having it has caused us big problems. Our society badly needs the sort of discipline military service can impose on headstrong young men who scoff now at family values and religious beliefs. When I was a kid in the 1950s, I wouldn't go scrumping for apples because I didn't want to get caught by the policeman and I didn't want my mum and dad to tell me off or get them into trouble. If we could only get back to that way of thinking, we'd be all right.

That said, it does seem the day of the hooligan appears to be receding. Stricter policing, the gentrification of football crowds and a welcome return of the desire to watch football for its own sake seem to have done the trick. So far as the English are concerned, hooliganism only seems to surface now when the controls are relaxed for a moment and a cause is involved, as was the case with the outbreak of trouble that brought about the abandonment of England's match against the Republic of Ireland in Dublin in February 1995. That dreadful episode, said to have been sparked off by extreme right-wing elements, should have been enough to alert us to the fact that football hooliganism has not gone away completely.

If I had any doubts about it, they were removed by a visit we had at the FA towards the end of 1995 from a policeman who specializes in the subject. He showed us all the weapons they had confiscated from the thugs, and it was a terrifying sight. You are talking about axes, sabres and razor blades in the match programme. Yes, razor blades in the match programme. Apparently, they slide half the blades into the pages of a closed programme and then strike out with it. The advantage of that kind of deadly, makeshift weapon is that, if you are spotted on the closed-circuit television which has helped the police so much to identify these criminals, it looks as though you are just hitting someone with a programme. Then, if a policeman gets too close for comfort, you just open the programme and let the blades drop. Sickeningly, there are usually two blades, it seems, because you can't stitch the kind of wound they inflict – two very close parallel cuts.

I thought to myself that if anyone saw that collection of weapons they'd never go to football again, and certainly never let their kids go. It was such an appalling sight, I wondered whether to show it to the England players. I decided to in the end because sometimes games are held up for 15 minutes or so when there's trouble getting the crowd into the ground. The players get upset at the delay and go berserk with the referee because they are all tuned up and ready to go. So I told them to cast their minds back to what they had just seen the next time their game is held up. 'Then,' l added,

'1 think you'll agree it's best to give the police that extra 15 minutes.'

One of the worst side-effects of hooliganism is that it has made it so much more difficult for the well-behaved football supporter to gain some recognition and respect from the football authorities. Although the genuine fan is in the majority, the excesses of the few have persuaded football's rulers to believe that no fans are to be trusted. That is plainly nonsense, and the sooner the notion is discarded the better. For, as I keep on saying, the game belongs to the fan. It belongs to him not in the sense that he should be able to interfere directly with the running of his team, but in the sense that he should have a big say in the way his club is run. People do think about the fan, but not enough. In the thrashing out of what the game's going to be, he should be represented strongly. I'm not quite sure how that can be brought about, but perhaps the media could help.

Chapter Seven

Europe

No one will have more influence on the future of English football than the FA's new technical director. I cannot stress enough the importance I attach to the appointment and, in particular, to finding the right man for the job. His power to change things will be, or should be, immense. It will stretch right across the vast expanse of football in this country, stopping short only of the England team itself. But if he does his job properly, the technical director will influence that, too, through the quality of the players his system produces for it. He will need massive powers because he is taking on a Herculean task. What he will be expected to do, in effect, is modernize an English game that has fallen at least ten years behind the times. That much is clear from the embarrassingly poor record of English clubs in the three European club competitions since the post-Heysel ban on them was lifted in 1990. But it is not only a question of bringing us up to date; the new supremo of English football must think of ways of putting us ahead of the rest of Europe once again.

If any one person can restore the dominance we used to enjoy over our continental rivals at club level, it is the technical director. Essentially, his job will be to coach the coaches: give them the knowledge to change our game. His guidance will be especially important now that UEFA are to introduce a standard, three-tier coaching licence for the whole of Europe. The top award will be tougher to get than the FA coaching badge, and applicants will have to know their subject inside out. That's no bad thing considering we are talking in England about giving fully qualified coaches access to boys of seven. Children as young as that must be in the care of people who know what they are talking about, and the coaches involved in that kind of work carry a heavy responsibility. It's a case of practice making permanent, my own pet variation on the old saying. Permanent rather than perfect because teaching youngsters the right way to play the game at an early age will stay with them for ever. It's like the old Jesuit boast: 'Give me a child at seven, and I'll give you a good Catholic for the rest of his life.'

It has become increasingly clear that we have been teaching the coaches the wrong things. So we have to modify the lessons and give them the sort of information that will enable them to spread a gospel worth spreading. It's important we are all going in the right direction, and I feel the Football Association have made a start in that respect by drawing the professional and 'amateur' sides of the game closer together. I'd like to think I've played my part in the process, as have Graham Kelly, the FA's chief executive, Don Howe, who has been acting as the FA's technical co-ordinator pending the arrival of the technical director, and Jimmy Armfield, the FA's main link with the professional game. Bridging the gap between the amateurs and the professionals was a necessary first step because Charles Hughes, the FA director of coaching, who was due to be replaced on retirement by the technical director, chose to have little to do with the professionals. Charles is a very intelligent man with a vast store of coaching knowledge, but he preferred to concentrate on the grass roots of the game.

The influence of the technical director will not be just a matter of coaching. He has to apply real vision right across the board. Other qualities are required, too. In his caretaker role, Don Howe has kept coming up against obstacles that show you've got to be a bit of a politician as well. So the technical director will need the charisma to get him into places where he can get his message across. Once in them, he'll have to be forceful and not wonder whether he should say something or not. People want to listen: they are there waiting to be told, to be directed. We mustn't assume that everyone knows what they want to do. Those who become coaches are good football people who care, but we've got to be up to date with everyone else in the world. It's not just a question of doing a good job in this country, but that would be a start.

I would like to think the technical director would be a strong enough personality to be able to persuade the leading professional coaches to change the way the game is played in the Premiership.

That would be part of the short term and long term plans I am always going on about. You campaign for change in the short term while producing the coaches who can make the change permanent in the long term. Whichever way the change comes, English clubs will never make the impact of old on Europe until it does. As Ruud Gullit said when he was working as a television pundit at the European Championship play-off game between Holland and the Republic of Ireland, English football has to make up its mind what it wants. There's nothing wrong with the Premiership, he pointed out. It's very exciting and very fast, with lots of mistakes. And if you don't want to know about Europe or the rest of the world, stay as you are because your league works and it's financially strong. But if you do want to compete with the big boys, you've got to change.

As I said earlier, as chief executive at Tottenham, I was part of the discussions when the old First Division of the Football League broke away and became the Premier League in 1992, and I was quite taken by its glitziness and the big television deal coming in at the same time. But no one thought it would be any different, and basically it hasn't changed too much. We've still got 11 v. 11 and the pitch is the same size. The only real change is that there is more money in the pot. The game's richer and faster, but richer and faster doesn't equal better in my opinion. Some of our football now is substandard, and a lot of the excitement in matches comes from mistakes. I think our technical ability is not actually as poor as people say, but the speed of our game puts it under unnecessary pressure. If the Italians and the Spanish played at our pace, I'm sure they would have the same problems controlling the ball.

Three points for a win, introduced back in the old Football League days, has encouraged more attacking attitudes in the Premiership (for the uninitiated, that is what the Premier League competition is called), and that's not a bad thing. Here, both teams want to get a goal. But instead of thinking they've got 90 minutes to win the match, they try to win it in the first five minutes. So we go at them and they go at us, and it's a toss-up who gets the first goal. It might be 15 minutes, it might be 20 minutes, but we get a goal. So there's a game going now, and I will come at you even harder or vice-versa. So it's going to go to 2–0 or 1–1. That's how it goes because there are risks being taken.

In Italy, the attitude is entirely different. Teams go out thinking that if they don't lose a goal, they don't lose the game. Basically, that thought is stamped on the front of their brains. So they bring everybody back and they are solid and they draw you in until suddenly, bang, they get you on the break. They are leading 1–0, but they still stay the same. They'll hold on to that lead or, bump, get you again on the break. You look at their results. You'll get big scores occasionally, but not very often. In the main, it's 0–0 or 1–0, and the narrowness of those scorelines is an indication of the difficulties our teams face when they meet Italian opponents in the European club competitions.

As it stands, Premiership football has become a great television sport, like darts and snooker. People around the world love tuning in to English football. Even in countries like Holland, where controlled, intelligent football is appreciated, they love watching English teams playing other English teams because the game is full of thrills and spills. It's to do with speed and mistakes, and it's reached such a state of frenzy you feel like suggesting they wet the ground and freeze it so the players can stagger and slither around trying to control the ball. Then we'll really have loads of mistakes, and we can all enjoy ourselves. Malcolm Allison said a long while ago that our game was in danger of becoming like Rollerball, the ruthless fictional game of the future in which anything goes, and that is the way we have been progressing for too long.

There were two main reasons for English football's drift into its present state. One was the five-year ban from the European competitions and the other a revival of the long-ball game popularized by Wolves in the 1950s. Unfortunately, those two damaging developments overlapped. Forced in on themselves again, as they were before Sir Matt Busby broke through the insularity of the Football League in the 1950s, English clubs found the long ball a quick and easy way to get results in domestic football. Not too many people objected to the trend because there was no European yardstick to show how crude and ineffective the long ball would be against more sophisticated opposition. Worse still, the clubs who insisted on playing the game properly forgot during the wilderness years how to handle the European competitions. Even Liverpool, who had dominated the European Cup in the grand manner and had refused to betray the traditions of their passing game, got rusty during their six years of banishment. They, of course, served an extra year as punishment for the direct involvement of their fans in the Heysel Stadium disaster.

Before I went to Barcelona in 1984, I said the long-ball game had put English football back ten years. I wish now I had said 15, because I think the damage was even worse than I anticipated. I hesitate to point the finger of blame at Graham Taylor because he and I have always got off on the wrong foot, somehow; but I don't see where else it can be pointed, unless it is at Charles Hughes, a major coaching influence at the FA since 1964. If Charlie was the high priest of the long-ball game, Graham was his disciple and I was the opposite. I was manager at Queen's Park Rangers and Graham was manager of Watford. He did a particularly good job there, taking them from the old Fourth Division to the First in five years.

Although Graham got as high as League Championship runners-up with Watford and Aston Villa, and took Watford to the FA Cup final, I just didn't think the way his teams played the game was the right way. It consisted of four basic principles: hit the ball to the back post if you are in their half; up the line if you are in your own half; get the midfield up in support for the knock-downs; and make the most of your corners and free-kicks. It was commercial, but it took all the imagination out of the game. It was like reading Harold Robbins as opposed to John Steinbeck. Robbins might have sold more books than Steinbeck, but there was no question which of them was the better writer in terms of quality. The excuse for the long-ball game, apart from Charlie Hughes's statistics about the number of goals scored from the least number of passes, was that it was a case of playing to the strengths of the English footballer. But don't tell me we can't play football like the continentals, because Liverpool proved otherwise when they were winning the European Cup four times between 1977 and 1984.

What I did like about Graham Taylor was that he kept the long-ball game within the rules. I always said that type of game would dictate the type of players we would have in English football; that is to say, 6ft 8in strikers who were good in the air and midfielders with leather lungs to enable them to get up and down. Graham also insisted on wide players who could dribble and cross, and there's plenty of room for all that in the game. Above all, there was none of the brute force and nastiness in his teams that some other devotees of the long-ball game used to enforce their directness. It always worried me where that style of play was going to go, and I feared it could develop into a monster. Once it became a question of big guys battling it out in the air, it was only a matter of time before it was elbows in the face. And that started to come, as an increase in the number of serious facial injuries proved.

Fortunately, the long-ball teams didn't sweep the board, otherwise I shudder to think what state our game might be in by now. George Graham's Arsenal were the nearest thing to a long-ball team that won major honours. They collected two League titles in 1988–9 and 1990–1 and the European Cup-Winners' Cup in 1993–4. They did not play it long all the time, though. As I pointed out in a previous chapter, the side that won the title in 1988–9 had some very creative midfielders and played right through the team.

It is a fact that Arsenal are the only English team to have done anything like well in Europe since we were readmitted in 1990. Manchester United won the Cup-Winners' Cup in 1990–1, but have failed consistently since then. Arsenal, on the other hand, won the Cup-winners Cup in 1994 and reached the final again the following year – only to lose to Nayim's freakish long-range goal for Real Zaragoza. Yet their success was based on a well-organized defensive system more than anything else. I think they did it mainly by having two outstanding central defenders in Tony Adams and Steve Bould and a back-five who were gritty. The two full-backs, Lee Dixon and Nigel Winterburn, also played very close to Adams and Bould. Then they had people like Martin Keown, Ray Parlour and Steve Morrow in front of them. They could call on a lot of people who wanted to defend and deny space. Other than that, they just hoped they would get a goal out of the blue, which they were fortunate enough to do against Parma in the 1994 final. George had some fighters who wanted to win, but you couldn't take the game forward the way he sees it, in my opinion.

The way forward, as I make no apologies for repeating, has been shown to us by Ajax. Only three club sides stand out for me in the history of European football. They are the exciting Real Madrid of Alfredo di Stefano and Ferenc Puskas that beat Eintracht Frankfurt 7–3 in 1960 to win the European Cup for a fifth successive time; the inspired, well-organized AC Milan of recent years; and, now, Ajax. The Dutchmen are the best I've seen for some time, along with the Brazilians who won the 1994 World Cup. In fact, they are probably as good a team as there's been in Europe. I saw their 2–0 Champions League win against today's Real Madrid at the

Bernabeu in 1995–6 on video and it could have been 6–0 or 8–0. They were so superior it was embarrassing. And you are talking about a serious team in Real Madrid. I mean, they've got outstanding international footballers like Redondo, Luis Enrique, Amavisca and Zamorano; yet Ajax had them running all over the place. Real just couldn't get the ball off them. What it proved was that it doesn't matter how many good players you've got in your team if you come up against the kind of know-how the Ajax players possess at a very young age.

That's because of the way they have been taught the game. Ajax are superb teachers of the young. When you study Dutch football closely, as I have, the thing that keeps coming through is the intelligence of the players. That is drilled into them at an early age and it is the key. It's not really a question of superior technique. Good technique in the young is important, but we shouldn't think it is the answer to everything. Technically, Ajax and the Holland team, who are practically the same thing, are no better than the Italians, the Spanish, the Germans or the Portuguese. But, despite their European Cup final defeat by Juventus earlier this year, they are dominating club football at the moment. That is because of the way they play, their system of play. It isn't something you can pick up easily. You think you've got it because the two full-backs play alongside the centre-half, they use two wide players and one striker drops off the other; but it's much more complex than that. Basically, it's a question of controlling the pace of the game from the back and waiting until players farther forward are in position to receive the ball. But every time you see it, you see something different. It requires a lot of study to prepare for a match against them because it's a bit like playing chess against a grand master. If you go there, he's got you; and if you go here, he's got you. So you've got to get him before he gets you.

The strange thing is that no one ever copies the way Ajax and Holland play. Barcelona are possible exceptions because their former coach, Johan Cruyff, used to be an Ajax player and Dutch international. It would be wonderful, then, to think English football might try to model itself on them. Obviously, you are not going to go from helter-skelter Premiership football to Ajax's mastery of the game overnight, though I doubt whether the crowds would object to that. After all, it's an attacking, entertaining game they play with plenty of goals. Plenty of goals at the other end, that is. People say Ajax are vulnerable at the back, but they don't give too many goals away. I don't think we could suddenly slow our game right down, though, and play tippy-tappy football. The fans wouldn't accept that. We'd have to do it in stages and change things gradually from the back.

That's what West Germany did when they moved Franz Beckenbauer from midfield to sweeper in the 1970s. Everyone in this country said they were wasting his creative talent in defence, but he was able to dictate the game from there because that is where the space is. Bobby Moore dictated the game from the back, too, and so does Danny Blind, the present Ajax sweeper. Alan Hansen used to do it for Liverpool. He would step out elegantly, get the ball, not give it away and endeavour to set something up. Commendably, Glenn Hoddle tried to get Ruud Guillit to do the same thing for him at Chelsea. Basically, what's required is a good footballer in the position, and I thought Mark Wright could do it for us until he got injured just before Euro '96.

Unfortunately, we have not taught all our best defenders to play with the right kind of intelligence and enterprise. At 17, Tony Adams was one of the most talented young players I had come across when I first saw him at Lilleshall. 'Who the hell is he?' I asked, and was told he was at Arsenal. Tony could do just about anything you wanted on a football field. So by now, at this late stage of his career, he should be hitting balls out wide and then going in to get on the end of a cross. But the fear factor in English football – 'You stay back there: don't start getting clever', and all that – prevented him developing his ability to the full. He's had a certain amount of success by not taking risks, so he thinks that's the right way to play. But he could have been so much better if he had been encouraged to develop the skill he obviously had as a youngster. Then, by now, you would be giving him eight or nine, instead of six or seven, for technique in that test of quality I was talking about earlier in the book. I think Tony's performances during Euro '96 proved beyond doubt that he was capable of so much more than people believed.

We've got good defenders, people who are capable of doing more than defend, but I don't blame them for not coming out from the back. The problem is that they have not been encouraged to do it. I tried to encourage them when they were with England, but they were reluctant to do it. Their natural instinct is to retreat. The difference is underlined by players like Philippe Albert, Newcastle's Belgian international defender. He'll suddenly accelerate upfield and people will ask what he's doing. But it's only the same as going upfield for a corner. If he gets caught out, he's got to get back. Until he does, someone fills in for him. Our defenders won't try that in open play because we are full of fear. Like the old adage says, there's nothing to fear but fear itself. Fear itself becomes a problem.

A lot of the detail that goes into our planning relates to defensive organization. That's because our game is so full of mistakes. Stopping goals is the easiest thing in football to do. You can do it with a couple of weeks' training. The hard part is linking it to the scoring of goals. But we've got to strive to make that link, because we owe it to the public to entertain. I know the Premiership is entertaining already, but I mean entertaining by design, not accident. We have to search harder in our minds for the solution to our problems, study more deeply. If a nation as small as Holland can do it, so can we. The first step, of course is to recognize that we do have a problem. Not until you admit you are sick can you start to get better. What the situation here needs is someone to win something playing like Ajax. Sadly, no one will take in what you are saying to them unless they see it for themselves. It's a shame, really, because if we had the intelligence, we'd say: 'Let's try it, let's do it, let's have a go!'

At least some clubs are making a conscious effort to move in that direction. The likes of Liverpool, Manchester United, Tottenham and Nottingham Forest have always remained faithful to the passing game, and they have been joined in recent seasons by Newcastle, Aston Villa and, of all people, Arsenal. If Bruce Rioch's successor as manager makes the right couple of moves now that the club has got a creative player like Dennis Bergkamp, they could be more entertaining than Tottenham. What I would especially like to see at the moment is Newcastle play Ajax. Kevin Keegan, Newcastle's manager, has built a very good team on the old Liverpool principle that you buy the best players you can for each position. Ajax, on the other hand, produce their own players and teach them to be world-beaters at a very early age. It would be very interesting to see what happened.

If we are not prepared to change the knockabout manner in which most of the game is played in the Premiership, the only way we are going to be successful in Europe again is by adopting a different, separate approach to European football. That's what Liverpool did back in the1970s and 80s. They realized very quickly that you couldn't afford to attack too freely against cunning continental opponents, especially away from home, and they gradually developed two distinct styles of play – one for English football and one for Europe. They learned how to be careful, how to keep possession, how to kill a game, how to nick a goal on the break. Because they were in Europe for an unbroken run of 21 years, and kept getting to the final stages of the tournaments, Liverpool were able to to add valuable bits to their knowledge all the time. Happily for them, too, they succeeding in persuading their crowd that modifications to the team's normal, all-out attacking style were necessary. Winning the crowd over is all-important in English football because, generally speaking, the man on what used to be the terraces is not happy if his team are not going forward at every opportunity. Mind you, it can't be difficult to approve of change when a team is as overwhelmingly successful as Liverpool used to be.

Other English clubs, such as Nottingham Forest and Aston Villa, learned from Liverpool and won the European Cup themselves during an eight-year period that must be classed as a special time in our post-war history, possibly the best we've ever had across the board. It hardly seems possible now, but Europe's premier club tournament was won seven times by the English between 1977 and 1984. Only Hamburg, with Kevin Keegan in attack, spoiled the sequence. It was an era of sustained domination still unmatched by any other country.

I have heard people trying to devalue the achievement on the grounds that the English did not carry the development of the game forward when they had the chance. But that's a silly argument in my opinion. How about Kenny Dalglish, Ian Rush and Graeme Souness? Are you trying to tell me those three great Liverpool players did not advance the art of attacking football while their club was lording it over the rest of Europe? And what about Mark Lawrenson and Alan Hansen at the back? They were as talented and inventive a pair of central defenders as Europe has seen. Tactically, too, Liverpool were always trying something different. Rush and Dalglish gave them split strikers, for a start. Away from home in Europe, too, they would deliberately employ the old WM formation. Not a lot of people know that now, and not a lot of people cottoned on at the time. In fact, I can't think of many European teams that were better than Liverpool in the way they played. In any case, which clubs from which countries *were* taking the game forward? The German sides definitely didn't advance the game, and European club football was very negative when the Italians were in control of it for the first time.

All things considered, then, I have no hesitation in saying that it is possible for us to get back to where we were. But it will take time because, in addition to the damaging effects of the ban from Europe and the popularity of the long-ball game, the other European nations have carried the game forward in our absence. Ajax's progress speaks for itself, while the Italians worked out from studying us that their natural flair needed to be bolstered by physical strength and good organization. You can see that in the way AC Milan play. Arrigo Sacchi, who used to be their coach and is now in charge of the Italian national team, quite admires certain aspects of English football. He copied the pressing game I introduced with some success at Barcelona, for example.

It is worth recalling at this point that, following their readmittance to the European tournaments, English clubs were hit harder than most by UEFA's rule restricting to three the number of foreign players that could be included in a team. Since the Scots, Welsh and Irish were classified as foreigners for this purpose, and English clubs had always relied heavily on Celtic imports, it meant some managers could not put out their strongest team. That applied particularly to Alex Ferguson's Manchester United as they struggled unsuccessfully to come to terms with the demands of the Champions League. But it was hardly the main reason for English failures in the revamped early part of the European Cup. Arsenal, Leeds and Blackburn, with far fewer problems in that respect, also failed to qualify for the later stages of the competition.

Everyone says Liverpool might not have won the European Cup four times if they'd had the three-foreigners rule to contend with, but that theory doesn't stand up if you examine the teams they fielded. Only the fourth time, when they beat Roma in Rome on penalties in 1984, would they have had problems putting out their strongest team. On the three other occasions they became champions of Europe, they were well within the three-foreigner limit. Nottingham Forest and Aston Villa might have needed some help from the two 'assimilated' players clause designed to soften the rule's impact on English clubs, but they would have coped quite comfortably with the restrictions when they too won the European Cup. Assimilated players are, or were, those who, though technically foreign, could be regarded as English because they had learned their trade in our game as youths.

At the time of writing, no one was sure whether the rule still applied. While UEFA's lawyers were trying to work out the implications of the Bosman verdict in this area, the governing body were hoping they could keep the rule in force until the end of the 1995–6 season at least. But if the European Court felt it was not legal, it's hard to see how they could enforce it. The mistake would be to imagine that a scrapping of the rule would somehow give English clubs an advantage in the European competitions. Don't forget that the continental clubs could then field as many foreigners as they wanted, and wealthy clubs like AC Milan have far more on the books than they are presently allowed to play.

So, it cannot alter the fact that we are in the position of having to learn our European lessons all over again. I tried to help by holding a meeting with the managers of the six English representatives – Blackburn Rovers, Manchester United, Liverpool, Nottingham Forest, Leeds and Everton – before they went into the 1995–6 European tournaments. Since Forest were the only ones who made it into the final stages, my intervention can hardly be counted a howling success; but I'm satisfied with the thought that I got the managers to address the issue of what problems they would face in Europe that were likely to be different from those they normally encountered in the Premiership. I'd also like to think that Liverpool played a lot more carefully as a result. In the end, I thought, they were a bit unlucky to be knocked out of the UEFA Cup by Brondby. Their tactics worked perfectly in the first round and almost so in the first, away leg of the second round. Where they fell down was in not getting an away goal. It's not much good being sound defensively if you don't score yourselves. You've got to learn how to do that. When I was in Europe with Barcelona, I was always driving home the value of the away goal and it kept getting us through.

I wasn't surprised Forest got through to the quarter-final, because Frank Clark, their manager and former left-back, is steeped in the counter-attacking creed of Brian Clough, the man who twice brought the European Cup to the City Ground (1978–9, 1979–80). While Forest's many rearguard actions were not pretty to watch, they never forgot how to hurt the opposition on the break. Their continued mastery of the counter-attacking game is quite exceptional, given that the crowds want Premiership teams to go forward all the time and that most other sides have lost the knack of soaking up punishment then breaking out suddenly. It was certainly disappointing to see Leeds, whose manager, Howard Wilkinson, did not attend the pre-tournament meeting, play in a very attacking, gung-ho way against PSV Eindhoven and lose. When we had another meeting with the managers after most of them had been knocked out, I think they realized we had to play a different sort of game in Europe.

There is not a shadow of doubt that playing as we do in the Premiership will get us nowhere. It will just make us easy pickings. The Republic of Ireland did fantastically well under Jack Charlton and I've no wish to put them down, but I have to say their 2–0 defeat by Holland in that European Championship play-off game at Anfield could have been a lot heavier. The Irish tried to play the Dutch the way we play our league football and they were just picked off, as easy as you like. Now the continentals have gone ahead of us again, we've got to catch up. Not only catch up, but overtake them. It's no good just copying something: that just gives you a poor imitation. What you have to do is copy, and then some. But it's going to be a big job to restore our credibility at club level. It's alongside what I've been doing with the England team. Then we've got to get it right for the future. It's about teaching players, and there are so many things that have to be taught. Essentially, it's a question of how to play football with intelligence in all areas of the field.

Technique, as I've said, is only part of the story. If you teach kids nothing but good technique, you are liable to end up with ball-jugglers like David Burnside, the former West Bromwich Albion player, who was so good at manipulating the ball as a youngster he used to give displays at half-time. David now works for the FA as a coach, incidentally, and is just the opposite to his old image in his views. It's as though he's rebelling against what he'd been taught and had mastered. 'You led me the wrong way,' he seems to be saying. 'I mastered it and it still didn't work. So I've gone the other way.'

Making the right kind of information available to the coaches and the kids is vital. It's like the story of Andy Roxburgh, the former Scotland coach, doing a coaching session watched by Rinus Michels, the legendary former Ajax and Holland coach. Roxburgh likes to demonstrate all sorts of tricky things, but Michels kept shouting out things like 'Rubbish!' and 'Wrong!'. He then added: 'Training is no good if it has nothing to do with the game!' which is absolutely correct. Unlike us, the Dutch are a people who are not worried about speaking their minds, and he put Andy on the spot. But he was right: coaching is not entertainment, it's not a matter of keeping the lads happy. It's about being effective and bringing about improvement.

There is certainly no reason for us in England to despair about the future. I think it's quite possible to get to the stage where all our players are as comfortable on the ball as the continentals. We've just got to teach them the right way at an earlier age. We've always had this fight with the schools over access, and it's nonsense. If you are a promising schoolboy footballer and the schoolteacher likes football, that's helpful. If he doesn't, you are struggling. If you want to learn to play the piano as a child, you go to a piano teacher outside of school. Similarly, if you want to learn how to play football, you have to go to the local football club as they do in Barcelona. They run 15 or 16 schoolboy sides there. If you are not getting the right coaching at school, you lose such a lot of possibilities as a player. If the schools don't like the idea of their pupils going to football clubs for coaching, they've got to let the coaches into the schools. As it stands, the whole situation is ludicrously antiquated. It's yet another example of our history as the founders of the game holding us back.

Although I am happy to think that England's success in reaching the semi-finals of Euro '96 has lifted the spirits of the whole nation, we are still going through one of the many periods of self-assessment and self-doubt there have been since a marvellous Hungarian team first shattered all illusions about our football supremacy in 1953. The Hungarians turned the football world on its head by coming to Wembley, where England had never lost to foreign opposition, and thrashing the self-styled kings of the game 6–3. Then, just to prove it wasn't a fluke, Ferenc Puskas, Jozsef Bozsik, Sandor Koskics, Nandor Hidegkuti and company hammered them 7–1 in Budapest the following year. This, too, against

England teams containing players as good as Stanley Matthews, Tom Finney, Roger Byrne, Jimmy Dickinson and Stan Mortensen.

But everything that goes around comes around, and we shouldn't forget we still possess certain natural advantages. There's our spirit and moral fibre, for instance. I could be wrong, but I think it was Adolf Hitler who said that if he could combine the organization of the Germans and the fighting spirit of the British Tommy, he'd conquer the world. There's our heading, too. That's a football technique, and we are as good as anyone, if not better, at heading the ball in either box. We will go for the header attacking or defending, and it frightens the life out of the Italians, the Spanish and the Dutch. To stop you, they'll pull you and push you, but you never see a penalty for it. A few penalties would let them know they can't do it any more. Our technical superiority at heading should give us an advantage, but it doesn't because we are at the mercy of unscrupulous players.

I honestly believe the technique of heading is going out of the game because referees and the football authorities are not taking strong enough action against the sort of defender who employs blatantly unfair methods to stop forwards jumping for the ball. That's where television should help. If the cameras focused not on the corner-kick or free-kick, but on what was happening in the box, you'd be amazed at what was going on. Instead, we watch the ball as it lands on someone's head. By then, the pushing and the pulling is over. If you did the same thing 30 yards out, you'd get sent off. But because it's only six yards from goal, the referees always cop out.

For all that, I welcome the influx of foreign players into English football. We were slow in this country to appreciate the value of being able to have foreigners in the team. When I was a manager in England before going out to Barcelona in 1984, I thought about foreign players in the same way as most other people. You know – they won't settle down, they won't play well in the cold weather. It was all negative. But when I went to Barcelona, I began to understand what an advantage it could be to have those three foreigners. In Spain and Italy they realized long before we did that most of the native footballers were of roughly the same standard. Therefore, it would give you perhaps a decisive edge to choose three outstanding players from anywhere in the world.

Now that we have finally caught up with the rest of Europe on this, the Bosman case has opened the floodgates to players from the European Community. What effect that will have on English football is difficult to tell. Although transfer fees are lower throughout most of the Continent than they are here, they are lowest in the old eastern bloc, which is not in the EC. That means the players most likely to attract cost-conscious English clubs can be restricted in number. Otherwise, the situation will probably remain much as it now. That is to say, a steady stream of Scandinavian imports enlivened by the occasional Brazilian, Italian, German, Frenchman, Dutchman, Spaniard or African. The number of foreigners per team is likely to rise, but not enough, I would hope, to block the development of promising young English footballers. It should help that the Bosman judgment will bring down transfer fees in the domestic market and make the home-bred player just as attractive financially as the foreigner.

In any case, it is a two-way street. Our players can go and join continental clubs if they want to when they are free agents at the end of their contracts. That kind of traffic is likely to be thinner, admittedly, if only because the wages in the Premier League are at least as good as anywhere else in Europe. In truth, our players are getting big money before performing in the proper way. And let us not kid ourselves: the big names who have been attracted here have not come to complete their education. They have come because the money is good and, perhaps, because our high-velocity football presents a new kind of challenge. I imagine they must feel a bit lost at times. Being as intelligent as they are, they are probably saying to themselves: 'Why aren't those players running there?' There was a big debate about Dennis Bergkamp not scoring when he first joined Arsenal, and not getting the space. But he needs other people to make that for him. So does Ruud Gullit, because the Dutch are used to playing in a different way.

I don't think Jürgen Klinsmann needed that kind of help. He's been to so many clubs in his career, he's got used to adapting to new styles of play. The Dutch are different, though, and I think the trick is to get about three of them together. That way, they can make a case for their style of football and maybe increase its popularity, spread the gospel. We must certainly make every effort to learn from the most talented foreigners who come into our game. That appears to be happening at Old Trafford, where Eric Cantona has become a guru to the many talented young English footballers on Manchester United's books. Similarly, Nicky Barmby cannot have helped but glean something from a class act like Klinsmann during the German international's one shining season with Spurs.

Barmby will definitely have benefited from training with, and playing alongside, that supremely professional striker. He is bright enough to have seen things Klinsmann does that he could add to his own game. And now he's got Juninho and Ravanelli to study at Middlesbrough. So he can see for himself that they are not men from Mars, and he will not be overawed by having to play against them in international football. They'll be on first-name terms, and he's not going to be frightened of them.

We also need to know more about what is going on in the world. Not just in terms of coaching methods and playing styles, but in the practical sense of knowing where the best players are to be found and how available they might be. This is another area where we are behind the times. Our clubs only seem to know through recommendation or an agent going out to get you a video. By contrast, Liverpool's Robbie Fowler has been on Ajax's database for some time as a player they reckoned could fit into their system. They reached that conclusion not just because of all the goals he's scored – you could get that out of a magazine – but from reports by their scouts. They really know what is going on elsewhere in the world. Likewise, Barcelona have paid representatives scouring the world for the finest talent. When I was there, I had reports on everybody – from Nigeria, from Russia, from everywhere.

Here, as usual, we just trust to luck. Unless your manager does a lot of travelling and has good contacts abroad, you have to rely on agents who make it their business to know where the best foreign players are and at what price. The situation is becoming more strained as the chairmen of English clubs realize that good players can be bought abroad at far lower prices than those in the Premier League. So, all of a sudden, they say to their managers: 'Look, you are being too parochial. We want you to know what's going on out there in Europe. What do you mean, you don't know anyone in Russia? Ajax, or whoever, have taken two Nigerians and a Russian, and it seems we don't know about them.' But they don't want anything to do with agents, of course.

There were complaints when we, at Spurs, had Frank McLintock and people going out looking for players on our behalf. I believe I'm a fair judge of a player and I sometimes think I'd like to be an agent myself. I can see the attraction in travelling the world trying to spot new talent; but there's an awful lot of downsides to it as well. Frank will tell you about the times he's been out there, spent money on plane trips, hotels, videos, etc., and then the manager he's acting for says: 'Sorry, I don't fancy the player.' So who's going to pay for that? The answer is nobody, and you can't take too many of those kind of losses unless you've got a lot of capital behind you. Frank has decided it doesn't make sense financially and has packed it in. They say he's getting all this money, but it can't be such a wonderful business, can it, if he can't make it pay?

How English clubs are going to find good foreign players without the help of agents like Frank is a matter for debate. Are the clubs prepared to set up the same kind of expensive operation themselves, for instance? In the end, I think, a lot of chairmen will decide that if they can save £2 million on one player, it's worth spending £500,000 a year on a scouting operation. For that, they can have four scouts providing them with the world-wide information they need when they want a new player. Those who are not willing to set up their own operation must be prepared to employ people to act on their behalf. And that means coming to a financial arrangement before the agent leaves this country. When I was at Barcelona employing scouts on an ad hoc basis, we'd perhaps agree to pay them their expenses and a bonus on top if we signed the player. You can't expect them to work for you without getting paid.

Whichever system English clubs use, they need to employ people who know what they are doing. That's because we are at the stage now where the Italians and the Spanish are taking advantage of us because they know we are prepared to pay almost as much for their players as we are for our own. As the prices they quote seem a little bit less to us, we are happy. But, in actual fact, they are selling players to us for much more than they would get for them in Italy. The transfers of Dennis Bergkamp (£7.5 million) and David Platt £4.75 million) to Arsenal were two prime examples. It might have sounded like sour grapes when George Graham said his old club had paid over the odds for them, but he was just speaking the truth. I know for a fact Arsenal could have had Bergkamp and Platt for £2 million less each because I was contacted about them myself. You see, playing in Europe and travelling out there, George would start to know people in Italian football. But without that kind of travel, how do you start to make contacts?

Although nothing will really change on the field until we start dictating the pace of the game from the back, the hope has got to be that a mass influx of top-class foreign footballers will raise standards through sheer weight of numbers. I'm not worried about young English players being crowded out because I believe true ability will always be recognized. But I don't think employing foreign coaches will provide a short cut to tactical change, necessarily. Aston Villa tried it with Josef Venglos, didn't they, and came unstuck. Venglos is a very good coach, and it wasn't entirely his fault the appointment didn't work out. When results started to go badly, the players were taking the mickey behind his back because his English wasn't good. Abroad, the players don't care what language you speak so long as they know you are good at your job. Then they'll give you all the respect you need. It's another of the cultural differences that divide us and yet another area where we need to put our house in order.

Our best hope of change, as I have said, lies in the appointment of a strong, knowledgeable, charismatic and far-sighted technical director. It won't be easy to find someone with the necessary qualities, especially now that candidates such as Howard Wilkinson and Roy Hodgson have withdrawn from the running. Dario Gradi, the manager of Crewe Alexandra, has done well with young players, but I don't see how they could put him in a position of such wide-ranging responsibility. Gerard Houllier, France's English-speaking technical director, was said to be a strong candidate and may seem the perfect answer to some. Bearing in mind the rather undistinguished record of French football, though, I'm not sure they can teach us the sort of things we need to know. If it's a foreigner you want, why not go to the very top and try to entice Louis van Gaal, another English speaker, away from Ajax? The trouble, of course, is that the FA are unable, or unwilling, to offer the sort of salary that would attract the best in the world.

Bobby Robson, to my mind, would have made the perfect technical director. He has credentials just about as good as you are going to get. As a former manager of England and Ipswich, he knows English football inside-out and cares for it with a rare passion. As a coach who has gone abroad and found success with PSV Eindhoven in Holland and Sporting Lisbon and Porto in Portugal, he could offer our game a real insight into what has enabled the Dutch and the Portuguese to become two of the most progressive nations in world football. As a combination of all those things, he would be bound to command respect. It is not a job for a young man, either, so Bobby's age – 63 – would have been nothing but an advantage. Unfortunately, Barcelona got in first.

Chapter Eight

England

Managing or coaching England has been called an impossible job, but it's not. It's difficult, but not impossible. Nothing's impossible if you put your mind to it. I stick firmly to that view despite the wrangles with the FA's international committee that prompted my decision to resign following the finals of the European Championship and all the attacks on me by certain sections of the media. In fact, I'd like to think I have done enough to prove that the job is not impossible, and have perhaps taken some of the fear out of it for other people. It has long been argued, for instance, that the man in charge of the England team can't hope to achieve much success because the English footballer is so inferior to the continentals in terms of technique. Then there is the alleged handicap of our club sides playing in a very British way and not sticking to a style everyone is familiar with, as is the case abroad. Yet I'd like to think we proved during Euro '96 that the English footballer is not the poor relation of Europe individually or collectively. Certainly, my players delighted me by the way they took on board, and put into practice, all the new and unfamiliar things I asked them to do. The one quality the English player is definitely not short of is adaptability, so Glenn Hoddle should have no difficulty in putting over his ideas, which are not that far removed from mine.

Of course I'm sorry not to have the chance to take England to the finals of the next World Cup. It's got to be the ambition of every national team manager to take part in the world's greatest tournament; and when I was appointed in January 1994, it was my hope that I would be able to go all the way through to 1998 in France. But it wasn't to be, and I'll just have to live with my decision to relinquish the job prematurely. At the same time, I hope the scale of what I am giving up will help to convey to you just how important I believe it is for me to clear my name. I have been accused of just about every kind of financial wrongdoing in the past two years, and I couldn't live with myself if I did not prove those accusations totally false. I was brought up to know right from wrong, and my good name means a lot to me. Unfortunately, I did not think I could combine a heavy programme of litigation with a World Cup qualifying campaign when I did not have the full backing of the FA's international committee. Some members of it were beginning to go a bit wobbly on me last year (1995), when I was in court for a only a few days in all. Although it has emerged since that the demand on my time might not be as great as first thought, when I took the decision not to continue as England coach it looked as if I would need several weeks in the latter part of this year to fight four major cases; and that, of course, was when England were due to be involved in World Cup qualifiers. Those four cases, by the way, are my claim for wrongful dismissal against Tottenham, my separate libel actions against *Panorama* and the *Daily Mirror*, and Alan Sugar's libel action against me. So I would have needed all the support and understanding I could get from the international committee in order to do the England job to the best of my ability. I must stress that I never had a problem with Sir Bert Millichip, the FA chairman, or Graham Kelly, the chief executive. Both of them backed me to the hilt from the beginning. I know the chairman wasn't too keen on employing me at first – 'Over my dead body' was the phrase he used – but he became so supportive in the end that he was telling the press he wanted to give me a contract that would not just take me up the 1998 World Cup finals, but a year beyond them as well. That was very flattering and gratifying, because I think it showed Sir Bert had enjoyed working with me and had been impressed by what I had done with the England team. Graham, too, kept repeating that he considered me the best man for the job and refused to over-react to the damaging stories about my business affairs that were appearing regularly in two newspapers, the *Daily Mirror* and the *Daily Telegraph*, and occasionally in one television programme, *Panorama*. As he pointed out, the FA were satisfied that nothing in my private life was interfering with my job as England coach, and that was good enough for them until such time as the allegations against me were proved or disproved.

You can't put a price on loyalty like that, especially when other, so-called colleagues are sniping at you behind your back. I refer, in particular, to Liverpool director Noel White, the chairman of the international committee, and committee member Ian Stott, the chairman of Oldham Athletic. Both of them were quoted in the newspapers as expressing concern about the sort of headlines I was attracting and the number of times I was appearing in court. There was also a suggestion from them that I should not be offered a new contract until such time as I had shown what I could do in the competitive context of the European Championship finals. In other words, the jury was still out on my ability as a coach so far as they were concerned. But if that is what they were thinking, why did they not speak to me first? What really annoyed me was having to find out about it in the newspapers.

On top of the disloyalty involved, their remarks were illogical and grossly insulting. Illogical because both White and Stott had been members of the sub-committee that appointed me and were made fully aware of the problems I faced off the field. I had certainly not hidden anything when I was interviewed by them. What they said was grossly insulting because I did not feel I had much to prove about coping with the pressures of competitive international football after winning the Spanish title with Barcelona in 1985, their first in 11 years, and taking them to the final of the European Cup the following year, when we lost to Steau Bucharest on penalties. Logic was lacking here, too, in that none of the Englishmen from whom the committee were preparing to choose my successor possessed any experience of being in charge of the England team for friendly internationals, never mind competitive ones! So what would they have gained from not renewing my contract until after the finals?

I was especially lucky because I was in Europe with Barcelona at the time English clubs were out of Europe. I had three years in a league that was a good training ground for the European competitions. Spanish football is so high-profile you get used to pressure on and off the field. So what chance do our managers have, going straight from the Premier League to that? Believe me, the Premier League is child's play by comparison. What was uppermost in my mind, then, was that someone was going to have to come in cold and tackle a World Cup qualifying game only eight weeks after the end of Euro '96. If I had done what Noel White and company wanted and waited until the European Championship was over, that's the sort of problem the FA would have faced immediately.

As it is, it won't be easy for Glenn; but at least I gave them six months to sort something out. In addition, I'll be glad to help if they want. If they don't, it's not a problem.

The bottom line here, I think, is that everyone at the FA was uneasy about the potential embarrassment my business affairs might cause them. That's why they only offered me a two-and-a-half year contract in the first place and called me the England coach instead of the England manager. I was prepared to accept it because I needed a job at the time and it's not every day of the week you are offered the chance to take charge of the England team. So it suited them and it suited me. If I'd still been at Tottenham, I wouldn't have taken the job. Making Spurs great again was the challenge I had wanted for the rest of my life. Sensibly, in the circumstances, the FA insisted on a get-out clause if anything untoward came of old or new allegations, and it was agreed the situation should be reviewed by both sides after six months. The review never took place, unfortunately. If it had, perhaps the FA could have tacked the extra year on to my contract that would have put me on a par with Bobby Robson and Graham Taylor. As Sir Bert pointed out, those England managers didn't go into any tournament fearing the sack because there was always that additional year beyond it to give both parties room for manoeuvre. If the contract finishes with the tournament, you end up with the FA looking for a replacement behind the manager's back, and the manager looking for a new job behind the FA's back. But what's the point of that? Let's be out in the open like all the other countries.

It was the lack of faith in my ability that annoyed me most, I suppose. The very fact that the international committee had appointed me England coach showed they thought I was the best man for the job; yet here some of them were, asking for further proof. Not surprisingly, then, I did not mince words when I had it out with White at a meeting also attended by Sir Bert Millichip and Graham Kelly at the Hyatt Regency Hotel in Birmingham last December, before the draw for the finals of the European Championship. Arguing that if the chairman of the international committee had any complaints to make about me he should make them to my face, I asked him if he had actually said what he had been reported as saying in the papers. When he denied saying it, I suggested he should make a statement to that effect and Sir Bert agreed with me.

No such statement was forthcoming, but I did add: 'What you are hoping to do is wait until the horse has crossed the line before you have a bet on it.' To his credit, White came to see me after I had announced my decision to quit and tried to clear the air between us. He insisted the chairman of the international committee should have the right to comment on anything related to the England team, and I refused to back down on anything I had said about him. In other words, we agreed to disagree. Nevertheless, White did come up to me after we had got to the semi-finals of Euro '96 and say: 'Well done!' That can't have been easy for him to do.

My misgivings about the whole situation had begun as long ago as October 1995, when I took England to Oslo for a friendly against Norway. The match, which ended in a goalless draw, gave me a lot of satisfaction from a tactical point of view, but was not pretty to watch. Unfortunately, interviewed straight after the game, I said I thought we'd done well without adding, as I believed myself, it wasn't much of a spectacle. Consequently, I was panned for what I said as well as for the boring way most journalists thought England had played. But that didn't bother me. Honest criticism I can take. What disturbed me much more was the reaction there had been to a story my co-writer, Colin Malam, had run in the *Sunday Telegraph* the day before we set off for Oslo.

It was to the effect that I had been approached by a representative of Inter Milan to see if I was willing to become the new coach of the famous Italian club. The approach had been made while I was on holiday in Spain with my wife, Yvette. The man in question, who phoned me at my hotel, asked if I would be prepared give up the England job and move to Milan for 'any money'. I said there was no chance of that because I was under contract to the FA for two years and believed in honouring such agreements. It was a perfectly true story; and I had mentioned it to Colin as an example of the temptations that can be put in your way only because we were discussing, for the purposes of this book, Don Revie's decision to take up a job in the Middle East in 1977 before his four-year England contract had ended. Aware of the information's news value, and thinking it might help to counteract the adverse publicity I had been getting from *Panorama* and the *Daily Mirror*, he asked for my permission to use it in his paper.

Unfortunately, Inter then issued a statement denying they had made an official approach to me. Technically they were right, because the approach had come from a middleman, not a full-time employee of the club. Almost certainly, they issued the denial because they were about to appoint another Englishman, Roy Hodgson, as their new coach. Inter would not have wanted, either, to have been found guilty of 'tapping up' a manager already in employment without first asking the permission of his employers. But that sort of thing goes on all the time throughout football, and only the naïve would think it doesn't. Nevertheless, perhaps Colin and I were wrong in not thinking through more carefully the possible consequences of the story, especially as I had promised the middleman I would not reveal his identity.

My enemies in the press had a field day with Inter's denial, of course. I was virtually accused of making up stories about being head-hunted in order to steamroller the FA into giving me a fat new contract. It was maddening, not only because the approach from Inter was fact, but because money was the last thing on my mind at that moment. I can't pretend I wasn't hoping for a significant increase in my annual salary of £130,000 – paltry by comparison with the top Premier League managers, never mind other national coaches around the world – but the main consideration was the length of my contract. Basically, I wanted to know whether I would still be in the job after Euro '96. I wanted to be able to plan ahead, and I felt the FA ought to be doing the same thing. I kept repeating that it was no good waiting until Euro '96 was over to see who was going to be the England coach, because the first World Cup qualifier would be only a matter of weeks away. I also pointed out that the Danish FA already knew their coach, Richard Moller Nielsen, would be leaving after the finals to take over Finland's national team, and could plan accordingly. Yet most people preferred to believe all I was doing was trying to twist the FA's arm over a new contract.

At least the Inter story did prompt Graham Kelly to bring up the subject of my future on that trip to Norway. As our talks continued right up to Christmas, I became increasingly aware I was not going to get the backing from the international committee I would need to cope with my impending court cases. Finally, Graham asked me to think things over during a week's holiday I took in Oman at the start of 1996. There was nothing to think over so far as I was concerned, since I had already made up my mind not to continue as England coach after Euro '96.

To be absolutely honest, I got the impression Graham was trying to find a compromise that would keep me in the job and the international committee happy. When he asked me if I would accept a one-year contract and a substantial rise, for example, I was staggered. That would have meant I could have left, or they could have got rid of me, halfway through the World Cup qualifying campaign. Graham's words were: 'I think I may be able to get that through.' But I wouldn't even consider it. So, when we were going to tell the media I was not continuing as England coach, and Graham and I and David Davies, the FA's director of public affairs, were trying to anticipate the questions we might be asked, I said: 'Oh, and what about the year's contract you offered me?' But Graham said: 'It wasn't an offer. I just wanted to see whether you would accept it.' 'What if I'd said yes?' I replied. 'Well,' he said, 'I think I could have got it through.' So I said: 'Therefore, it was an offer.' 'No, it wasn't,' he insisted. 'OK,' I agreed, 'it wasn't an offer.'

I think Graham was trying really hard to solve the problem, but he was being hampered by the undue influence FA committees have. A chief executive should be an all-powerful administrator, but the committee structure of the FA was stopping him working as he would want to work. There were obviously people behind the scenes who weren't prepared to go along with him. I think Graham was put under pressure by the publicized objections of Stott and White to the idea of the chief executive offering me a new contract without consulting the international committee first. The truth is that, if they had offered me two years more, I would have stayed on. Money didn't really come into it. Unfortunately, I think there were people on the international committee, who were looking for excuses not to extend my contract.

That's the trouble with committees. The people on them often feel they have to say something to justify their position. There's no common sense in having committees, in my opinion, but the whole of the FA is run by them. I think the ruling body would be far more effective and quicker off the mark if key decisions could be made by smaller groups of people or even individuals. I certainly believe nobody but the chairman, the chief executive and the England coach should have the power to make public statements about the England team and other related matters. And if the circumstances of my departure help in some small way to break down the antiquated structure of the FA, I'd feel my two years in office did achieve something that might make it easier for my successors to do the job.

Still, my problems were as nothing, I suppose, to those of Walter Winterbottom when he was the first England manager in the early years after the war (1946–62). Walter could hardly cough without referring to an FA committee first. A panel of selectors picked his teams for him, and it was not until 1953 that he was even allowed to make recommendations. But that was normal then. Managers were fairly anonymous and the chairmen wielded all the power. So if that was the way things were conducted everywhere, you just got used to it and got on with it. You would certainly find that kind of arrangement hard to change while you were in the job. I'd think Alf must have changed it before he took the job. As a manager, you are at your strongest in your first three months or so. Even if you are successful, they get used to you after five or six years. I reckon it's when you first come into a job that you can get things done.

Walter did reasonably well, considering the handicaps he had to work under. Reaching the quarter-finals of the 1954 and 1962 World Cups offset to some extent the acute embarrassment of losing to the United States in the 1950 tournament. But, in all honesty, you would have expected more from England during a 16-year period when they could call on outstanding players such as Stanley Matthews, Tom Finney, Wilf Mannion, Tommy Lawton, Stan Mortensen, Nat Lofthouse, Duncan Edwards and Neil Franklin. In fact, Winterbottom's biggest achievements were probably in his secondary capacity as director of coaching. A former teacher as well as a former Manchester United wing-half, he offered English football its first organized instruction in the arts and crafts of the game on a variety of levels. As someone who values coaching above most things in football, I willingly pay tribute to him for getting things under way like that.

In some ways, managing or coaching England in the last 50 years has been a mirror image of developments in the game at large. Alf Ramsey (1962–74), who took over the job when Winterbottom resigned after the 1962 World Cup, reflected the rise of the strong-willed, self-reliant, charismatic manager at club level by demanding, and getting, the right to pick his own teams. After a short and jolly period under caretaker-manager Joe Mercer, the next up was Don Revie (1974–7), who, as I've said, scandalized the nation by bailing out before his contract had expired to take up a well-paid job in the United Arab Emirates. That unfortunate episode was an example of the wealth becoming available in the game at the time and the effect it could have on people's judgment. The scholarly Ron Greenwood (1977–82) was chosen to succeed Revie. While the FA were probably attracted mainly by Ron's reputation for integrity after the Revie affair, their choice could also be seen as belated recognition of the value of good coaching. Bobby Robson (1982–90) fell into much the same category as Ron, but Graham Taylor (1990–4) was rather different in that he owed his appointment to success with the long-ball game at club level.

I don't know enough about Alf Ramsey's tactical skill to comment, but there's no doubt he knew how to put a team together. The one he won the World Cup with in 1966 wasn't the one he started out with, despite what some people have said. He began with wingers, or at least one orthodox winger in John Connelly, Terry Paine or Ian Callaghan, then decided to turn it round because he didn't think the system was functioning in the first few games. Some players came in very late on as well. Martin Peters, Alan Ball and Geoff Hurst only had 18 caps between them before the start of the tournament. But Alf certainly got it right in the end, and I thought it was a tremendous achievement to win the World Cup even though we had the advantage of playing at home.

I actually thought Argentina were the best team in that World Cup. I spent a week up in the Midlands, where the Argentines were based for their first-round matches, and I thought they were terrific. We only won our quarter-final against them 1–0 with a late goal from Geoff Hurst, and they'd had to play with ten men for a long time. The guy who was sent off for dissent, Antonio Rattin, was a very good player, and they had another outstanding mid-fielder in Ermindo Onega. Alf called them animals, and he wasn't very far away from the truth. They could be nasty, but they could play, too. We may have been a little fortunate to have beaten Argentina, but you need a bit of luck if you are going to win a major tournament – as I found to my cost. England certainly deserved to win the final against West Germany. There's always that argument about whether Geoff Hurst's shot was over the line or not, but I don't think it matters. We were much the better side on the day. All-in-all, I don't think England had too much luck in 1966. They just played well on the right days.

Luck certainly deserted Alf at the next World Cup, when a stomach upset robbed him of Gordon Banks, the best goalkeeper in the world just then, for the quarter-final against West Germany. It didn't seem much of a handicap in the first half while England were leading 2–0 and playing the Germans off the park, but it became cruelly apparent when the old foe started to put on the pressure in the second half. Two substitutions changed everything, West Germany sending on Grabowski for Libuda on the right-wing and England replacing Bobby Charlton with Colin Bell in central midfield. Grabowski ran a tiring England defence to death, while the departure of Charlton freed Franz Beckenbauer from a marking job and released him to do terrible damage. Peter Bonetti, my old Chelsea team-mate, was blamed for at least one of the three goals with which West Germany won the game, but it was his first appearance in goal during the tournament and the ball does fly a bit in the thin air of Mexico. Alf, too, was heavily criticized. It's probably right that he should have replaced the exhausted Terry Cooper at left-back, rather than Martin Peters, with Norman Hunter, but I can see how he would have wanted to try and save Peters and Charlton for the semi-final. None of us can be right all the time, and it just goes to show how important decisions of that kind can be in the heat of battle. Some believe Alf's 1970 England team was even better than the one that won the World Cup, but I wouldn't agree. There was no Jack Charlton in the side for a start, and I think he was a bigger influence than people realize. There may have been slightly better players in the 1970 team, but I think the mix in 1966 was much more effective. Even so, it shows what a good manager Alf was to keep the continuity going like that.

I won my two senior England caps under Ramsey. He picked me to play against Belgium and Holland in 1964. I was chosen for a third one, but I got injured and Johnny Byrne came in. He played well and stayed in. I didn't get a cap while I was at Tottenham, where I didn't do very well, and missed out on the 1966 World Cup after getting into the initial squad of 40 players. Then, when I was at QPR, I heard Alf was thinking of bringing me back because I was playing the best football of my career. I was about 30 then, though, and I think he decided it was a bit late. Alf and I both come from Dagenham, although our accents are slightly different. We were literally streets away from each other, and I remember trying to curry favour with him through a guy my dad knew. This bloke used to live next door to Alf and was a very good friend of his. So I though it would get me in with Alf to mention the neighbour. 'Mr Pritchett (or whatever his name was) sends his regards,' I said. 'He used to live next door to you.' At which, Alf just coughed awkwardly and left without saying anything. I don't think he cared to be reminded of his Dagenham roots. There was never a lot of communication from him, I found. He didn't really say anything to me, but I've got a lot of admiration for the way he handled the whole thing. He was very controlled and completely unswerving in his beliefs.

He got criticism from the media, but nothing like the sort of stuff people in his position get now. It almost becomes the bigger issue, doesn't it? He was always very bitter, though, about the way the FA got rid of him. He felt he'd changed the England set-up, made it successful, and then they wanted him out. It was the same with Jack Charlton. They reckon the reason the FA of Ireland let him go in the end was that they wanted to get their power back. Jack puts his foot down, and they know they are not going to, say, Brazil. So they can't have a nice trip out there and get gifts. Brian Clough always reckoned directors were at their worst when you were successful, because they want some of the credit and the praise. It's the power and the glory again. But when the team is struggling, they want the manager there because they want to be out of the limelight and he might just know how to put it right again.

Like Ramsey, Don Revie was one of the new breed of successful, high-profile club managers, but he will be remembered with nothing like the same respect. That's largely because he left before his contract was up and while England were fighting to qualify for the 1978 World Cup. To go like that was bad, there's no getting away from it. All you can say about his England performance is that it left a lot to be desired. That's not opinion, it's fact. He used a huge amount of players, and the team didn't qualify for either the European Championship or the World Cup. You can't leave halfway through your contract, either, unless the FA want you to. And at that particular time it was touch and go, so he should have seen it through. I'm afraid his bottle went at England level. It certainly looks as though he couldn't take the criticism, because the *Daily Mail*, in their exclusive story about Revie's defection, quoted him as saying: 'Nearly everyone in the country seems to want me out. So I am giving them what they want.'

But I don't like thin appraisals of people. It's very simple to say he was this, that or the other. Good friends of mine liked Revie, and the Leeds players always spoke well of him. So if there was that much respect and affection for him, there must have been a lot more to him. In fact, my suspicion is that he was an OK bloke. It sounds like there was a lot of the giver in him. I know he was always very kind to me and made me feel very important. Perhaps these things don't happen today, but when I was a player it was very flattering when another manager spoke to you or recognized you. I was always very impressed by him. I am also told that Professor Sir Harold Thompson, the FA chairman at the time, was not the most likeable of men or the easiest to get along with.

My liking and respect for Ron Greenwood, Revie's permanent successor, should have become apparent by now. He was an intelligent coach when that was a bit of a rarity in football and he was a good person. But I think the greatest service he did England was providing Alf Ramsey with the fully-educated trio of Martin Peters, Geoff Hurst and Bobby Moore. Although Ron was a tactician, I don't think England did a lot of tactical stuff under him. He might have decided it was safer not to confuse the players. But I think you've got to try and lay down some fundamentals. Otherwise you are going to struggle to get a cohesive team out of people just turning up. Significantly, in view of the way Ajax have become Holland to all intents and purposes, Ron tried the ploy of including a lot of people from the same club for his first match, a goalless draw at Wembley with Switzerland. There were six Liverpool players in the side plus Kevin Keegan, who had just been transferred to Hamburg. It didn't work too well, and that's largely because Liverpool's most influential players at the time were three Scotsmen, Kenny Dalglish, Graeme Souness and Alan Hansen. Still, it was only on goal difference that Ron failed to get England to the finals of the 1978 World Cup after picking up the reins from Don Revie. In effect, Italy qualified because they beat Finland 6-1 at home when we could only manage a 2–1 win against them at Wembley. It was that close with a very good Italian team, who finished an impressive fourth in the world in Argentina. Ron then went on to take England to the finals of both the 1980 European Championship and the 1982 World Cup, but without making much of an impact. The European Championship was marred by crowd trouble at the game against Italy in Turin, while

England were handicapped at the 1982 World Cup finals in Spain by the unfitness of Keegan and Trevor Brooking. If I remember rightly, Ron was so fed up with the criticism he was getting in the papers, he would have resigned after a World Cup qualifying game in Hungary if the players hadn't talked him out of it. So we've all been through the mill, one way or the other.

None more so than Bobby Robson, Greenwood's successor. In fact, Bobby had a bit of a nightmare until right near the end of his eight years in the hot seat. He failed to qualify for the finals of the 1984 European Championship, lost in the quarter-finals of the 1986 World Cup to Diego Maradona's 'Hand of God' goal and took some bad blows in the finals of the 1988 European Championship. On top of all that, the press were constantly having a go at him – and not always because of his team's performances. I sympathize because Bobby was the first England manager to have his private life dragged into public view by the tabloids.

I always remember going to Italy in 1980 for the finals of the European Championship and getting to know Bobby at Asti, near Turin, where Ron Greenwood and the England team were based. The FA had taken all the coaches in the England set-up then – Howard Wilkinson, Don Howe, Dave Sexton, Bobby and me – to Italy as a thank-you for working for them. Dave and I had just won the Under-21 European Championship, in fact. They were all good, friendly guys and we used to have sing-songs in the coach that carried us about. Bobby came over as a particularly warm sort of bloke, but he was very naïve in many ways. To be honest, I never thought he'd come out of his troubles. People forget he lost his first job as manager of Vancouver Royals because the club went bust, then he was sacked after nine months as manager of Fulham, his old club, and had to go on the dole. He'd lost his way so much, he was almost suicidal. Then it all just sort of seemed to come right for him. Bobby Keetch, who played with Bobby at Fulham, always reckoned he was a lucky devil.

What I always liked about Bobby Robson was that he was a really decent human being. So I was really pleased it went well for him in the end. Eventually, I think, he got through to the players who worked under him. They liked him and sympathized with him. I don't know that much about his football abilities, to be truthful, but he always put his players first. He was very honest with them and very protective. He also understood them quite well. That's what you are there for, really, as a manager or coach. A big part of your job is to take away as many of the pressures as possible, because there are enough of them on the players in a game as it is. Bobby's reward with England was reaching the quarter-finals of the 1986 World Cup and then going one better four years later in Italy. In 1990, I thought we were a bit fortunate to come through some of those games, especially the ones against Belgium and Cameroon. The game is so finely balanced at that level, it's just the little edge you need – the corner that breaks for you, the shot that goes in off a post. It really is that tight. But once we got to the semi-finals, we were unlucky to lose on penalties. England could easily have beaten West Germany, as they were then, and won the World Cup. Argentina were no great shakes in the final, if you recall. Bobby stayed with the players in that 1990 team for a long time, and he got the benefits of his loyalty and patience in the end.

The problem for Graham Taylor when he took over from Bobby was that the England team needed rebuilding. But there was more to it than that. Graham faced a really difficult conundrum because he had to decide whether to stick to what had got him the England job in the first place – his success with the long-ball game at Watford and Aston Villa, which he knew inside out – or try to be a bit more sophisticated. To have made it work, he should have remained true to his beliefs and played the ball long to a 6ft 6ins centre-forward in the Ross Jenkins and George Reilly mould. The trouble with being the manager of England, though, is that the country wants you to pick the best players, and the best players wouldn't want to play the long-ball game. Skilful players like Paul Gascoigne wouldn't have wanted to know about that, but he couldn't really refuse to pick Gazza, could he? I know he left him out of the odd game, but I mean on a regular basis. So he sort of compromised, made a mess of the 1992 European Championship finals and failed to qualify for the 1994 World Cup.

It's impossible to tell whether Graham would have been successful if he had remained true to his beliefs. It's unlikely because that kind of direct football doesn't seem to have proved effective at the top level of the game. Norway have persevered with it. They play with big, 6ft-plus strikers in Jan-Aage Fjortoft and Jostein Flo. The Republic of Ireland did the same and did pretty well but they didn't make spectacular progress in European Championships and

World Cups. They were teams you would be able to do something against. They've become less successful as time's gone on and opponents have worked out how to counter their tactics. We've never seen any real success from it anywhere, thank goodness.

One reason Graham got the job, I'm sure, is that he was an FA man. So was Bobby, really. That is to say, unlike me, they look comfortable in a blazer. Let's face it, the FA wouldn't have chosen me if they could have helped it. Without doubt, I got the job only because of a dramatic change of attitude at Lancaster Gate. Irked, I think, by all the jibes about their 'amateurism', they made a conscious effort to consult the professional side of the game about the appointment. I'm flattered to think I was the nomination of my professional peers, but I realize I would never even have been considered but for Graham Kelly who has been the driving force behind the campaign to modernize the ruling body of the English game, and the game itself. Yet, despite all Kelly's efforts, I fell victim in the end to the enduring, outdated, committee-driven nature of the FA.

You may not agree, but I think the FA have had fewer problems from me than from many of my predecessors. If the court cases and the newspaper stories were going to be a problem, they should have been a problem from the beginning. The test for the FA was whether they could support me through thick and thin. If they couldn't, that was their problem, not mine. If I'd given them a shock six months down the line and told them I'd got four big court cases coming up, fair enough. But, having laid everything on the line from the start, I've not got the slightest worry about that side of things.

Basically, as England coach, you've got to know what you want to do tactically. You've got to have no doubts about what you are after, even if it's a poor system of play. Then you've got to sort out the players you want. Above all, I was looking for intelligence. If two players were equal in ability, but one picked things up quicker than the other, I'd have him. The ability to pick up things quickly is a big asset because you've only got a short period of time to work with the players. The England coach hasn't got the time to develop good habits. You've also got to know your own mind over the selection of players. You can't pick a player, or leave a player out, simply because someone else says you've got to. It should be incidental what other people say. I may read something in a newspaper, accept the writer has made a good point and put that in my thinking; but, when it comes to the crunch, I'm going to do what I'm going to do. Just to keep my mind absolutely clear, I didn't read the newspapers before an England match. But I wouldn't be deterred from what I wanted to do by the press, the man next door or the shopkeeper.

As for the job being impossible, I've found it no better and no worse than I expected. I've watched how it's gone on before, how my predecessors have had to handle things, and it's definitely a crazy job. It's a job that's full of frustrations and the odds are loaded against you. But if you've got any competitiveness in you, you think there might just be a chance you can win. I remember Bobby Robson saying it took him two years just to understand what the job was about. I understand what he means, because you may know about systems of play and this, that and the other, but you've got to go different ways about it.

You lack regular contact with the players, for a start. I missed the day-to-day involvement you get at a club, but found I had gained the thinking time you don't normally have as a club manager. Travelling time as well. I was able to familiarize myself with players from abroad and what they were doing. In fact, I'm probably more of a rounded manager now than I was before. It's just a very different kind of job. You make your plans, then you get players withdrawing because of injury and you have to make them all over again. It's frustrating, too, to have to wait a month or so for your next fixture. I didn't enjoy that. Yet I grew to enjoy more of the other side of the job than perhaps I did in the beginning. In short, I liked being England coach. It would have been even more enjoyable if I could have made some of the other, non-football stuff go away.

One thing I made a point of not complaining about was the loss of players through injury. Apart from being a futile exercise, complaining doesn't solve the real problem, which is to find adequate replacements for the missing men. It's something you might have to do in the middle of a tournament, so you might as well get used to doing it as well as you can. Withdrawals have always been the bane of an England manager's life, but I have to say the problem has eased a little since I became coach in 1994. The Premier League's willingness to allow free weekends before major international matches has helped to reduce the risk of injury to England players and has provided more time to work with the squad. Those concessions have been invaluable, though I think there is still room for improvement in the relationship. The Premier League and the Italian League have become so commercial and popular, and the prizes so big, you feel they are only concerned with the clubs. I've been a club manager and I understand that.

The central question English football has to address is: do we want a strong and successful national team? If the answer is yes, then we've got to do it properly. There's no point in having one if the clubs are going to make it difficult for players to join squads or get-togethers, which I've proved to my own satisfaction are invaluable. Other nations, even new ones like South Africa, will take their national team away for a month or two months for tours or special training. But their football associations have the power to tell the clubs what to do. That's the difference. You can understand the clubs here not wanting to lose their players or see them get injured. OK then, let's be honest and say we want the best league in the world and are not too bothered about the national team. If that's the case, you are only playing at being an international force. You are not giving the man in charge of the England team and his players the chance to excel. It would be a great shame because we are a very proud nation, and that's why we get so upset when the national team doesn't do well. We feel we deserve better. Our expectations are far greater than anyone else's because too many still cling to the outdated belief that we have a natural superiority over most of the football world. There was that day in June 1995, when we played Brazil, the world champions, the England rugby team were playing Australia, the potential world champions, and the cricket team were playing the West Indies, the world champions. How dare we be so arrogant as to think we should win those sort of games! But we do think that.

For all those reasons and more, I think being in charge of the England football team is a job for an experienced, older man. You also need someone to do it for 8–10 years. Because you have so little time with the players, you require a longer period to get your message across. Age shouldn't come into it. Look at the guy Brazil have re-appointed, Mario Zagalo. He's 66. As I keep saying about good coaches like Don Howe and Dave Sexton, who are over 60, you are not asking them to play in midfield. As long as the knowledge is still there, the mind is all that matters. Ideally, too, the guy in charge of the England team should have had some experience of working abroad. Bobby Robson, for instance, would have been a better England manager, I believe, if he had been at PSV Eindhoven in Holland and Sporting Lisbon and Porto in Portugal before the 1990 World Cup instead of after it. He's probably a much better coach now than he was when he was with England. I certainly feel I'm a much better coach than I've ever been. That's because I've worked in the English League, worked in the Spanish League and been in charge of the England team. I've also had more time recently to think about coaching and tactics.

What we need, above all, is a system for appointing an England manager or coach. We've got to find one and stick to it. We've got to find out what's right for now and for the future. There was a lot of sense in the old German system of grooming the assistant coach and then promoting him when his boss stepped down. I know it wasn't infallible and they had to bring in Franz Beckenbauer to get them out of trouble in 1984; but they didn't do too badly out of it if you look at the two World Cups and two European Championships they won before that hiccup in the managerial supply line. In any case, Beckenbauer was such an outstanding character that he turned the breakdown into a virtue and won the World Cup again. It was a case of making emergency repairs to get the system back on-line.

Ajax may have to do something similar in the foreseeable future. Their admirable system for appointing a first team coach is threatened by the decision of the current youth team coach, Co Adriaanse, to stay exactly where he is. In the past, the youth team coach has always gone on to take charge of the first team. But Adriaanse says he doesn't want to do that, and they've promised him a job until he's 65. That means if Louis van Gaal, the present first team coach, leaves, they've either got to unblock the system by cutting out the youth team coach or go outside and bring someone in until such time as he goes and the line of succession starts flowing again. Nothing's perfect, but if we look back over the years we've got to say the Ajax system is better than most. At least they've got a sensible, logical system for appointing their coach, which is more than you can say for most clubs in this country, not to mention the national team. I did my best to put into place the personnel for a line of succession. It wasn't by accident that I brought two younger men, Bryan Robson and Ray Wilkins, into the England coaching set-up. The idea was that they should be groomed for the future by learning the job alongside older, more experienced coaches. That's how Bryan came to be working alongside me and Don Howe with the senior side and Ray began helping Dave Sexton with the Under-21s. By the time this book is published, it will probably have become clear whether Glenn Hoddle has retained any of my backroom staff, or whether they have elected to stay on. If he makes wholesale changes, nobody could blame him for wanting his own people around him. It just seems a great shame, though, to waste all the experience that was built up during my time in charge. But 'twas ever thus with England, as our relatively modest record in the major competitions shows.

Chapter Nine

The Future

English football is going nowhere unless we get the right people in positions of authority and back them to the hilt. I'm thinking particularly of the FA's new technical director and make no apologies for returning to the subject. It is of overwhelming importance, in my opinion. His job will encompass the whole of English football, and it will be his responsibility to ensure all the different parts of the game move forward in the same direction. Asking for a definition of his role is a bit like asking what the Prime Minister does. You name it, and it's his job to do it. That's how big his sphere of influence will be. It will stretch from coaching children to helping the England coach, and take in such things as women's football along the way. While the technical director will be responsible ultimately to the chief executive, Graham Kelly, his power to transform English football will be almost limitless.

It's not just a question of duties and responsibilities, either. We are talking about someone capable of leading a crusade. Someone who can point out where the game is going wrong and inspire it to strive for improvement. Someone who can put English football back on top of the world game. He has to lay out his plans for the future, then go out and make sure his blueprint is put into practice. He's got to push for money for better facilities at all levels of the game, get good coaching into the schools and stop the sale of school playing fields. The decision to replace the retiring director of coaching, Charles Hughes, with a technical director presents a wonderful opportunity to revitalize our domestic football and it would be criminal to waste it.

Charles has spent a lot of time amassing an enormous amount of knowledge during the 13 years he has been in office. Unfortunately, he has kept most of it to himself. I think he, a former school-

179

teacher, fell out with the professionals years ago and turned to the grass roots of the game instead. Really, he should have challenged the pros. I think they would have respected him for having a few arguments with them. Everybody's got a thirst for knowledge, and I don't think they were against him because he was a former schoolteacher. In fact I think the technical director could be a former anything, if he was prepared to get in amongst the pros. Filling the void between the FA and the professional game is the important thing. Both sides have wanted it filled for a long time, I and others have started to bring them closer together and it's just amazing it's not been done before now.

Charles's reign has not been all doom and gloom, by any means. The fact that professional clubs now have access to boys as young as nine is down to the hard work he put into persuading the schools to be more accommodating. He also played a big part in launching the FA's national school at Lilleshall, which must be counted a success. They said it would take ten years to get the benefits, and that's about how long it's taken to produce players like Andy Cole, Nicky Barmby, Sol Campbell and Ian Walker, all of them now operating at the top end of the market. At the school, of course, the pupils combine an academic education with specialized football coaching; but the problem is that it's only for a selected few. In Holland, thousands of youngsters are able to combine the two things because their schools release them after their morning studies so they can go to their football clubs at 1 p.m. The comparison shows how far we have still to go if we want to catch the Dutch up in terms of teaching kids the right way to play the game.

It is in that area the technical director's influence will be particularly vital. As I've said, the coaches are now more important than the players. It's like saying the parents are more important than the children. The way they mould them, the way they teach them to go in the right way is very important. If the coaches give them bad information, they are going to be playing the game badly at an earlier age. So we've got to make sure that we are all singing from the same hymn-book and spreading the same gospel. This is why the technical director needs to get the education programme for these new UEFA coaching licences absolutely spot-on.

I've said for a long time the day of the coach hasn't really arrived yet. Coaching has tended to be something of a dirty word among the press and the public because they believe, correctly in lots of cases, that coaching can coach ability out of people. But it can also coach it into them. The good coaches, like those in Holland, have shown they can make their work very productive. Good technique, attacking football, entertaining football, goals: all the things we want they can provide with coaching and teaching. To get the glory days, to get goals, to get drama, we need good teaching.

More specifically, we need four-a-side matches so that the players have get more touches of the ball and concentrate on practice. There are also certain principles you have to cover. They include teaching people how to get out of tight corners, teaching defenders how to deal with one-on-one in situations where we always want cover, and teaching them how to come out and play from the back. I cannot stress too much the importance of first-class teaching. In fact, I've been thinking for a while of setting up a football school to coach players and coaches myself. I get letters from people all the time asking where they should go to get coaching information. I was hoping to open the school if I got enough finance from leaving Tottenham, and it might still be something I would consider as a job for the future.

Ideally, I think, the technical director would have to have a football background. That's because his job would be rather like overseeing a football club on a grand scale. The same principles are involved. You've got young players and you.have to do your scouting. You have to be *au fait* with coaching and how to teach players and coaches. You have to make sure it's viable: you are looking for success from the England team in the short term as you would be from the club side. Then you've got the long-term investment in the youth team. It's the same as at a club, but on a wider basis. There's more of it and there are more people, but you still face the same problems and challenges.

An ability to organize would come pretty high on the list of qualifications for a technical director, as would experience of working at all levels of English football. You've got to be able to understand everyone's problems, in other words. The technical director would certainly have to have some knowledge of the top end of the game. Otherwise, he might find it difficult to retain the respect of the England coach, especially if the two of them were to fall out. It's also absolutely essential the two of them should get on well. Mutual respect would be more likely, I think, if the technical director were also of fairly advanced years. All of which brings me back to the conclusion that Bobby Robson would have been the ideal candidate.

One of the things I'd like to see the technical director pressing for is the privatizing of the proposed new national stadium. They were talking about putting £100 million from the National Lottery into financing a national stadium, be it Wembley or in Birmingham or Manchester or wherever. But I say they've got it the wrong way round. That £100 million should be spent on providing football facilities for youngsters up and down the country. I think there would be plenty of private money for a national stadium because it would be a great investment. They could turn it into a lot of profit. So that would take care of itself, whereas a private investor might not want to put money into facilities for youngsters. The technical director will have less full-time professional football to contend with in the foreseeable future, I am certain. I expect economic pressures to reduce the traditional four divisions of English football to just two, Premier League 1 and 2, with the others going part-time. As I've explained already, I don't think that would be a bad thing because it would enable part-timers in the Second and Third Divisions to improve their earnings by taking a job outside football.

The only difference would be that they trained in the evening instead of the morning. That's what a lot of Scandinavian footballers do now without reducing their level of fitness. Nor do I believe it would reduce the supply of talent from below on which the big clubs have come to rely. It doesn't matter what the lower leagues are called, the top clubs will still scour them for potential talent. It will still be there. It won't have gone abroad or drowned in the sea. If you are still not convinced, look at the former part-timers who have made it into the England team, Ian Wright, Les Ferdinand, Stuart Pearce and Tim Flowers among them. Some players are late developers.

Youth development programmes will be kept alive, as I have already suggested, by the practice, common abroad, of clubs in the top division using a nursery club as a breeding ground. Three of the sides in the Spanish second division are, in effect, the second teams of Real Madrid, Barcelona and Athletic Bilbao. That's partly because they struggle in Spain to find enough clubs to make up two viable divisions. Yet that comparatively small number of full-time professional clubs does not seem to have affected unduly Spain's ability to put out an effective national side. The Italians, too, have nothing much beyond their second division. The truth is that most national teams are drawn almost exclusively from their country's top division.

What is essential, I feel, is that a system of promotion and relegation should remain. It would be fatal to close the door to the clubs trying to make it into the big time. A lot of the clubs presently at the top would want to see the door closed because they are frightened of coming out. But competition is what has made our League great. Even if it's only one team that goes down and one that goes up, you've got to give the great mass of clubs at the bottom some incentive to climb the ladder.

The future, though, will belong to the big clubs rather than to national teams. Club football will dominate to the detriment of international football. Friendly internationals, certainly, will become of secondary importance, but World Cup games will still be too big for the clubs to ignore. So there will be a dividing line. You may or may not get your players for friendlies, but they will be guaranteed still for World Cup matches and possibly the European Championship. Meanwhile, the European club competitions will become more important, especially the European Cup.

The Bosman verdict, of course, has added to the crushing economic pressures on the smaller clubs. It makes it more difficult for them, though not impossible, to keep afloat financially by selling their players to bigger clubs at a considerable profit. Yet that can hardly be counted a good enough reason to deny the professional footballer the basic human right to move freely to another club at the end of his contract. Not that the right appears to have been granted in every case by the judgment of the European Court of Justice.

As I understand this complicated issue, an English footballer can move at the end of his contract to a club in another European Community country without a transfer fee being necessary. Yet a fee must be paid if he moves to another English club in the same circumstances. In other words, if I'm playing for Arsenal, I can go to Paris St Germain for nothing at the end of my contract. But Aston Villa might have to pay £2 million if I go to them. That seems so incredibly unfair to me that I'm sure it would be shot down immediately if there was a player who wanted to challenge it.

Unless it 'is shot down, that rule will force the English footballer to go abroad in increasing numbers. If he goes to Paris St Germain he can get perhaps half that £2 million fee for himself. Nor do I think it would do any good here to phase in complete freedom of contract over three years, as the FA are suggesting. If player X is 30, he's not going to be prepared to wait around for three years before he gets a move. His career will be over by then, and he'll want to cash in right away. It's just another example of the sort of muddle you get when you try to compromise.

What is certain is that it is make-up-your-mind time for the clubs who say they don't want to pay £8 million for players and don't want complete freedom of contract, either. Sorry, but you have to have one or the other: you can't wriggle out of both. Players' values are going to fall so quickly that those clubs who include their players as assets on the balance sheets are likely to suffer in double quick time. What is going to be interesting is the effect on the two clubs who are public companies, Manchester United and Tottenham. I don't think the players are valued on the books at United, but they are at Tottenham. The player's value is written off gradually over five years, but the change in the market-place could happen a lot quicker than that.

What I don't see happening is the development of the Champions League into the full-blown European League people have been predicting for years. I can't think what you would gain, because you've got it already, in effect. All the leading champions of the domestic leagues in Europe are playing in a league competition. So I think we are getting the best of both worlds. Our champions are able to play the best in Europe on a home and away basis, but they can still take part in their own domestic competitions. The alternative might not be quite so attractive as some imagine. Would Liverpool fans, for instance, prefer to watch their team play Real Madrid or Everton twice a season? Personally, I think they'd miss the local derby.

More important, so far as English football is concerned, is the task of sorting out the fixture congestion that clogs up our game. The Coca-Cola Cup (League Cup) for a start, ought to be played on a one-match, knock-out basis and be over by Christmas. You could start it pre-season almost. You are looking for games then, anyway, and you could start the tournament the week before the season began. Failing that, there should not be a League Cup at all.

I'd knock it on the head, to be truthful, rather than keep reducing the size of the Premiership to make more room in the fixture list. After all, the League Cup only came into being in 1961 as compensation for a proposed cut in the size of the old First Division that has taken more than 30 years to implement on anything like a permanent basis.

A winter break is one of my hobby horses, I know, but I think it would help to ease the fixture congestion. If you had a three-week break in the winter and a four-week break in the summer, you could cater for most things. You could rest your players, and get the injured ones fit again, during the mid-season break, and that might enable clubs to carry smaller squads. In addition, the overall extension of the season would enable you to fit in more fixtures. That's becoming increasingly important as football edges ever closer to becoming a year-round sport. The introduction of the summer-based Inter-Toto Cup, which so embarrassed English football at the end of the 1994–5 season and cost it a place in the UEFA Cup, is a case in point.

Basically, we are out of step with the rest of Europe. I can understand the fears of the clubs about cash flow problems because there are no matches taking place, but you are playing at a time just after New Year when people have spent all their money on the festivities anyway and everyone wants a rest. Another consideration is that a shorter summer break, three or four weeks instead of six or seven, would reduce the likelihood of players returning for pre-season training overweight.

What we are talking about, really, is bringing the game up to date. If we want to do that, I would suggest, we have to consider the possibility of having line judges and two referees. The line judges I am thinking of would adjudicate on just two things – whether the ball was over the line in disputed attempts to score a goal, and whether a foul was committed inside or outside the penalty area. Like the third umpire in cricket, they would have the benefit of slow-motion television replays from cameras sited along all the relevant lines. The right of interpretation would remain with the referee, in that he still decides whether the foul was deserving of a penalty, and the line judge would simply tell him whether the offence had been committed inside or outside the penalty area. The umpire in tennis sits high above everyone, but still relies on line judges to tell him whether the ball is in or out.

The game now is so fast and so important that you cannot afford to have a rough idea of whether the ball was, or was not, across the line, or whether a tackle was inside or outside the penalty area. You actually want to be in line with what's happening. That's partly the job of the linesman, I know, but it's just not humanly possible to be in line with everything all the time. I don't think it would slow the game down to call on the line judge in disputed cases. How many times would you have to call on him? Once every four games, perhaps? And how long would it take to come to a decision – 30 seconds? As far as I'm concerned, it doesn't matter how long it takes so long as justice is done. You can be in or out of a cup or a major competition, and lose an awful lot of money and prestige, because the referee or linesman has made a mistake. Romania would certainly agree, I'm sure, after being denied a crucial Euro '96 goal when Dorinel Munteanu's spectacular shot bounced down off the bar and, as the slow-motion replays proved, inside the goal-line.

Using TV cameras to adjudicate in these cases would enable the the spectator to see for himself what had happened. I'm not in favour of the instant replays on a big screen that Tottenham now supply, because you don't want to incite violence at the ground itself and I can understand why Kevin Keegan objected to them when Newcastle played at White Hart Lane last season. I'm thinking more of the guy watching the game live at home or catching up with the recorded highlights later. Mind you, if TV evidence were an accepted part of the refereeing, there would be less of a problem with instant replays at the ground.

I want to see football experiment with two referees, too. Many good judges, Don Howe among them, believe the game is now so fast that one referee cannot hope to keep up with the play no matter how fit he is. The suggestion is that we should have one referee for each half of the pitch. A lot of people say it wouldn't work. So let's see if they are right. Let us go into the part-time leagues and try out ideas such as line judges and two referees for a part or the whole of a season. FIFA did it with the kick-in, so what is there to lose? If these ideas don't work, they don't work, and that's it. There's no downside so far as I can see. If you try 10 or 12 experiments and only one or two come off, you've made the game better, more entertaining and more professional. Anything, within reason, that improves it for the fan has got to be worthwhile. And it could be that employing line judges and two referees would prove a better solution to the refereeing problem than bringing in full-time officials.

There are other changes I would like to see, starting with a new points system for wins and draws. While teams are rewarded for a goalless draw with one point, they'll settle for that. But if you say there are no points for a 0–0, you force a change of attitude. That's the only way you'll get them to attack more. Three points for a win and one for a draw was a start in that direction, but the figures just don't add up when you draw. If there are three points to divide between two teams, what happens to the third one? Does it just disappear into thin air? There is something wrong there. It's not logical. Although the system encourages teams to go for the win, it ignores the fact that one point for a draw is the same reward as before. If you check, you'll find that if you followed the old classic formula for success of winning at home and a drawing away, you'd still end up in the same place in the table. There might be the odd exception, but that's how it would work out in general terms. How, then, about four points for a win and two for a score-draw? Although we all know a goalless draw can be thrilling, the result is against the whole purpose of the game. So you don't get any points for it. People will say that teams would arrange that someone on each side scored a goal so that they could get two points each instead of none. But if we've got to rely on misdemeanours to settle matches, we are not going to have a game. It's the same as a goalkeeper chucking in a goal.

Even if two teams were to reach such an agreement, there would come a moment when one team was a goal in front. Could the other side then rely on their opponents to let them have a goal back? After all, they are going to get four points if the score stays like that. I vividly remember going to the swimming baths when I was at school. You and your mate stood on the edge and said let's go in together. Then there was that awful moment when you were jumping in and he was still laughing on the side. It's the same principle with this business of draws. I don't think you could arrange something like that.

There's another proposal I have, though I don't think I've explained it too well when I've brought it up with UEFA. Perhaps there's a language problem. It's to do with penalties, and I can't understand why everyone I explain it to doesn't think it's a wonderful idea. Maybe it's just that I've got it wrong. Anyway, what I noticed during the finals of the last World Cup was that not one penalty was ordered to be taken again. That's not only during the games themselves, but in the many penalty shoot-outs as well. The point I'm making is that goalkeepers are moving too soon and referees are not penalizing them for it. But I know of a way, I think, to stop that kind of illegality without requiring any action from the referee. It's simple. The rules say the goalkeeper cannot move before the kick is taken and the kicker cannot stop in his run-up. But what happens if you say the goalkeeper can move whenever he wants and the kicker can stop in his run-up if he wants to? If the kicker can do that, the goalkeeper won't move early. And if the goalkeeper doesn't move, the kicker won't stop because he'll look silly. So there's a better chance of scoring, and that's the way it should be. We've given the advantage back to the attacking team. At the moment, the advantage is with the goalkeeper. The defending team have made a mistake of some sort, yet the goalkeeper gets the benefit of the doubt. The answer is to let the kicker stop. The 'keeper won't move until he has hit the ball, and if he does move, the kicker will make a fool of him. If it's done right, the problem's solved, but nobody seems to want to pick it up. I've tried it in training, and it's worked just as I've said.

Something else I've tried is an alternative to penalties. They are shoot-outs, but not like the ones they had in the old American soccer league. There, it was an attacker running at the goalkeeper from 30 yards and trying to score inside 15 seconds. It was a good idea and better than penalties, but it was still unsatisfactory, inasmuch as that particular situation doesn't often happen in a game. I'd like to take something out of the game and put it into the penalty situation. In my version, the kicker starts with the ball two yards ahead of a defender. What you've got then is a player breaking towards goal with a defender chasing him. To score, he's got to shake off the defender as well as beat the goalkeeper, and it's really exciting. You may succeed in taking the ball round the 'keeper, for instance, but the defender can come and clear your shot off the line. We used it to settle drawn practice matches in England training and stop them going on too long.

What annoys me about rule changes is the way they are introduced with a fanfare of trumpets, then forgotten about as time goes on. Outlawing the tackle from behind is a case in point. That

FIFA clampdown helped to make the 1994 World Cup finals a great tournament, in my opinion. It was one of the reasons the ball was in play more in that World Cup than in the previous one. I think I worked it out at six minutes more per game on average. Another reason was the way they got injured players off the field as fast as possible. They quickened the game up not with speed of play, but with content. They kept it ticking over.

The clampdown also forced defenders to be more skilful. They couldn't get the ball just by hacking somebody down from the back. They had to stay on their feet and do it with skill and organization. As a result, attacking players got more room and a lot of goals were scored. The success of the campaign stemmed from the referees' strict interpretation of the new rule, and it was not relaxed as we went into the 1994–5 season. It looked terrific then, but now it all seems to have been forgotten. Tackling from the back is back again. And the referees, instead of holding a meeting every three months to discuss what they are going to do about it, have a purge and book ten players when there's not been a tackle in the game. So inconsistency creeps back in and we've completely lost the impetus of what was a very helpful campaign.

Forcing defenders to stay on their feet and become better players was one of the beneficial effects of the synthetic surfaces that were installed so controversially at four Football League clubs, Queen's Park Rangers, Luton, Oldham and Preston, in the 1980s. Even on natural grass, going to ground is where a lot of players get injuries. Artificial turf also made people be careful with their passing. If you hit one in the general direction of a team-mate, as you could afford to on natural grass, it would run out of play. It was like making a snooker shot: you really had to take care over it. So, from a learning point of view for youngsters and for training generally, those pitches were major assets.

As I was co-author of *They Used to Play on Grass*, the football novel that predicted the coming of the plastic pitch, and manager of QPR in 1981, when we put down the very first one in the League, you could hardly expect me not to mention the subject in a chapter about the future. Actually, I don't think the synthetic surface has got much of a future now unless the manufacturers can produce one that's as sophisticated as the real thing. That will be very hard to do if only because Premiership clubs have improved their natural pitches out of all recognition. You don't get heavy grounds with big brown areas any more. Of course, clubs stage reserve games somewhere else now because television wants a perfect playing surface for the big games.

I have to say the manufacturers of our Omniturf pitch at QPR did not live up to their promises. What had appealed to us was their assurance that, as they went along, they would be able to produce artificial grass that was almost indistinguishable from the real thing. They said it would take a stud and the bounce would be the same as on natural grass. And that was where the let-down was. They never really progressed, and I don't know whether they will in the future. As I understand the situation, the manufacturers of these plastic pitches needed to install as many as possible to fund the research required to improve the product. So once the Football League banned artificial pitches in the old First Division in 1991–2 there was little hope of advancement in this country. I'm surprised, though, that more progress has not been made in America, where money is more plentiful and there have been complaints from the players about the greater risk of injury on synthetic surfaces in the gridiron game. They can put men on the moon, so producing a superior kind of artificial grass should not be beyond them.

Talking of America reminds me of my only complaint about the 1994 World Cup finals. I can't see that playing at noon in searing temperatures is the ideal way to get the best out of footballers. We nearly exploded with heat just watching the games, but I doubt very much whether the players were even asked it they wanted to play in such conditions. Yet, as I pointed out at the start of this book, the player is the most important piece in the whole jigsaw. If they had worked it out and played the tournament exclusively on the cooler east coast, the rest of the world could still have got the games comfortably on television and the weather would have been more suitable for playing football. We know the world is watching and there's a lot of money involved in the TV coverage, but did we do the product justice? It might actually have been counter-productive. The most important thing is that the product is great. The most important thing, that is, after letting the players have their say.

Whenever I think of the future, I keep coming back to the importance of the FA's new technical director. We desperately need someone in that job who can pull us round. I'm not thinking purely of the good of the game, either. Unless we can give our kids something to believe in, something to aim for, I don't know what they are going to grow up into, I really don't. There's a hate-filled part of our society that wants to fight, wants to destroy. Because cynicism now rules, no one seems to dream any more about what they want to be when they grow up. There's no impetus in society, no incentive to better yourself. We go back to football's problems of no imagination and no vision. We live for the day: we've got a short-term policy. All most people ask is, can I get by tomorrow and the next day? That's the way the vast majority have lived down the years, but now we are like that at the top end of the market, too.

We are now in a period where, like football, we've got to shape our future. You only have to hear or read the horrifying daily stories about rape, murder and general brutality to realize we are no longer the fair-minded, bowler-hatted, pinstripe-suited race we used to be known as. The bulldog breed, the salt of the earth. We are something far less attractive now, and I don't think I'd like to know what people abroad think of us. Possibly the first picture that jumps into their minds is of a shaven-headed thug with a football scarf tied in a knot round his waist drinking lager. In short, a lager lout. I just don't think we've got any imagination anywhere, be it in football or in life. Our future is a mess and our national identity is in the melting pot. I don't expect the technical director to sort all of that out by himself, but he could make a start on it. That's how important the job is.

Chapter Ten

Euro '96

Euro '96 was, without question, the high point of my whole career. I had some great moments with Barcelona, like winning the Spanish title and getting to the European Cup final, but nothing to compare with what happened in June, 1996. I'll never forget those wonderful occasions at Wembley when we overcame Scotland, Holland and Spain, then took Germany to the wire in the semi-final. In addition to the deep professional satisfaction those successes gave me and my players, there was the elation of knowing we had captured the imagination of the nation and brought back the feel-good factor missed for so long by football fans. The volume of support we received was quite extraordinary. I cannot remember a packed Wembley generating so much noise and national fervour – not even at the 1966 World Cup final. In fact, the din was so great it was impossible to shout instructions to the players. If there was anything I wanted to say or any changes I wanted to make, I had to wait until half-time to do something about it. It didn't hinder us in any way at all – just the opposite, in fact – and it was a small price to pay for an incredibly exciting and fulfilling experience that will be very hard to better wherever I eventually pick up the threads of my football career.

England's stirring deeds in the 1996 European Championship can be traced back beyond my appointment as coach in January, 1994. They had their roots in the tactical work I was doing as manager of Queen's Park Rangers, England Under-21 coach, Barcelona's coach and Tottenham's manager in the late 1980s and the early 90s. That's where I began to develop most of the ideas with which I tried to modernize England's approach to international football during my two and a half years in charge. I'm talking now about things like split strikers, the 'Christmas tree' formation and my version of three-at-the-back. But those ideas would have been unworkable without the co-operation of the players. Their response to the unfamiliar tactics and challenges I presented them with was absolutely magnificent, and I cannot praise them highly enough. By reaching the semi-final of Euro '96, and getting so close to the final, I believe we proved that the much-maligned English footballer is quite capable of competing success-fully in the game's most exalted circles provided he is given the right sort of direction. I have no doubt in my mind that England were the best team in the tournament, and I would contend that we, derided not so long ago as technical and tactical dinosaurs, showed the rest of Europe how the game should be played in the future.

Before I took over, I always had this picture in my mind of an England where everyone was a yard late, everyone was rushing and not quite getting there. And the opposition were playing the ball around us. So I set out to stop our opponents having too many people with too much room in the wrong areas of the field. I had a little motto: 'If you can't outplay them, outnumber them.' If it was true the continentals were technically better than us, I was deter-mined to try and get more players than the opposition wherever the ball was. I also felt that, because we had fallen so far behind in international terms, we had to have a real gamble and take a giant leap forward. The alternative was to take pigeon steps and catch up slowly. I decided to go for a really attacking formation, and it was the biggest gamble I've ever taken.

My initial approach to the problem was to imagine I was in one of those brainstorming situations and had my pick of the best play-ers there have ever been. So I started off thinking ten Peles and a good goalkeeper would be wonderful. Then I switched to England in 1966 and wondered about having ten Bobby Charltons. It was a question of separating the fantasy from the reality, of course. When I asked myself whether I could afford to play ten Peles or Bobby Charltons, the answer had to be no. Common sense demands that you have some defenders. But how many? That was the key to it.

Normally, if you wanted a good defence, you'd have six Jack Charltons and four Bobby Charltons in the team. But what about five and five, or even four Jacks and six Bobbys? If I could make four and six work, I knew I would get goals from it. That's when I looked at Ajax and saw that sometimes they had four at the back, and sometimes three, depending on how many attackers the opposition had. So I began to shape my defence the same way. That, really, was the basis of the tactical jump we made. It meant I could afford the luxury of fielding six attacking players – McManaman, Anderton, Sheringham, Shearer, Gascoigne and Redknapp or Platt – without giving the opposition too many goal-scoring chances.

The first step was to introduce split strikers. The idea there was to give the opposing defence a marking problem. Now, they've got a decision to make. Do they push out, or not? If they are playing four at the back, they won't do that. If it's three, they might. It's one of those 'If we do this, will they do that?' situations. I was sure we could create a lot of room by playing one of the strikers deeper, and that Teddy Sheringham, Nicky Barmby and Peter Beardsley were the three players who could exploit it. I knew Alan Shearer would play up front and that I would have to find a partner for him, but I didn't know at that stage it was going to be Teddy. David Platt coming from deeper was another option I considered, but I never expected to get the sort of criticism I did over the general idea.

I was using split strikers before Ajax. That's how I played at Barcelona. I tried it with Steve Archibald and Francisco Carrasco first. Archibald was up front, with Carrasco coming in and using the wide areas. Then I did the same thing with Sheringham and Barmby at Tottenham when we started to get a good team there. So I was already re-styling the front end of my teams: there was no need for me to copy anything. There were all these articles in the papers about me copying Ajax, but I wasn't copying anything. I'll admit I took two or three principles from Ajax's style of play, but I didn't copy it slavishly because I was already moving in that direction myself.

The changes I introduced, I introduced gradually over a period of about 18 months working backwards through the team. All I wanted to do for the first few games was enable them to feel good about themselves again. You know – get a few results, don't give any goals away. When I took over, the spirit of the players was optimistic, but in a rather lightweight way. So it was good to see their self-belief grow with every game. I'd thought a lot about what I was doing and I was moving closer all the time towards what I wanted. So it really annoyed me when journalists like

Patrick Collins, who is at the top of his profession, said I was no nearer to finding a system or a settled team.

Although the deeper of the split strikers gave me an extra man in midfield, I found the opposition, especially good passing teams like Romania, were still getting a bit too much room in midfield. Then, in September, 1995, we played Colombia, who are as good as, if not better than, Romania at the possession game. So I thought I had got to do something about that. I had to go over the top with things defensively or attackingly to find out how far I could go. I think we improved it a lot and didn't get outplayed in the middle of the park. I had Jamie Redknapp and Paul Gascoigne in there because I thought those two would keep the ball better than anyone. So we were getting a bit better in that vital area. It didn't matter how quick or aggressive we were, they were going to play around us if we were outnumbered.

I felt we'd got the split strikers right – even though Alan Shearer wasn't scoring, I always felt he and Sheringham looked full of chances as a partnership – and we'd got the central midfield right, but we still needed to get the outsides of the team right. So I decided to play people who would go at full-backs. What I wanted was width to get crosses in, especially if we had good headers of the ball like Shearer and Sheringham as our spearhead. I also wanted width to stretch the opposing defence and create space for us to get through the middle. Switzerland had big problems with us in that respect when they came to Wembley for a friendly in November 1995, and so did Bulgaria at the same ground four months later.

I still wasn't happy, though, about the wingers going at opposing full-backs, then passing them over to a defender when the full-backs went forward themselves. So I began to wonder whether the wingers could go all the way with the full-backs and whether we could come up with something different from 4–4–2 just to throw the opposition a bit. Finally, I decided that if the opposing full-backs wanted to run, our wide players would have to go with them. You might say that's a lot of work, but the winger is not going to have to go any further than the full-back. And if the full-back can go that far, so can the winger. It's a game of cat and mouse. They have to decide whether they are going to mark each other or not.

Then, after Christmas 1995, came the final step. It was to

introduce the sort of back three favoured by Ajax. That is to say, a central defender flanked tightly by two full-backs. It became essential then for the wingers to go all the way with the opposing full-backs, otherwise your back three get spread. The idea wasn't without other problems, of course, since Mark Wright, the experienced Liverpool defender I had chosen to play in the middle of the three, got injured in the friendly against Hungary only three weeks before the start of Euro '96 and had to pull out of the squad. To the surprise of his many critics, however, Arsenal's Tony Adams proved a magnificent replacement.

Only recently recovered from a cartilage operation himself, Tony deserved a medal for playing right through the tournament despite the pain from his knee. How he got through all those games I don't know. Amazingly, he became more and more dominant as the tournament went on. Playing him in those circumstances wasn't enough to do him any damage, we were told, and we wouldn't have allowed him to play had we thought there would be any risk. John Crane, the Arsenal doctor, is also the England doctor and he kept his club in touch with the situation. Even so, Tony had to go through a lot to play and has had to undergo surgery since. I told him not to make himself a hero unnecessarily, but he was really heroic – sensational, in fact. Not only that, but he was playing in a position not many people thought he had the skill to cope with. I spoke to him about that, and he was tickled pink with what he had achieved.

It wasn't three at the back all the time, of course. Our defensive formation, like Ajax's, was determined by the number of attackers our opponents used, in the sense that we made sure we always outnumbered them. Basically, I wanted a set-up that was flexible enough to change from three to four, or vice-versa, as required. To do that, I needed a midfield man who could drop back into defence or a defender who could step out into midfield. Paul Ince gave me the first option and Gareth Southgate the second. Ince, the former Manchester United midfielder, had struggled to settle in Italy at first following his transfer to Inter Milan. He had also pulled out of the Umbro Cup in the summer of 1995 because of the negotiations for the move and his involvement in the court cases that followed Eric Cantona's assault on a Crystal Palace fan.

The tournament against Brazil, Sweden and Japan was an important stage in my team-building, and I thought Ince should have been there. Anyway, I decided to leave him out of the England reckoning for a while to see what he was made of. Happily, he responded with great determination and character. He soon became a dominating presence in the Inter team, and I was only too glad to have him back in the England fold once he had sorted himself out. A commanding figure playing just in front of the back line, Ince was one of the main reasons we were able to make our new flexible defensive tactics work. So, too, was Southgate, the versatile Aston Villa defender who made his name as a midfielder at Crystal Palace. He did not win his first cap until the game against Portugal in December 1995, but he took to international football like a duck to water.

If you get full-backs to push in, play as wing-backs, they will never get you the supply of crosses in that a winger would. OK, so you could say you are not going to get wingers who can defend as well as a full-back. But if you can find midfield players who mark their men, you only have half the problem. As long as they are defending wide, the worst thing that can happen is that the opposing full-backs can get in a cross. What we had was wingers going with full-backs, not wingers going with wingers. If the opposition play wingers, I bring my central midfield player back and tell my full-backs to mark the wingers. So it suits every situation.

It was quite an adjustment, really, from the way the players were used to playing. Even though more and more English clubs are adopting a three-man defence, it is with three recognized centre-backs and two full-backs pushed in as wing-backs. What you have to do is make sure they have confidence in you. There are some players who adapt better than others, and that was the point of introducing the younger players early. So by the time they came through, they would be ready. My greatest enemy was time. I was just concerned whether I would have enough games and get-togethers to make it work. I was criticized for introducing the defensive part of the system so late, but I was sure in my own mind that the players were ready for it by then. I think they were always pleased they went along with what we wanted to do. I don't think we'd have done as well as we did in Euro '96 if we had conformed.

When I explained the new defensive set-up to the players, they were a bit worried about having fewer men at the back. But I explained that the ball wouldn't get into our defensive third so often because we'd stop it in midfield. To prove it, we staged a game with one team playing with three at the back. Sure enough, they won. 'That's not bad,' they thought. The full-backs asked me if I wanted them to attack, but I said: 'No, just sit. I want the wingers to stay with their full-backs; and if Gazza's not marked, give him the ball. The next bit we've got to do is try and get the ball inside the full-backs.' They said they thought it was a bit adventurous, but I assured them they would find it all right. When I asked the two full-backs how they found it after we had tried it for the first time, they said: 'We thought we could have got forward a lot more.' I said: 'Do what? Can you imagine what the reaction would have been if I'd said I wanted the wingers to go up and down and the full-backs to attack. You'd have gone ballistic!' But it just shows what can be done with that system.

The younger players will go with what you say. Experienced players will question what you say, and quite rightly. But if they had been really against what I wanted to do, I wouldn't have done it. No way. It was all very well me wanting to try something different, but it wouldn't have been any good if the players didn't have open minds about it. There were a lot of experienced players in my squad, people like David Platt, Tony Adams, Paul Gascoigne and Stuart Pearce, and once you get people like them to accept what you are trying to do, the others will follow. There's no doubt I was helped in my experiments by the fact that England had to play nothing but friendlies on the way to Euro '96. In other words, it's not the end of the world if you lose a friendly. But it can be very negative if you come unstuck in a friendly just prior to the tournament, so I think we still had to be brave to do what we did.

Our preparation for the big event was wound up with a trip to the Far East that provoked criticism from beginning to end. For a start, nearly everyone seemed to come to the conclusion that it was madness to take the players on a 16,000-mile round trip to Beijing and Hong Kong so close to a major tournament played in England. It would have made much more sense, argued the critics, to have prepared with games in Europe. What they overlooked, or chose to ignore, was the oft-repeated explanation that the Football Association were anxious England should complete their Euro '96 preparations as far away from Europe as possible, so that the risk of an embarrassing outbreak of English hooliganism on the eve of the tournament could be minimized. In other words, the FA wanted us to play in places where the hooligans would find it difficult to follow.

We had three options to begin with. The other two were South Africa and America, but neither could give me the two games I wanted. I told the South Africans I would like one game in Johannesburg and one in Durban or Capetown, because I felt we would have had to do a lot of coaching in Johannesburg if we'd stayed there all the time. Politically it would have been expected of us, and we would have been perfectly happy to do it in other circumstances; but I thought it might bring unnecessary pressures to bear on the eve of a major tournament. The American option, taken up by Scotland, was not a great deal different to our trip in terms of the travelling time. In fact, it was more difficult because you normally suffer more from jet-lag when you are coming forwards in time, as you are when travelling from the States to Britain.

In any case, modern sport is all about global travel. Brazil, for instance, think nothing of hopping on a plane to fly over 5,000 miles to play a game in the Middle East, then getting back on the plane and going home. And what about tennis players on the grand prix circuit? I was listening to the radio during Wimbledon fortnight, and I couldn't help chuckling when I heard what their itinerary is like. They are in California one minute, then they go to Hong Kong, Australia and France before fetching up at Wimbledon. How can you play world sport sitting still, or just travelling for an hour and a half? I think it was naïvety and ignorance that made so many people critical of our trip to the Far East.

No one was willing after Euro '96, though, to say it did us no harm physically. I had a bit of banter about it with Gary Lineker, because he was one of those who claimed it had been a bad decision to take the players on such a long trip just before the start of the tournament. I said to him: 'Why don't you admit you were wrong? Did we play for 120 minutes in two games on the trot in five days? Did we look less fit than anyone else? Did we look less relaxed than anyone else? So why criticize the trip? I think your problem was that you were imagining how it would have been eight years ago, when you were a player. It's definitely different now.' There always used to be this talk about how English footballers were more tired than anyone else when it came to the finals of a major tournament because their season was longer and harder than anyone else's. But our performances in Euro '96 proved that, despite the rigours of an English football season and a long trip to the Far East, the English footballer can be as fit as anyone in the world if the right amount of thought and preparation is applied to the situation.

We chose China and Hong Kong in the end because they could guarantee us two games and because I was impressed by the rate at which Chinese football is developing. In fact, the FA should be thinking about taking England back there, or somewhere nearby, at least three times in the next six years in preparation for the finals of the 2002 World Cup, which is to be shared by Japan and South Korea. The Chinese are certainly going to catch up very quickly. Lazio and Sampdoria had played in Beijing before us, so the Chinese seem to have a strong tie-up with Italy. They obviously feel the Italians are the best opponents to be playing against. It gives them a benchmark for what they are doing, and I think that's wise of them.

Our 3–0 win in Beijing was beneficial in all sorts of ways. Southgate really blossomed in that game – he was outstanding. The young Neville brothers, Gary and Philip, also shone. Gary certainly showed what he could do. I think it was the first time he and Tony Adams had played' together. The 1–0 win in Hong Kong also had its benefits, even though it wasn't successful as a match. It enabled me to involve all the players and give them a game.

There were insinuations all along that the only reason we went to China and Hong Kong was money. The financial incentive for going happened to be good, but that was not the real motivation; we went to get two more games. And the more I look back, the more I think I was right to take England there. The players and I could not possibly have taken another ten days at the Burnham Beeches Hotel, nice as it undoubtedly is. The pressures of living in a goldfish bowl for a month were quite severe enough without extending the period any further. Not only that, but everything we had set out to do in China and Hong Kong worked as well as, if not better than, we had hoped.

Everything except the Cathay Pacific flight home, that is. Some nine hours after we had landed, the airline alleged that two of the mini-television sets which are built into the backs of business-class seats and a seat tray-table had been damaged in the upper deck section of the jumbo jet, where the players were sitting during the 14-hour journey from Hong Kong to London Heathrow. Although no pictorial evidence of the alleged vandalism was ever produced, Cathay Pacific claimed it would cost £5,000 to repair the damage and the FA paid up without any argument. The conclusion everyone jumped to was that, because the flight home coincided with Paul Gascoigne's 29th birthday, the players had been involved in a wild party on the upper deck.

Yet nothing really happened on the plane. If I told the whole story, no one would believe it. The truth would certainly exonerate the players. Unfortunately, I cannot set the record straight because it might lead to the sacking of a member of the Cathay Pacific staff. All I can say is that those newspapers which accused Robbie Fowler and Steve McManaman of causing the damage have got a big problem. I don't know whether those two are going to continue with their legal action, but they would wipe the floor with their accusers in court if they did. I wasn't there on the upper deck myself, but guys I just don't believe would tell lies all say the same thing. I questioned certain players individually about the incident and they all told me the same story.

Only a small number of them were involved, anyway, because most of the squad were fast asleep during the flight home. I know that for a fact because more than one FA official visited the upper deck at different times. Ted Buxton, my assistant, went up there at one point to sort out a complaint from a stewardess who claimed Gazza had been abusive to her, but that was the only sign of trouble so far as I was aware. There was certainly no noise coming from the upper deck. I was determined myself not to go to sleep until about seven hours into the flight so that I could stay in line with English time. During that period, Gary Newbon, the ITV sports interviewer, and I had a long chat at the bottom of the stairs leading up to the upper section of business class. We didn't hear a sound from up there, yet nobody bothered to interview Gary when I invited the press to ask him for his version of events. Colin Malam was sitting near the bottom of the stairs, too, and he confirms that if there was a party going on, it must have been an unusually quiet one.

Much was made, too, of the visit by a handful of players to the China Jump Club in Hong Kong on the last night of the trip to the Far East. The pictures that appeared in the papers of them, their clothes torn and having tequila poured into their mouths while strapped into an old dentist's chair, were unfortunate, I'll admit.

But they were not doing anybody any harm, they were not causing any trouble and they were not breaking curfew. They had been given the night off, and they all returned to the hotel by the 2 a.m. deadline I set. Not only that, but the bulk of the squad did not even leave the hotel. From the hysterical reaction back home, though, you'd have thought they had all raped and pillaged their way through Hong Kong. Again, Gazza took most of the criticism because it was his birthday and he figured most prominently in the pictures.

I was annoyed by the reaction because it was made to look as though discipline was slack in the England squad. Yet I've never had any problem on that score throughout my 20-year career as a coach and manager. I am fairly easy going, but the players know there is a line they mustn't cross. I used to say to them, 'If you were with your wife and young children and there was a bunch of 12 guys swearing and effing and blinding and slamming doors, would you like it? No? Well don't do it to anyone else then. If you want to do it, go and do it somewhere else.' I hate that sort of thing so much, I once put a player on the transfer list for verbally abusing a waiter while we were abroad. I also suspended the German international Bernd Schuster for a year at Barcelona. That was his punishment for walking out of the stadium in a huff after I substituted him during the 1986 European Cup final against Steau Bucharest. It was irresponsible behaviour because, had we won – not lost – on penalties, he could have cost us the game if he had been selected for a drugs test and not been available. As for the drinking side of it, you've got to use a bit of psychology. If you ban players from going to a pub after Thursday, say, they'll go to one 30 miles out of town so you don't find out. You've got to try and make them understand why they shouldn't go out, and let them build up a conscience about it. I remember reading a magazine article about Vietnam, and they were saying that the day of the sergeant-major has gone. It's the same in football. Leadership now has to be more skilful than that. Saying don't do it because I say so doesn't wash any more. You've got to be one of the boys, but not quite. That means they can talk to you, tell you what their problems are, but you've got to be slightly removed. They've got to be comfortable with you, like your company in some ways and not want to lose it. That's how you make the relationship grow.

But I have to say the fuss over the night out in Hong Kong, and then over three players being spotted in an Ilford nightclub during the 36 hours they were given off after the Switzerland game, was out of all proportion to the 'offences'. They were put in perspective later by the tales we heard about the drinking exploits in some of the other camps. At one point, it seems, every night was party night for the Czech Republic; and they got to the final! I'm not suggesting we should relax our attitude to drinking. In fact, we had a ban on alcohol throughout the week, and the players adhered to it strictly. But I just wish the media would not react so hysterically to what they interpret, mistakenly for the most part, as footballers letting the side down.

In terms of psychology, the torrent of criticism directed at the players over the China Jump Club and Cathay Pacific incidents was not without its advantages. I have to be honest and say I saw it as an ideal opportunity to forge the spirit of togetherness in the squad that had been one of the objectives of the Far East trip anyway. It wasn't too hard to do, because I could see we were all upset about the way it was going and we all know that is the sort of thing team bonding is about. You feel hurt and aggrieved and develop an 'I'll show you' attitude. When criticism is unjust and hurtful, it does make you fight. If you are guilty of doing something, it's hard to respond in a positive fashion, because you've just got to hold your hands up and accept the blame. I was criticized for introducing a policy of collective responsibility for the Cathay Pacific damage, but I could do that with a clear conscience because I knew nothing out of order had occurred on that flight home.

The united front certainly got us to where I wanted to be a lot quicker than normal. The Italians and other teams have done something similar in the past, but it has usually involved a media blackout. To be fair, we never refused to co-operate with our newspaper, television and radio people. Most of us did our press conference stints every day, which pleased me. We discussed the situation and I made it clear we still had responsibilities to the public, who wanted to know what we thought. I also pointed out that it was not necessarily the guilty newspapers the players would be punishing by refusing interviews. We decided to take it a step at a time, but fortunately the mood of the whole nation turned round anyway with each successful game we played. Gazza, McManaman and Fowler were the exceptions because they had been blamed directly for the trouble. They were raging about it and refused to speak to anyone. But, on the whole, I think we showed a lot of tolerance and handled it well.

Gazza did well to say, in effect, 'I'm not being rude, I just want to be quiet. I've been hammered out of all that. I just don't want to get involved in all that again.' I was happy because it helped him concentrate. He has to deal with things that do throw him. No one could take all that he has to contend with. You just have to hope people can grow with it, as the Klinsmanns and the Linekers have. But even they never had people following them around in case they slipped up. Lineker, a very popular character, will take care of things and do it right, so they'll leave him alone. But Gazza's let his guard drop a couple of times, so they keep following him to see if he'll do it again. What people don't understand about Paul is that he is completely different from his public image. Everyone thinks he's a big shot who couldn't care less if you told him off. But he is not like that. He hates to let you down.

The fuss over the players' alleged misbehaviour was so great that it completely overshadowed the selection of my final 22 for Euro '96. I had announced the squad just before we left Hong Kong, and it necessitated the painful process of telling five of the players who had gone to the Far East with us that their services would not be required. Basically, I always knew what I wanted from day one, which people may or may not believe. It was a blend of intelligence, technical ability and a determination to win whatever the circumstances. And the people who thought I was wandering blindly through all those friendly matches might be interested to know that I retained seven of the players – Seaman, Ince, Adams, Platt, Gascoigne, Shearer and Anderton – I used in my first game, the 1–0 win against Denmark at Wembley in March 1994. That, incidentally, was one of the few times I was able to pick a team with a clean bill of health. There might have been even more survivors from it, too, had Graeme Le Saux and Gary Pallister not been ruled out by injury. After three months in the job, I was going to write down my final team, barring injuries, have it witnessed and put it away to show to the cynics should the need arise. But I didn't need to in the end.

What I would like to do is offer a word of praise and thanks to all the players who were involved in the build-up to Euro '96 right from the first game. That includes those who were unfortunate or injured or whatever. But, in particular, I'm thinking of the five who were left out of the squad at last knockings. It was reported that I didn't find it difficult to cut the party down to 22, but that gave completely the wrong impression. What I had meant by that was, once I'd thought it through and decided what had to be done, then it became a simpler task than before. What I definitely didn't mean was that it didn't bother me to leave five players out. I want to clear that up.

I was wrestling with selection problems all the time. Have I got enough midfield players? Have I got this, have I got that? Did we have a left-sided player? We would have had one if Le Saux had not broken his leg so unluckily. The way I was going, Graeme could have been left-back, left-half or left-wing. He was that important to us. We had Jason Wilcox, and he came into the reckoning. I always wanted three wide players, but Darren Anderton and Steve Stone could both play in central midfield as well as on the wing. That's why I knew I could trim my midfield up and include an extra defender.

Martin Tyler, the Sky Television commentator, said the only criticism he would make of my squad was the omission of Wilcox, because he was left-sided. I replied to the effect that I knew lots of left-sided players, but it was not going to solve my problem. Wilcox, another of the players in the squad who had been out a long, long time because of injury, had a very promising game against Hungary. But I thought the Hungarians were very poor, to be honest. So I had to go on my judgment of ability in the end. Hopefully, Jason will do it for England in the future. Once he gets another season under his belt, I'd think he'd be a different proposition.

Newcastle midfielder Robert Lee was very unlucky to be one of the five. I like Robert and think he's a good player, but it was just that choices had to be made between people who were only a cigarette paper apart in ability. What all the discarded players got out of it was great experience. Wilcox, for instance, earned an international cap and travelled with the team. Ugo Ehiogu, the young Aston Villa defender, got his first senior cap, so he'll be off and running. I think he will be a really good player in the future. Wisey (Dennis Wise) has done really, really well for me, but again I could only afford to have four central midfield players.

Peter Beardsley was the tough one. I've got so much respect for him and Stuart Pearce. That's why I tried to be up front with both of them as much as I could. When I first started, I wasn't sure how long Pearcey could continue to do it for England. I told him he was not going to be my first choice at left-back, and asked him what his feelings were about that. To his credit, he said he would take any chance he got – which turned out wonderfully for him in the end following Le Saux's unfortunate injury. But so far as Peter was concerned, I had Teddy (Sheringham) and Nicky Barmby to do the same job as him.

So, we tackled the first major tournament to be held in England for 30 years with the following squad of 22: goalkeepers: David Seaman (Arsenal), Tim Flowers (Blackburn Rovers), Ian Walker (Tottenham Hotspur); defenders: Gary Neville (Manchester United), Tony Adams (Arsenal), Gareth Southgate (Aston Villa), Steve Howey (Newcastle United), Stuart Pearce (Nottingham Forest), Sol Campbell (Tottenham), Philip Neville (Manchester United); midfielders: Darren Anderton (Tottenham), Paul Ince (Inter Milan), Paul Gascoigne (Glasgow Rangers), David Platt (Arsenal), Steve McManaman (Liverpool), Steve Stone (Nottingham Forest), Jamie Redknapp (Liverpool); forwards: Alan Shearer (Blackburn), Teddy Sheringham (Tottenham), Les Ferdinand (Newcastle), Nicky Barmby (Middlesbrough) and Robbie Fowler (Liverpool).

That was immediately reduced to 21 when Steve Howey, having fought his way back to fitness after hamstring trouble, turned his ankle on a training run near his home in the north-east. UEFA, in marked contrast to their generosity when the Germans complained they were running out of players for the final, said Howey would have had to be knocked down by a car for us to be allowed a replacement. So I told him he should have kept hobbling till he found a road! It was all rather ironic, considering it had been my campaign which had resulted in the squads being increased from 20 to cope with the demands of 16-team tournament, the first time the finals had been so large.

On paper, our first game in Group A did not seem too daunting. We had beaten Switzerland comfortably 3–1 in a friendly at Wembley seven months earlier, and nothing that had happened since then suggested they were going to be a bigger threat to us: just the opposite, in fact. The decision of the Swiss FA not to retain Roy Hodgson, the Englishman who had transformed their national team into a real force and got them to the finals, looked as though it might upset the applecart. Artur Jorge, the Portuguese who replaced him, is a good, experienced and successful coach, but there was every possibility that the players might struggle to adapt to his methods in the short time available. Two of their most famous and talented players didn't need to bother. Jorge created a real stir by leaving Alain Sutter and Adrian Knup out of his 22.

Even so, I always knew it was going to be a difficult game, the first one. It wasn't just our first competitive game for nearly three years, but the first game of the tournament. And when did you ever see a good opening match? There are peculiar tensions and pressures at work and the crowd was a bit subdued. I think that might have been because they'd had two and a half hours of entertainment during the opening ceremony. The spectators might have been tired, I don't know, but a lot of people said it was a strange atmosphere. Perhaps they were nervous, too. We did all right in the first half, when Alan Shearer ended his England goal-drought with a powerful strike, and David Seaman and all the boys felt we had a tackle on all their chances in the second half. Although Kubilay Turkyilmaz was a bit of a handful, there was nothing clear-cut, really, and we should have scrambled through 1–0 and had the points to give us a platform to go forward.

Instead, we had a harsh penalty given against us late in the game, when Pearcey was adjudged to have handled a shot by Marco Grassi. Turkyilmaz gave Seaman no chance of saving that kick and we had to settle for a draw. I'm not disputing that Stuart handled the ball, but there's no doubt in my mind there was no intent on his part to do so. If you recall, he was right on top of Grassi trying to block the shot, and he had turned his head away to avoid being hit in the face. The ball struck his hand, which was up alongside his face, but I don't see how he could possibly have handled intentionally when he was not even looking at the ball. You've got to see it to handle it!

People claimed we ran out of steam in the second half and tried to suggest the trip to the Far East had taken its toll, but I don't think that was the reason we fell away after the interval. We examined the possibility and I mentioned it to the players, but another look at the game on video satisfied me that something else was responsible. It was the old business of the last thing you learn being the first thing you forget under pressure. In any case, we proved later it wasn't a question of fitness. If we were out of gas, we would have been out all the way through the tournament. We certainly wouldn't have got fit in time for our next game, against Scotland, a week later. That week gave us the time we needed to iron everything out, and I thought we were fine by the time we faced the Scots the following Saturday. I think we would still have got there with four days' preparation, but it was nice to have the extra day or two.

What also happened was that all the criticism we got for failing to beat Switzerland made us that much more determined to do well. We knew what points we had to get right and went through them all thoroughly with the players. What pleased me more than anything was the training and the preparation during that week between the first two games. Everything we wanted to cover, we covered. I would have liked to do some other things that were perhaps more entertaining, but Don Howe and Bryan Robson did the ball-work with them and I used my time with the tactical side of it.

Scotland presented an entirely different challenge. Because they were another British side and because we, the oldest rivals in world football, had not played each other for seven years, there was a real danger of our players treating the game as something separate from the tournament rather than as part of it. I tried hard to guard against that kind of approach, and stressed they must regard it as just another game and not something special.

A lot of people thought we started poorly against the Scots, but I don't think that's fair. We did what we set out out to do. I'd been banging on to the players about having 90 minutes to win the game, which is always the attitude adopted by the best teams, like Liverpool. You've got to see what's happening first. From the 'lovely moves' point of view, yes, you can criticize them; but I think we stopped all the things Scotland had to throw at us in the first half. In fact they might have had a better chance or two in the second half, even though we overran them. That second half, I thought, was fantastic from our point of view.

In the first half, we tried to curb their enthusiasm. Let 'em run, let 'em run, then see how it goes. About 15 minutes before half-time, I felt we weren't quite right – I'll give you that; but I wouldn't say we were poor. We were playing the game the way we had planned. It was like the way Croatia had played against us in the friendly at Wembley a couple of months before Euro '96. In the first half, they were very dour. Then, in the second half, they tried to win the game.

At half-time I made the decision to take Pearce off and bring Jamie Redknapp on. The reason was that, with Southgate coming into central midfield, we had two anchormen there. I was happy for Paul Ince to break forward, as he can, with Gareth holding, or vice-versa. What we were trying to do was get our central midfield to run their players away so that the people at the back could have more space to pass the ball. The trouble was that Gareth was getting ahead of the ball and receiving it with his back to the game. Although he did pretty well, he was finding himself in awkward positions and I thought the fluency just wasn't there.

So I decided to change the system. I felt it would be better with Southgate going to the left side of the back-three, in place of Pearce, and Ince moving into the very centre of midfield. Then I brought on another Gascoigne-type player in Redknapp. It really made a difference. It gave McManaman a looser role and enabled him to link up with Redknapp like he does at Liverpool. Jamie's used to sticking the ball to him early, and that's what led to the first goal. Jamie got it to Steve early; the Scottish defence thought he was going to dribble, but Gary Neville came up on the outside and McManaman laid it into him. Good cross, Shearer's head, goal! It was an outstanding example of how we moved opposing defences about. If you look at it again, you will see how the attack is shifted back and forth across the field until we find the opening we are looking for. I wanted someone to manipulate the ball, and Redknapp did exactly that. Jamie was very unfortunate to twist his ankle in that game jumping for the ball; but he's definitely one for the future. He's got lots of confidence and he likes playing with Gascoigne. They played so well together in China, if you recall.

Then, about 15 minutes from the end, we had a penalty awarded against us for the second match running. It was for a sliding tackle by Adams on Gordon Durie, and I thought it was justified. This time, though, Seaman hurled himself to his right and deflected Gary McAllister's spot-kick over the bar. It was a good save, and something that made it a lot easier for us to win the game, but I wouldn't go along with the view that it turned the tournament for us. Unlike the Swiss penalty, this one was given early enough for us to do something about it. I feel confident we would still have beaten the Scots even if McAllister had scored, a belief Gascoigne's tremendous goal soon afterwards tended to support.

A couple of minutes after the penalty, Seaman found Anderton on the left with a long clearance. Seeing Gascoigne making a good run inside the full-back, Anderton did exactly the right thing by knocking the ball in to him first time. Colin Hendry had come across to make a challenge, but Gascoigne lifted the ball over him with his left foot, then volleyed it into the bottom corner with his right as he ran round the flummoxed Scottish defender. It was not only the best goal of the tournament, but the best in the last two or three major tournaments. If Romario or Marco van Basten had scored it, everyone would be raving about it still; but, being English, we tend to give only grudging respect to wonderful demonstrations of individual skill like that. When the goal went in, incidentally, a picture flashed into my mind. It was of Richard Littlejohn, the *Daily Mail* columnist, who had cruelly dubbed Gazza 'fat boy'. I could just see Littlejohn throwing his cream buns and Greyfriars cap into the air.

Gazza always gives you that touch of the unexpected the opposition don't like. After his goal against Scotland, certainly, our opponents were making plans how to play against him. That was good for us, because it gave other players more room to do some damage. But the poor guy just can't win in the eyes of some people. First we were accused of being over-reliant on him, then there were calls for me to drop him from the team because some thought he wasn't doing the business. It seems the critics are always looking for a reason to have a go at him. But as far as I am concerned, he did everything I expected of him. It was a remarkable achievement to get himself back into tournament fitness after all his injury problems, and he made a full contribution to the team effort – as he always does. He is a giver. All he wants is for his team to be successful.

Gazza seems to have a problem with referees in Scotland, but something no one mentioned during Euro '96 was that he got only one yellow card in five games at a very high level of competition. So he obviously learned from his mistakes at the finals of the 1990 World Cup, where he would have missed the final because of two yellow cards. Not this time, though. Everyone kept saying he was a time-bomb, but no one mentioned how well-behaved he was during the competition. So it's not just a question of his behaviour off the field: you've got to talk about his behaviour on it, too.

If we were to look back on Gazza's career now, and it was over, I would say he's done enough already to be classed as one of the all-time greats of English football. I thought he did tremendously well for England in 1990 and he did a lot for us this time, too. He's a rare mixture of lots of players. He's got a Dave Mackay type of build, for instance, but he can manipulate the ball like George Best. The difference is that the tabloids weren't as merciless in George's day as they are today. I've dealt with the Schusters and the Maradonas of this world, and other players of great talent, and I would say Gazza is in that class.

People say I'm the expert at handling him, but it just seems like good old-fashioned common sense to me. I think as long as you don't bullshit him, he's OK. Sometimes, you have to have a go at him because he's picking his nose or looking at something else when you are talking to him. At other times, you have to understand his problems, and he appreciates you taking the time to do it. He's different from other players only in that he's probably got a wider variety of behaviour patterns.

While our win against the Scots put us in a strong position in Group A, we still needed to beat Holland three days later to be absolutely sure of reaching the quarter-finals. A point would have done but, as I stressed at the time, playing for a draw can be a very dangerous game. So, I was confronted by the exciting and demanding task of devising a plan to beat the team I most admire in Europe. That's not strictly true, in that Ajax are the team I most admire in Europe. But there were so many current and former Ajax players in the Dutch team which competed in Euro '96, the difference between them was minimal. After all, Holland only qualified for the tournament in a play-off with the Republic of Ireland after coach Guus Hiddink had finally committed himself to playing the Ajax way.

Unless you look at Ajax for hours and hours, and start to realize how clever they are and why they are doing certain things, you will never unravel the complexity of their tactical plan. Even the smallest thing matters. You may not think so at first, but it does. Fortunately, because I was so fascinated by their unusual tactics, I had put endless hours into studying them. In fact, I flatter myself that no coach in Euro '96 could have been better prepared than I was to take on Holland. Not only that, but I really believed we could do what Ajax and Holland do, and do it better because we had better players. I was convinced of that despite the ridiculous claims of Louis van Gaal, the Ajax coach, and Ruud Gullit that no foreigners could master the Ajax way of playing because you need to learn it from a very young age. What about Jari Litmanen, Nwankwo Kanu and Finidi George, then? They are not Dutch, but it didn't take them long to adjust to playing for Ajax. What their system of teaching young players does is enable them to get into the first team at an early age. But I don't think it's impossible to teach it to other people. If artists can copy Van Gogh successfully, I don't see why we can't copy a few of Ajax's principles. It's not rocket science we are talking about, after all. Johan Cruyff improved on it at Barcelona, and I think it can be improved further.

If you are doing what the Dutch do only half as well as they are doing it, you've got a problem. It's no good copying it if you are going to be second-best at what they do. But I always thought that if we gave it 100 per cent, and didn't do it grudgingly, our wide players (Anderton and McManaman) were better than theirs (Jordi and Richard Witschge) and our strikers were better than theirs. Yes, you read that correctly. I didn't think Patrick Kluivert and Dennis Bergkamp would be as effective as Teddy Sheringham and Alan Shearer because Sheringham and Shearer had the edge in the air. I was also confident we were as strong as them in midfield and at the back.

The upshot of all this was a decision to dust off the 'Christmas tree' formation the media had become obsessed with soon after I took over as England coach. I coined that name for it because the shape of the formation – 1–4–3–2–1 – gave it the outline of a pine tree. I had only used it two or three times during the 20 friendly matches leading up to Euro '96, but some football writers – Harry Harris prominent among them – seemed to think it was a permanent fixture, the way they went on about it all the time. So I can't pretend it didn't give me a lot of satisfaction, and amusement, to replant the Christmas tree against Holland without any of the media men noticing.

I had always intended to use some sort of 4–3–3 formation in that game, but I wasn't sure whether to play the wingers wide or not. I decided against it because the Dutch full-backs, Michael Reiziger and Winston Bogarde, don't want to attack. So we didn't need the wingers to go all the way back with them. Normally, Sheringham doesn't play deep enough when defending, so he had to stay right up in attack or take the full-back up to the halfway line.

Once the game started, we had them all over the place tactically. They weren't sure, for instance, who should pick up McManaman, who was playing alongside Sheringham in support of Shearer. Witschge marked him to begin with, but realized that wasn't working and passed him over to Bogarde. Sheringham, meanwhile, kept dropping very deep – so deep that Reiziger didn't know whether to follow him or stay where he was. It confused the Dutch almost as much as it confused some English observers, who complained Sheringham was dropping too deep! The reason Teddy usually comes back is to make sure we still outnumber the opposition in midfield if Ince has to drop into the back three. The good thing about Teddy is that he can come out of very deep positions laying the ball off and still be up in the box by the time the winger gets in a cross. In fact, it was in that way, I think, he started the move that led to Anderton's great scoring chance against Germany. Abroad, no one would be concerned about such tactics, but here we have to ask why he is playing so deep. Don't people think we have thought these things through?

The rest really is history. We just played Holland off the park and scored four times in the first 62 minutes without reply. Alan Shearer put away a penalty after Danny Blind had tripped Ince at the end of a clever attacking move. Sheringham scored with a header by making room for himself shrewdly at a corner. Shearer blasted home a lovely, disguised square pass from Sheringham, and then Teddy wrapped it up by pouncing on the loose ball when Edwin van der Sar, the Dutch goalkeeper, could not hold a fierce shot from Anderton. Kluivert, who had come on as substitute, got a late goal for Holland, but it wasn't much by way of consolation for a real drubbing. Even Guus Hiddink had to admit we had been superior to them in every aspect of the game.

As a performance by England, it was close to perfection. You don't often get that close to it, especially when you are playing the Dutch. They were full of Ajax, or ex-Ajax, players, yet we took them apart. I'm looking forward to sitting down at some later date with a glass of champagne and a cigar and watching it again on video. It will warm the cockles of my heart on a cold winter's night. But I expect they'll say I was lucky. People have tried to devalue the win by arguing that it was an inexperienced, sub-standard Dutch team we beat. Inexperienced some of them might be in terms of international caps, but most of them have appeared in two European Cup finals and two World Club Championships. Much was made, too, of the rifts in the Dutch camp, but they have always thrived on that sort of thing before. It was conveniently forgotten that Holland had started the tournament as second favourites behind Germany and took France, a team fancied by many to win Euro '96, to penalties after we had slaughtered them. I certainly cannot remember anyone beating Ajax or Holland by the sort of score we managed. Our trouble is that we are too reluctant to celebrate victory and too eager to downgrade our own achievements. It is one of the reasons we do not progress as a football nation.

Our immediate reward for thrashing Holland was that it enabled us to play our quarter-final game at Wembley, where the fantastic support we were getting from crowds of over 76,000 was becoming such a valuable asset. As winners of Group A, we met the runners-up in Group B, who turned out to be Spain, another team I knew a lot about. They were a good side who were unbeaten in 20 matches before they met us. They hadn't lost since the quarter-finals of the 1994 World Cup, where they could have beaten Italy. They could have beaten us, too, and people say they thought we had a bit of luck in an incredibly tense match. The fact is, though, that we allowed them only two real scoring chances in the whole of the 120 minutes the game was played. We were all right once we got to grips with Sergi's runs down the left-hand side by changing our tactics at half-time. We were the better side in the second half and during extra-time, I thought. Not by a great margin, but enough to have deserved our win.

What threw us out of our stride against Spain was the surprising decision by their coach, Javier Clemente, to alter his defensive system. They had always used a back-four before, so I played Teddy Sheringham up there with Shearer. But this time they used a back-three, with Sergi breaking forward from left-back. I could not believe it, because Clemente, whose tactics I know well from my days at Barcelona and from countless videos of Spain's matches, only ever tinkers with his midfield and front players. Teddy should have responded to the switch by staying on the right side of the centre half, but he came out to try and help us defend. He was dropping back because we were being outnumbered. Sometimes, as a player, you can't work out what the problem is. All you know is that it's uncomfortable, and the best thing is to get behind the ball and start again. Otherwise, you could lose a goal, and that's even more uncomfortable.

The trouble was, Teddy was going all the way back, which left Anderton narrow and Shearer isolated. McManaman also came back, which meant Gary Neville was pushed in and we were defending with four against two, which was one too many. In the end, Spain only gave us problems tactically for a 25-minute spell and Sergi didn't actually do us any damage. As I said to the players at half-time: 'If you do the right things, he won't hurt us. If you keep him wide, he is only going to get in a cross; and I'll back us on crosses.' So I gave them a licence not to worry about failing. I also pushed Neville on Sergi, told Teddy to get back upfield again and put McManaman in the 'hole', where he plays for his club. I just told Steve to do what he does for Liverpool, and asked the other players to get the ball to him quicker.

That's not the whole story, to be honest. Originally, I was planning to lay a type of trap. It would have involved Neville playing alongside the centre-half when the ball was in Spain's back third in case they attacked with a long forward pass. But, as the ball was coming forward, Gary would start going out wide and McManaman would have to come back only two-thirds of the field. Steve would then pass Sergi over to Neville and be in position to receive the ball when we got it. If we had stuck it into him quickly, there was no one in their side who could have picked him up until he had run the length of the field and around their backs. However, the players didn't look as though they were too sure what I meant. So when Don Howe suggested we should just push Neville in on Sergi, that's what we did. It was a better solution than mine because it was just as effective and simpler.

The match wasn't supposed to go the full 120 minutes because UEFA had had the bright idea of introducing sudden-death extra-time for this tournament. But instead of encouraging us and Spain to go for the 'golden goal' that would have ended the contest there and then, the first experience of the new system had an inhibiting effect and made both of us more cagey than we would normally have been in the extra period of play. I was happy before extra-time started. I said to the players: 'Keep that steely edge, that belief we are going to win it. Don't succumb to tiredness and just make sure we are doing the same things as before, because now we are the better side.' That's all. I kept it simple. I don't believe in long speeches, especially at moments like that when they are not really listening. Nevertheless, worrying more about giving a goal away than scoring one was a pattern that was to be repeated in other matches before we and Germany finally threw caution to the winds in our semi-final. So, eventually, we and Spain were forced to settle the contest with the dreaded penalty shoot-out.

Much as I dislike penalties as a way of deciding matches, I have to admit they can lend a touch of drama to the occasion. That was particularly true when Stuart Pearce stepped up to take the third of our five spot-kicks. Because Alan Shearer and David Platt had tucked away their penalties expertly and Fernando Hierro had hit the bar with the first of Spain's, we were leading 2–1. Therefore, it was vital Stuart did not miss if we were to keep our noses in front. But it was even more vital from his own point of view, because he had been carrying for six years the agony of his damaging miss in the penalty-shoot out that decided the 1990 World Cup semi-final in West Germany's favour. In fact, it was unbelievably brave of him to volunteer to take one of the kicks in the first place. No one could blame him, then, for reacting with clenched fists, wild eyes and roaring mouth when his penalty found the net. I've never seen a reaction like that from a penalty-taker before. I've seen celebration, but that was sheer, bloody relief. All the pain from 1990 came off him and out of him, and I was so thrilled for him. It was really marvellous to watch, and I still laugh when I see that picture now. He's such a competitive bastard.

With Gazza scoring from our fourth penalty, we won the shoot-out 4–2 when Seaman dived to his left to save Spain's fourth kick, taken by poor Miguel Angel Nadal, a good player who deserved a better fate. Together with his penalty save from Scotland's McAllister and the exceptional saves he made in open play from Switzerland's Grassi, Scotland's Durie and Holland's Bergkamp, Seaman's heroics against Spain established him without doubt as the best goalkeeper in the tournament. It was quite an achievement considering that Denmark's Peter Schmeichel and Portugal's Vitor Baia were regarded as being in contention for the title of best goalkeeper in the world at the start of Euro '96. But I don't want to start saddling David with the burden of that title. It wouldn't be fair.

Beating Spain meant we would meet Germany in the semi-finals, again at Wembley. So, it was very nearly 1966 all over again. Nearly, but not quite. This time, the result went Germany's way in a penalty shoot-out. It was a terrible way to go out, and one we didn't deserve. We made more of the scoring chances after Shearer had put us ahead in the third minute and Stefan Kuntz had equalized 13 minutes later, but the ball just wouldn't go in the net. In fact, we had more chances against the Germans than I've ever seen any team have. We hit a post, we just missed the goal, we did everything but score. It wasn't a question of great saves by their goalkeeper or anything. We actually got past them and should have won it. Our only consolation was that Shearer's goal, his fifth of the tournament, made him the leading scorer of Euro '96. That wasn't bad going for an international striker who had not scored for two years before we played Switzerland on 8 June. But, as he and I kept telling everybody, there was no need to panic, the goals would come. Natural goalscorers like Alan just don't lose the knack. Fortunately, too, he was strong enough mentally to deal with his long barren period without losing confidence in himself. In the end, he proved himself a world-class striker.

It was a great team performance against Germany and one that we had prepared for well. They had a good 20 minutes in the first half of normal time, but I don't think Matthias Sammer, their influential sweeper, was much of an influence on that game. Our problem was that we didn't know how to hold on to our lead for 20 minutes. I think we were a bit shocked at scoring so early, went back into our 'the last thing you learn' syndrome and let them back into the game. We had collapsed after Brazil equalized against us in the Umbro Cup, so what pleased me was that the players now went back on to the front foot against Germany and got it right for the rest of the first half. That encouraged them to believe they could win it. We were outstanding in the second half, I thought, and perhaps even better in extra-time.

We decided to go for it in the extra period, which no one else had really done up to then. When I was talking to the players just before the game, I had said: 'Let's be positive. Let's try and get this game won.' That's all I said. If you start saying: 'Let's go for it!', you'll get everyone going forward and that's just what the Germans want, because they like to suck you in and then hit you on the break. But it was always in the back of my mind to have a go at them. In the end, I thought to myself: 'If we can finish this off, so much the better.'

Sadly, it wasn't to be. Darren Anderton hit a post when he seemed certain to score the first 'golden goal' of the tournament, but I wouldn't blame him for that. Anderton is underestimated, in my opinion. He can play just about anywhere in the team and do an excellent all-round job for you. Although people say he didn't quite hit the heights in the tournament that they thought he might, we got a pint of milk out of a half-pint bottle there. He'd been out for seven months because of injury, but I knew he knew what I wanted. He's intelligent and I knew he would last the distance. Another two weeks and he would have been right back at his best. In his last game, against Germany, I thought he was terrific. He was just coming right. He needed the time and the games. I took a gamble on him, but I didn't see it as one. I just think he's so naturally fit, he doesn't have to train. There are certain players you only have to talk to, and they'll do it for you. Now I'm looking forward to seeing a great Darren Anderton in the future.

People kept suggesting I have favourites, but you must go with your real feelings about players. You have to decide whether they are good enough or not, regardless of what others say. I believed in Shearer, Sheringham and Gazza when other people were questioning their ability, and I'm happy to think they proved me right. I don't think there was anything to prove with Anderton. Up to Euro '96, he scored five goals in twelve games; and that, for a wide player, is outstanding. That kind of record doesn't need any confirmation from me. I didn't see it as showing loyalty to those players. So far as I was concerned, it was simply a question of believing they were the best-equipped candidates for their positions and for the type of football I wanted to play, and sticking to it.

So it was back to the penalty shoot-out, this time without a happy ending. Since even the first ten penalties couldn't separate us, all of them ending up in the net, it had to go to sudden-death again. Gareth Southgate had bravely volunteered to take our sixth penalty, but he failed to beat the German goalkeeper, Andreas Köpke, who had dived the right way. All that was needed then to complete Southgate's misery, and put us out of the competition, was for Andy Möller to score from the Germans' sixth penalty, which he duly did. Gareth was distraught and no amount of consoling from Stuart

Pearce, Tony Adams and, admirably, Jürgen Klinsmann, could alleviate his distress. I think he felt a bit better when we all opted to go back to our hotel at Burnham Beeches instead of going home, had a few drinks and talked long into the night.

The wiseacres, of course, were soon saying I was wrong to let Southgate take the sixth penalty. They argued that I should have insisted on a recognized marksman like Ince, Anderton or McManaman going before him. But I'm not going to get into all that. So far as I'm concerned, it's a much better arrangement to have someone volunteering to take a penalty than to have to force another player to do it. Not only that, but I do not intend to embarrass any of the players by revealing who was willing to take a penalty and who was not. In any case, the further you go down a list of penalty-takers, the more likely it is there will be a miss. But we ought not to be subjecting people to this kind of pressure. Penalties put too much strain on the one player. It could ruin his career if he's not a strong character. I don't think it will in Gareth's case; but if you feel for the rest of your life everyone could have had a winners' medal but for you, it's a hard thing to get over.

When I was angry with the press at the start of Euro '96, I said to them: 'Well, now you are giving them so much stick and have treated them so shabbily, they are out there to be judged on what they do. They are not just writing about it.' Maybe, in my anger, I didn't express myself as clearly as I might have done. What I meant to say was: 'Hold on a minute. Don't make yourselves superior. These are just ordinary human beings. They are guys who have been playing for their country and they live on the hard edge. Millions are watching them and expecting.' That is why I think it appropriate at this point to quote a well-known piece by Theodore Roosevelt, the former American president. It applies to the whole of the England squad, but to Gareth Southgate in particular. It reads as follows:

It is not the critic who counts; not the man who points out how the strong man stumbles, or where the doer of deeds could actually have done them better. The credit belongs to the man who is actually in the arena, whose face is marred by dust and sweat and blood, who strives valiantly; who errs and comes short again and again; because there is not effort without error and shortcomings; but who does actually strive to do the deed; who knows great enthusiasm, the great devotion, who spends himself in a worthy cause; who at the best knows in the end the triumph of high achievement and who at the worst, if he fails, at least he fails while daring greatly. So that his place shall never be with those cold and timid souls who know neither victory nor defeat.

There was also some criticism of me for not using any substitutes during the Germany game, our second 120-minute contest in five days. But that's a decision also affected by the possibility of penalties. If you've got your best penalty-takers on the bench, you've got to put your subs on. In our case, I had to keep them on the field. We were still making chances as well. If you are not doing that, you have to try and repair your game. But if it's working, why repair it? So-and-so on the bench is always better than someone on the field, isn't he? However, my first choices were not suffering fitness-wise. I looked at Gazza and thought he was bound to be tired, but all of a sudden he was the one in the box nearly scoring a goal. He came out and went back in there for a second time. Then he did it again. So what was I supposed to do? I know people will point to the fact that I brought on three substitutes against Spain, but the circumstances were different. Apart from anything else, I had to replace Sheringham with Robbie Fowler because Teddy had suffered a dead leg. Robbie, incidentally, would have taken the fifth penalty in that shoot-out, had it been necessary.

It is high time, though, that we found an alternative to penalties as a means of deciding important games. People are talking about playing for another half-hour or taking players off the pitch at intervals. But if you look at a boxing match that goes the distance, they don't have another ten rounds or stick their chins out and say 'You have a swing at me and then I'll have a swing at you.' They try to analyse the content of the contest, and I think that's the clue. Football has to find a way of awarding a points verdict. I thought first of suggesting the number of corner-kicks as a tie-breaker, but that might just encourage teams to play the ball long in the hope of forcing a corner. The best way, I think, would be to calculate the amount of possession each team has. That could be possession all over the field or just in the attacking third. Sky Television have shown the measurements can be carried out instantly, and I'm sure it would help to encourage attacking football as well.

We are giving forwards the benefit of the doubt now over off-side – or at least we are supposed to be – and we've got to give every incentive to the team that is prepared to attack. Because, I've got to tell you, Germany won Euro '96 with a defensive strategy. Quite honestly, I wouldn't want to buy a season ticket to watch them every week. I would with Holland because they can win things and entertain. That, as we established in an earlier chapter, is the perfect combination. You can't go forward quickly at Germany, though. They'll just get the ball and break at you. That's what Sammer's there for; he hides at the back. We pulled them around more than anyone else; but that might not be quite so necessary if they knew that possession, especially in the attacking third, could decide the game. So my suggestion is that we play a normal period of extra-time – no sudden-death or golden goal – then use the amount of possession each side enjoys as a tie-breaker. If that still doesn't separate the sides, perhaps we could fall back on the number of shots at goal or on target.

I don't know if the statisticians of Euro '96 ever totted up all the figures about possession for each match, but if they did I'm sure England would come out somewhere near the top. As it was, we were second only to Germany in terms of goal difference. We had scored eight goals and conceded three by the time we were knocked out at the semi-final stage, while the Germans' record at that point was 8–2. I don't think we come out of the comparison at all badly when you consider that Germany are experts at tournament play and had a pretty battle-hardened squad. It was certainly not a bad record for an attacking team like mine.

I had wide players, wingers if you like, playing like full-backs. They weren't really full-backs because they never marked wingers. That is a very, very important point. They only ever played against full-backs, so it was not the extravagant strategy everyone thought it was. But it does mean I was able to have six attacking players in my team. People think that if you have that many attackers, you must be at risk of losing goals. But it's the same as Ajax. Everyone thinks they are vulnerable because they only play three at the back, but the facts are that they don't give away many goals (except to England, of course!). And there are reasons why they don't. Why is it that when you've got wingers playing back there and perhaps just good footballers at the back, they don't give away goals? Well, that's the secret – they have a system that works.

I thought about using wing-backs because it's more solid. It's a change from four at the back, but not too much of a change. On the other hand, I don't think you are going to make the same number of chances, or score as many goals, as my team at the top level. You reduce yourself to maybe four attackers as opposed to six. That's the problem Glenn Hoddle will have as England coach. He will use wing-backs, and I don't blame him because that's what he knows and what has worked for him at Swindon and Chelsea. But what if it could be proved to him that he would get more scoring chances playing my way? Would he change? I doubt it, and I think he would be right to stick to what he knows. It just seems to me that, having caught the rest of Europe up, we'd be taking our foot off the gas. Opposing teams might not create more scoring chances against an England team using wing-backs, but that same England would not make the number of chances we made against the top sides, the Spains and the Germanys. I'm not saying we were twice as good as Germany, or twice as bad. But we are definitely in the same bracket now. We've proved we deserve to be there. Never mind that we were at home: it makes no difference at that level of the game. When it comes to expertise, I believe the players at the top of English football are good enough to compete with the best if the direction is right. Although there is still plenty of room for improvement overall, we do have players of the highest calibre. In fact, I think the best of our players are as good as anybody's. I certainly would not have changed those in my squad for any other group.

Although nobody seemed to grasp what they were seeing in Euro '96 – virtually a revolutionary system of play by England – I remain convinced my concept of the way the game should be played is the way forward. Some unnamed coach, supposedly a friend of mine, was arguing in *The Sunday Times* that English football had to copy the Germans to progress, but that's nonsense. They use wing-backs and they are taking the game backwards, in my opinion. I thought they were fortunate to beat Croatia and fortunate to beat Italy, too. Even their win in the final was unsatisfactory, the winning goal creeping inside a post like that after a couple of deflections. It was all right for Germany, but it was an anti-climax to end the tournament with.

They were even more fortunate to beat us; but that is so much water under the bridge now. I'll rest content in the thought that we had a team full of leaders and competitors and people who responded to what we wanted to do. That was hugely satisfying in itself. What we did well was to have a team with an abundance of attacking players in it that gave very few goals away. We made a lot of chances after Christmas 1995, once I'd got where I wanted to be in terms of team-building. It didn't matter who we played, they were impressed by the fact that we didn't give many goals away. We also made a lot of opportunities and scored a lot of goals; but what was more satisfying was the quality of our play. The football we played gave the country excitement, unity and a team to be proud of.

I was certainly very proud of my whole team. That is to say, not only the players, but the technical and medical staff as well. The achievements of those who actually played need no further comment from me, but I would like to record my thanks to those who saw little action or did not get on the field at all. They must have been very disappointed and frustrated, but they never indulged their own feelings at the expense of the team. I appreciated it, even if they might not have appreciated it themselves.

As for the technical and medical staff, I think their contributions vindicated my efforts to recruit the best people I could for every job. My two principal coaches, Don Howe and Bryan Robson, were a good partnership and great allies. Don's massive experience and steadiness were supplemented by Bryan's ability to get close to the players. The link he provided between me and them could not have been bettered. Mike Kelly, too, played his part. He's not only the best goalkeeping coach I've ever worked with, he was always offering shrewd observations that made me think about what I was doing. Then, as back-up, there was Ted Buxton, my eyes and ears and a really genuine man.

Doc Crane won the affection of us all for the way he organized the medical attention with great humour, while David Butler and Alan Smith, the two physios, worked tirelessly at any time of day or night to make sure we had every possibility of players being fit not only for games but for training. Plus they had other duties alongside the kit-man, Martin Grogan. Others played a valuable, unseen part, too. Michelle Rogers, the international secretary, was one. She had to be a bit broad-minded at times, though the players never overstepped the mark in her company.

I also want to pay tribute to my own secretary at the FA for the work she did for me during those two and a half years. Frances Hart was never fortunate enough to be in the glory line, but she was always a terrific team player behind the scenes. So was David Davies, the FA's director of public affairs. He held together the tough job of dealing with the media that was carried out, on almost a daily basis during Euro '96, by himself and his staff.

I've always believed that, while you cannot guarantee winning anything as a coach, you've got to leave a team better than when you started. I flatter myself that I've done that wherever I've gone. Whatever people say about my abilities as a coach, I would say just look and you'll see I've always given people – the players, the supporters – some fun and a better football team. I hope you agree. Thank you and goodbye. Or should it be au revoir?

Bibliography

Barrett, Norman: *The Daily Telegraph Football Chronicle* (Carlton Books)

Barret, Norman (ed): *World Soccer from A-Z* (Pan Books)

Busby, Sir Matt: *Soccer at the Top* (Weidenfeld & Nicolson)

Dunphy, Eamon: *A Strange Kind of Glory – Sir Matt Busby and Manchester United* (Heinemann)

Football Association: *The Official Football Association Yearbook* (Pan Books)

Fynn, Alex and Guest, Lynton: *Out of Time – Why Football Isn't Working!* (Simon & Schuster)

Gibson, John: *Kevin Keegan, Portrait of a Superstar* (W.H. Allen)

Glanville, Brian: *The History of the World Cup* (Faber & Faber)

Green, Geoffrey: *Soccer in the Fifties* (Ian Allan)

Harding, John: *For The Good Of The Game, The Official History of the Professional Footballers' Association* (Robson Books)

Hart, Graham (ed): *The Guinness Football Encyclopedia* (Guinness)

Hodgson, Derek: *The Manchester United Story* (Arthur Barker)

Korr, Charles: *West Ham United* (Duckworth)

Lasche, Ian: *Rothmans Book of Football League Records 1888–89 to 1978–79* (Queen Anne Press)

Lawrenson, Mark: *Mark Lawrenson, The Autobiography* (Queen Ann Press)

Mayes, Harold: *The Football Association World Cup Report, 1966* (Heinemann)

Pawson, Tony: *The Football Managers* (Eyre Methuen)

Ponting, Ivan: *Tottenham Hotspur, Player By Player* (Guinness)

Rogan, Johnny: *The Football Managers* (Queen Anne Press)

Rollin, Jack: *Rothmans Football Yearbook* (Headline and Queen Anne Press)

Rollin, Jack: *The Guinness Record of the World Cup 1930–94* (Guinness)

Soar, Phil, Tyler, Martin and Widdows, Richard: *Encylcopedia of World Football* (Marshall Cavendish)

Steen, Rob: *The Mavericks* (Mainstream Publishing)

Tyler, Martin and Soar, Phil: *Encyclopedia of British Football* (Collins)

Venables, Terry: *The Autobiography* (Michael Joseph)

Venebales, Terry: *They Used to Play on Grass* (Hodder & Stoughton)

Venables, Terry: *Venables' England, The Making of the Team* (Boxtree)

Young, Percy M: *Centenary Wolves, 1877–1977* (Wolverhampton Wanderers)